Impacts of European Territorial Policies in the Baltic States

Urban and regional development in the Baltic States and other Central and Eastern European countries has experienced rapid changes since their re-independence at the beginning of the 1990s. Meanwhile, urban and regional planning institutions and organizational cultures in the Baltic States have only changed rather incrementally, despite various national and European pressures for reform. As a consequence, the effects of European cohesion and structural policy measures have been quite modest, and the ability of the planning systems in the Baltic states to manage contemporary trends in urban and regional development has become increasingly limited. This book focuses on these issues and tensions of spatial planning and development in the Baltic States and their distinctiveness compared to other European countries. It provides an overview of the historical and cultural context of spatial development, a discussion of the processes of Europeanization of spatial planning in the specific context of the Baltic States, and an analysis of whether these processes may be leading to policy convergence in the region.

This book was published as a special issue of *European Planning Studies*.

Garri Raagmaa is Associate Professor at the University of Tartu, Estonia. He has published three books and over sixty articles about regional planning and development, regional innovation, regional identity and leadership issues.

Dominic Stead is Associate Professor at Delft University of Technology, The Netherlands. He has researched and published widely on a range of issues related to urban and regional governance, including more than fifty journal articles, twenty-five book chapters and three edited books.

Impacts of European Territorial Policies in the Baltic States

Edited by
Garri Raagmaa and Dominic Stead

LONDON AND NEW YORK

First published 2015 by Routledge

2 Park Square, Milton Park, Abingdon, Oxfordshire OX14 4RN
711 Third Avenue, New York, NY 10017

Routledge is an imprint of the Taylor & Francis Group, an informa business

First issued in paperback 2018

Copyright © 2015 Taylor & Francis

All rights reserved. No part of this book may be reprinted or reproduced or utilised in any form or by any electronic, mechanical, or other means, now known or hereafter invented, including photocopying and recording, or in any information storage or retrieval system, without permission in writing from the publishers.

Notice:
Product or corporate names may be trademarks or registered trademarks, and are used only for identification and explanation without intent to infringe.

British Library Cataloguing in Publication Data
A catalogue record for this book is available from the British Library

ISBN 13: 978-1-138-91561-9 (hbk)
ISBN 13: 978-1-138-08532-9 (pbk)

Typeset in Times New Roman
by RefineCatch Limited, Bungay, Suffolk

Publisher's Note
The publisher accepts responsibility for any inconsistencies that may have arisen during the conversion of this book from journal articles to book chapters, namely the possible inclusion of journal terminology.

Disclaimer
Every effort has been made to contact copyright holders for their permission to reprint material in this book. The publishers would be grateful to hear from any copyright holder who is not here acknowledged and will undertake to rectify any errors or omissions in future editions of this book.

Contents

Citation Information	vii
Notes on Contributors	ix

1. Spatial Planning in the Baltic States: Impacts of European Policies   1
   Garri Raagmaa and Dominic Stead

2. European Integration and Spatial Rescaling in the Baltic Region: Soft Spaces, Soft Planning and Soft Security   10
   Dominic Stead

3. New Spatial Patterns and Territorial–Administrative Structures in the European Union: Reflections on Eastern Europe   24
   Jussi Sakari Jauhiainen

4. The Engagement of Territorial Knowledge Communities with European Spatial Planning and the Territorial Cohesion Debate: A Baltic Perspective   42
   Neil Adams, Giancarlo Cotella and Richard Nunes

5. From Conditionality to Europeanization in Central and Eastern Europe: Administrative Performance and Capacity in Cohesion Policy   65
   John Bachtler, Carlos Mendez and Hildegard Oraže

6. Urban–Rural Interactions in Latvian Changing Policy and Practice Context   88
   Laila Kūle

7. Europeanization and De-Europeanization of Estonian Regional Policy   105
   Garri Raagmaa, Tarmo Kalvet and Ragne Kasesalu

8. Urban Policies for the Creative Industries: A European Comparison   126
   Külliki Tafel-Viia, Andres Viia, Erik Terk and Silja Lassur

Index   147

Citation Information

The chapters in this book were originally published in *European Planning Studies*, volume 22, issue 4 (April 2014). When citing this material, please use the original page numbering for each article, as follows:

Chapter 1
Editorial: Spatial Planning in the Baltic States: Impacts of European Policies
Garri Raagmaa and Dominic Stead
European Planning Studies, volume 22, issue 4 (April 2014) pp. 671–679

Chapter 2
European Integration and Spatial Rescaling in the Baltic Region: Soft Spaces, Soft Planning and Soft Security
Dominic Stead
European Planning Studies, volume 22, issue 4 (April 2014) pp. 680–693

Chapter 3
New Spatial Patterns and Territorial–Administrative Structures in the European Union: Reflections on Eastern Europe
Jussi Sakari Jauhiainen
European Planning Studies, volume 22, issue 4 (April 2014) pp. 694–711

Chapter 4
The Engagement of Territorial Knowledge Communities with European Spatial Planning and the Territorial Cohesion Debate: A Baltic Perspective
Neil Adams, Giancarlo Cotella and Richard Nunes
European Planning Studies, volume 22, issue 4 (April 2014) pp. 712–734

Chapter 5
From Conditionality to Europeanization in Central and Eastern Europe: Administrative Performance and Capacity in Cohesion Policy
John Bachtler, Carlos Mendez and Hildegard Oraže
European Planning Studies, volume 22, issue 4 (April 2014) pp. 735–757

CITATION INFORMATION

Chapter 6
Urban–Rural Interactions in Latvian Changing Policy and Practice Context
Laila Kūle
European Planning Studies, volume 22, issue 4 (April 2014) pp. 758–774

Chapter 7
Europeanization and De-Europeanization of Estonian Regional Policy
Garri Raagmaa, Tarmo Kalvet and Ragne Kasesalu
European Planning Studies, volume 22, issue 4 (April 2014) pp. 775–795

Chapter 8
Urban Policies for the Creative Industries: A European Comparison
Külliki Tafel-Viia, Andres Viia, Erik Terk and Silja Lassur
European Planning Studies, volume 22, issue 4 (April 2014) pp. 796–815

Please direct any queries you may have about the citations to
clsuk.permissions@cengage.com

Notes on Contributors

Neil Adams is Senior Lecturer in Spatial Planning in the Department of Urban, Environment and Leisure Studies at London South Bank University, UK.

John Bachtler is Professor of European Policy Studies and Director of the European Policies Research Centre at the University of Strathclyde, Glasgow, UK. His research expertise includes regional and industrial development in Europe, encompassing the regional policies of Member States and Candidate Countries and the structural and cohesion policies of the European Union.

Giancarlo Cotella is an Assistant Professor at the Politecnico di Torino, Italy. His research focuses on EU Territorial Governance and in particular on the mutual influence occurring between European Spatial Planning and the spatial planning systems of the various Member States.

Jussi Sakari Jauhiainen is based in the Department of Geography and Geology at the University of Turku, Finland, and in the Institute of Ecology and Earth Sciences at the University of Tartu, Estonia.

Tarmo Kalvet is a Senior Research Fellow in the School of Innovation and Governance at Tallinn University of Technology, Estonia.

Ragne Kasesalu is a Senior Consultant for Advisio Ltd., based in Tartu, Estonia.

Laila Kūle is based in the Faculty of Geography and Earth Sciences at the University of Latvia, Riga, Latvia.

Silja Lassur is based in the Estonian Institute for Futures Studies at Tallinn University, Estonia.

Carlos Mendez is a Senior Research Fellow in the European Policies Research Centre at the University of Strathclyde, Glasgow, UK. His research has focused on EU Cohesion policy and the regional development policies of Portugal and Spain.

Richard Nunes is a Lecturer in the School of Real Estate and Planning at the University of Reading, UK. His interests relate to design, planning and governance, especially where it involves the integration of urban ecosystem services into development planning processes and urban policy decision-making tools.

Hildegard Oraže is senior expert for European Cohesion policy (ERDF, ESF), cross-border and transnational cooperation at Metis GmbH, a European consultancy company based in Vienna, Austria.

NOTES ON CONTRIBUTORS

Garri Raagmaa is Associate Professor at the University of Tartu, Estonia. He has published three books and over sixty articles about regional planning and development, regional innovation, regional identity and leadership issues.

Dominic Stead is Associate Professor at Delft University of Technology, The Netherlands. He has researched and published widely on a range of issues related to urban and regional governance, including more than fifty journal articles, twenty-five book chapters and three edited books.

Külliki Tafel-Viia is based in the Estonian Institute for Futures Studies at Tallinn University, Estonia.

Erik Terk is based in the Estonian Institute for Futures Studies at Tallinn University, Estonia.

Andres Viia is based in the Estonian Institute for Futures Studies at Tallinn University, Estonia.

Spatial Planning in the Baltic States: Impacts of European Policies

GARRI RAAGMAA* & DOMINIC STEAD**

*Department of Geography, University of Tartu, Tartu, Estonia, **OTB Research Institute for the Built Environment, Delft University of Technology, Delft, The Netherlands

ABSTRACT *Baltic societies have been transformed rapidly since the beginning of the 1990s, whereas planning institutions and organizational cultures in the Baltic States have only changed rather incrementally despite various national and European pressures for reform. As a consequence, the extent of Europeanization of spatial planning has been limited in the Baltic region, and the effects of cohesion and structural policy measures have been quite modest. This paper focuses on these changes in spatial planning in the Baltic States and is divided into three main parts. The paper begins by describing the historical and cultural context of spatial development in the Baltic States. Second, it discusses processes of Europeanization of spatial planning in the specific context of the Baltic States, and third, it considers whether these processes may be leading to policy convergence in the region.*

1. Introduction—Spatial Changes and Planning in the Baltic States

Dramatic economic and political changes have taken place in the Baltic States over the last two decades, which have resulted in new institutional structures and a great deal of new physical development. The fall of communism required the construction of entirely new institutional, economic and political systems (Downes, 1996). The extent of change has been much more profound than other former republics of the Soviet Union. Rapid economic restructuring and the introduction of open trade policies resulted in huge changes in the Baltic economy. The 1990s and early 2000s was a period of great expansion and growth in the region: the annual rate of economic growth regularly increased by double digits and the rate of unemployment dropped to some of the lowest levels in Europe.

By 2008, however, the impacts of the global economic crisis were being felt: the economy declined rapidly, unemployment grew sharply and a large outflow of population from economically weaker regions occurred, posing substantial challenges for regional development.

Spatial planning in the Baltic region faces a number of common issues and challenges. Since the 1980s various types of old economic activities folded (largely in former collective farm centres and monofunctional industrial/mining/military settlements), leaving behind large areas of derelict land, abandoned housing and underused infrastructure. New economic activities emerged mainly in larger urban regions, often in poorly planned locations in the suburbs along major roads, giving rise to urban sprawl. Tens of thousands of urban residents moved out of inner cities to new low-density suburban residential areas or rebuilt/extended houses in garden districts (Kule, 2013, Leetmaa et al., 2012). While cities retained relatively strict land-use regulations and building codes, suburban municipalities were often far less demanding, and virtually any kind of development was permitted in order to attract new residents and tax revenues (Pucher & Buehler, 2005).

Spatial planning in Central and Eastern Europe (CEE) differs from Western Europe in terms of rapidly changing economic, organizational and political landscapes, lower levels of trust in the role of government (van Dijk, 2002; Jauhiainen, 2013; Mason, 1995), the position of planning in society (Maier, 1998) and the fact that spatial planning has had a longer history in Western Europe (Adams, 2008). Due to their general association with the communist regime, planning and respectable spatial policies enjoyed minimal support in CEE countries in the 1990s (Nedović-Budić, 2001; UNECE, 2000). Some extreme new right planning apologists (politicians) in the early 1990s even declared that their task was to provide liberation from the rule of the planners. Nevertheless, planning was generally recognized as one of the pre-conditions of accessing European Union (EU) funding in the CEE (Adams, 2008).

As a result of efforts to secure access to EU funding, attempts to emulate certain elements from western models of planning were made in the Baltic States and various examples of policy transfer in the area of planning can be found (Stead et al., 2008) despite some recognition that the doctrine and values of planning cannot simply be imported (Raagmaa, 2009). According to Jaakson (2000), western European planning ideas were often legitimized and presented to Eastern Europe as a culturally and socially superior model, and based on the presumption that Western planning models were appropriate because the newly independent States were moving towards market economies. Planning officials attempted to apply planning doctrines from elsewhere, but this was very often problematic since policy learning and administrative changes require a great deal of time and resources to achieve, especially when the legitimacy of planning is not considered a priority. Whereas the change of communist institutions took place rapidly in the Baltic States, their replacement with new institutions for planning has been a much slower process (Balchin et al., 1999; Raagmaa, 2009).

2. The Europeanization of Spatial Planning

Since the 1990s there has been an increasing perception that transnational influences on spatial development are growing and that such trends are accentuated by the processes of European integration (Sykes, 2008). Planners across Europe are increasingly involved in trans-boundary cooperation networks and inter-regional collaboration initiatives

(Dühr *et al.*, 2007). The transfer of ideas, practices and principles within Europe is diverse in nature: transfer can be top-down, bottom-up and/or horizontal (see, for example, Marshall, 2005).

Various cases of the Europeanization of planning can be identified. The EU's INTERREG Programme is a prime example which has facilitated cooperation between regions and actors, and has acted as a stimulus for Europeanization (Lähteenmäki-Smith *et al.*, 2005; Waterhout, 2007) supporting the emergence of transnational spatial planning practices, the diffusion of certain spatial ideas across European countries and changes in the domestic patterns of spatial planning and regional policies, both in terms of approaches and institutional capacity (Böhme *et al.*, 2004; Dabinett, 2006; Dabinett & Richardson, 2005; Giannakourou, 2005; Janin Rivolin, 2003; Janin Rivolin & Faludi, 2005; Pedrazzini, 2005; Tewdwr-Jones & Williams, 2001). Other examples include the PHARE Programme in CEE countries across a broad spectrum of areas, including administrative reforms and infrastructure and environment policies (Pallagst, 2006; Stanilov, 2007). Whilst there is no EU competence in spatial planning, the EU has played a key role in the promotion of a "European spatial planning agenda" (Colomb, 2007), discursively shaped by certain normative concepts and "spatial planning ideas" (Böhme *et al.*, 2004; Jensen & Richardson, 2004). In the Baltic States, the EU has also helped to shape the nature of new institutions and align professional cultures as in the case of the management of EU programmes (see Bachtler *et al.*, 2013).

Most of the studies on the Europeanization of spatial planning put forward arguments that the process is taking place in different places and in different ways (Böhme, 2002; Dabinett & Richardson, 2005; Giannakourou, 2005; Sykes, 2008; Tewdwr-Jones & Williams, 2001; Van Ravesteyn & Evers, 2004; Waterhout, 2007; Waterhout & Böhme, 2008; Zonneveld, 2005). Likewise, Börzel (2002) and Héritier *et al.* (2001) claim that Europeanization leads to differentiated outcomes depending on context. In the Baltic States and other CEE countries, the process of Europeanization has arguably been faster, and the extent of change is more profound (Batt & Wolczuk, 1999; Grabbe, 2001; O'Dwyer, 2006). Various reasons have been suggested to explain this, such as the openness of national elites to EU influence (Batt & Wolczuk, 1999), different starting points in terms of institutional development (Batt & Wolczuk, 1999), and lower levels of institutional resistance compared to "old" member states (Goetz, 2006; Grabbe, 2001).

Despite the wide range of potential facilitators of convergence, hard evidence for policy convergence in the area of spatial planning is difficult to find and various authors remain sceptical about the extent to which European planning systems or planning outcomes are actually converging. De Jong and Edelenbos (2007) indeed question whether the increase in intensity of cross-national comparisons and transnational exchanges necessarily lead to policy convergence of planning systems. Fürst (2009) is unconvinced that policy convergence is taking place in spatial planning, stating that conjecture about convergence seems "to be based on thin grounds" (p. 31). Discussing the convergence of development patterns in CEE, Nedović-Budić *et al.* (2006) argue that the built environment changes incrementally, and is still heavily influenced by local culture and politics. Meanwhile, Adams (2008) presents a case both for and against the convergence of different planning systems in Europe, arguing that, while there has been some convergence towards more collaborative and communicative forms of planning within Europe, certain other aspects of the planning process, such as implementation, monitoring and review, show few signs of convergence.

3. Limited Europeanization of Spatial Planning and Policy

Various explanations have been suggested for the lack in or limited degree of policy convergence in spatial planning. Fürst (2009), for example, contends that spatial planning processes are relatively slow to change and are restrained by high transaction costs. He argues that policy systems generally change only if the pressure is very strong or if ignoring the need to change will be met by severe sanctions. Most planning systems are not usually in this situation: the pressures are not strong enough and resisting change does not incur sanctions or other costs. Here the CEE and especially Baltic structures differ: transition and several post-transition shocks created a high level of stress.

Healey and Williams (1993) allude to factors like local institutional structures, path dependency, culture and local socioeconomic conditions constrain policy convergence when they contend that "[t]he diversity of planning systems and practices in Europe is the result of the specific histories and geographies of particular places, and the way these interlock with national institutional structures, cultures and economic opportunities" (p. 716). Similarly, Adams (2008) contends that differences in socioeconomic conditions, cultures and histories between countries form considerable barriers to the convergence of approaches to planning. Hamedinger et al. (2008, p. 2671) argue that "there is no evidence of EU-wide convergence of governance structures at the local and regional levels", which they suggest is due to "mediating" or "filtering" factors, such as domestic institutions, political cultures, the distribution of competences and legal procedures. Planning systems have a path dependency and a continuity of institutions and cultures (Jauhiainen, 2013), and practices from the past still have a considerable impact on current affairs (Kule, 2013; Raagmaa et al., 2013). Newcomers to policymaking for the creative industries have also found that path dependencies have a restricting character (Tafel-Viia et al., 2013).

These path dependencies have very real costs. Non-metropolitan regions in the Baltic States lost around a quarter of their population and employment over the past 20 years, which have not only led to greater regional polarization but also to a sharp decline in local and regional administrative capacity that has hampered strategic planning and hindered the effective use of local human and natural resources. Since the breakup of the Soviet Union, there has been little concern among the national ruling elites in the Baltic States about the management of spatial development and growing spatial inequalities—long term planning practices have generally been abandoned and little attention has recently been paid to regional economic restructuring. On the other hand, however, national and regional statkeholders are increasingly involved in international collaboration on spatial development (Stead, 2013), and the development of tools for implementing territorial cohesion policy (Bachtler et al., 2013).

To date, the Baltic States have not been very active contributors to European Cohesion Policy debates (Adams et al., 2013) and do not have strong "territorial knowledge communities". Despite pressure from Europe, Baltic officials and/or politicians have found ways for selectively applying European spatial policy principles and implementing their personal agendas (Raagmaa et al., 2013). This culture of "double standards" (see also Raagmaa & Kroon, 2005), or policy action mismatch, was born during the socialist period and in practice means that the reality can be rather different from the rhetoric. The EU Baltic Strategy conference ("Partnership between the state, universities and local governments to boost Estonia's role in the EU Baltic Sea Strategy") held in

January 2012 in Tallinn provides one specific example. The official speeches were generally positive and uncritical, whereas the expert interventions and informal discussions were highly critical and many participants voiced concerns that the strategy does not work and several projects have been much less beneficial to the Baltic States than previously expected. The tone of the publication distributed at the conference was overwhelmingly positive, and only contained one slightly critical remark about the institutional capacity of smaller local authorities.

Attitudes towards the EU have shifted substantially over the course of time in the Baltic States. Before accession to the EU, CEE administrations and political elites were attentive to European agendas, they were keen to learn from Western counterparts and were determined to deliver democratic and administrative reforms (Bachtler *et al.*, 2013; Jauhiainen 2013). After accession, however, the main focus was the absorption of EU grants: "double standards" in policymaking became more prevalent. A combination of previous behaviour, new EU rules, and local agendas (often reflecting the interests of business elites) appeared. This new situation put a brake on various plans for institutional reform and Europeanization more generally. As a result, certain old bureaucratic structures remain that have not changed significantly since the Baltic States joined the EU.

4. Convergence of Spatial Policy in the Baltic Region?

Theoretical debates about policy convergence in relation to spatial planning (and empirical evidence) are still in their infancy and have not yet reached firm conclusions. The question of whether European planning systems are converging is subject to differing views. There are various factors and trends that would appear to be promoting policy convergence in planning (facilitating factors), but at the same time there are other factors that work against convergence (inhibiting factors). These factors are discussed in more detail elsewhere (Stead, 2013). The brief overview of some of the recent debates and opinions concerning policy convergence and spatial planning as presented above serves to highlight some important points relating to further analysis on policy convergence.

Firstly, policy convergence has been defined and examined in a range of different ways, which help to explain some of the differing conclusions on whether convergence does (or does not) occur. When discussing and analysing policy convergence, it is important to be clear about what is being measured and how, since it can, for example, refer to policy goals, policy content, policy instruments, policy outcomes or policy styles (see Bennett, 1991), and the trajectories of these different dimensions do not necessarily follow each other. Thus it may happen, for example, that policy content is converging but policy outcomes are not (which is one of the conclusions drawn by Adams, 2008).

Secondly, the concept of policy convergence clearly has a time and relational dimension—it concerns the trajectory of change over time and how this trajectory compares (or relates) to one or more reference cases. The trajectory may not necessarily be linear. It is therefore, important to recognize that the chosen reference case(s) and period of analysis heavily influence any conclusions about the extent to which convergence may or may not have occurred.

Thirdly, a major problem of evaluating the evolution of policies and procedures is related to information sources. Evaluations based on official reports from government bodies, implementing agencies or their beneficiaries may not provide sufficient information about change or provide a full picture of the effect of spatial policies on the ground. There is also a tendency for managerial evaluations of policies and procedures to focus on formal changes (institutional arrangements, policies and rhetoric) rather than the reality (interpretation of policy and concepts and implementation).

A fourth issue arises from the terminology used in policy documents. Local politicians and civil servants are not necessarily familiar with basic EU documents. As Jauhiainen (2013, this issue) recognizes: "The core acquis is a formal legal hard element, but its implementation varies in Eastern Europe". Similarly, spatial policy goals and concepts are interpreted differently across Europe (see also Waterhout & Stead, 2007), which can affect the choice of policy instruments used to address these goals and concepts.

5. The Contributions in the Special Issue

Each of the contributions in this volume address issues concerning the Europeanization of spatial development and/or spatial planning in the Baltic region. Together, they help to provide a more detailed picture about whether there are indications of policy convergence in spatial development/planning in the Baltic States. Most of the papers were first presented at the conference on "Socioeconomic spatial systems and territorial governance" held in March 2010 at the University of Tartu, Estonia. The conference was dedicated to the memory of Professor Salme Nõmmik, a highly distinguished scholar in the former Soviet Union who worked at the Department of Geography in the University of Tartu from 1946 to 1988 (Tammiksaar *et al.*, 2013).

In the first paper, Jussi Jauhiainen adopts a governance perspective to analyze changes in spatial patterns and territorial-administrative structures shaped by EU spatial policy mechanisms and practices. He concludes that spatial patterns and territorial-administrative structures in Europe change slowly, being influenced by path-dependent legacies and the recently emerged uncertainties of the EU, turning the Europeanization of spatial planning into a more cyclical rather than top-down process.

Dominic Stead discusses how European territorial cooperation and development strategies in the Baltic region are contributing to spatial rescaling in "soft spaces", and how these strategies can be seen as a form of soft planning and as a means to promote soft security policy. He concludes that the direct impacts on spatial rescaling are limited, as might be expected for non-statutory arrangements. Nevertheless, these strategies are supplementing and perhaps even supplanting other existing policy spaces. The strategies are helping to promote more "regionalized" policy agendas for European territorial cooperation and are involving various regions outside the EU's external borders.

John Bachtler, Carlos Mendez and Hildegard Oraže assess the role of administrative capacity in explaining the performance of eight Central and Eastern European countries (EU8) in managing and implementing Cohesion Policy between 2004 and 2008. They argue that the EU8 have a substantial amount of administrative capacity for implementing Cohesion policy, but suggest that effective benchmarks against which to measure and monitor the state and progress of administrative performance and capacity is a critical task.

Neil Adams, Giancarlo Cotella and Richard Nunes explore the evolution of territorial knowledge channels in the Baltic States, and the extent and nature of the engagement of actors' communities in European spatial planning. They conclude that territorial knowledge communities in the Baltic States are weak and fragmented, their activity increasingly directed by policy pragmatism and political expedience that has become evident in a reassertion of economic priorities. Participation in EU level discussion is extremely varied: very active in the case of Poland and Hungary and almost absent in the Baltic States.

Laila Kule discusses the development of Latvian urban-rural policy through history and concludes that although certain collaborative models have been challenged during times of change, they have been re-established in similar forms time and time again. Kule argues that coordination between administrations and policy sectors remain key hindrances to the development of more integrated urban-rural partnerships in Latvia.

Garri Raagmaa, Tarmo Kalvet and Ragne Kasesalu address path dependencies in governance, spatial policy-making in their account of the Europeanization of regional policy in Estonia. They conclude that significant change occurred when Estonia acceded to the EU: national regional policy programmes were reduced and a selective application of EU principles occurred. However, the institutional framework remained largely unchanged and EU cohesion policy measures were often used to achieve personal agendas, setting Estonian regional policy apart from other approaches in Europe.

Finally, the paper by Külliki Tafel-Viia, Andres Viia, Erik Terk and Silja Lassur deals with path dependencies: this time in terms of policies for creative industries and their "ideal types". The success of these industries is clearly related to distinctive features created through history, which have become exploitable amenities. The 50-year separation from western Europe, has for example, provided the Baltic States with specific architectural and cultural features. Developing creative industries often requires new types of approaches and a significant amount of open-mindedness, which has posed problems for traditional governance models in Estonia.

Acknowledgements

Most of the papers in this special issue were first presented at a conference, organized in honour of Professor Salme Nõmmik and hosted at the University of Tartu in 2010. This special issue is dedicated to Professor Nõmmik and her contribution to scholarship in the field of economic geography and spatial development policy.

References

Adams, N. (2008) Convergence and policy transfer: An examination of the extent to which approaches to spatial planning have converged within the context of an enlarged EU, *International Planning Studies*, 13(1), pp. 31–49.

Adams, N., Cotella, G. & Nunes, R. (2013) The engagement of territorial knowledge communities with European spatial planning and the territorial cohesion debate: A Baltic perspective, *European Planning Studies*. doi: 10.1080/09654313.2013.772735.

Bachtler, J., Mendez, C. & Oraže, H. (2013) From conditionality to Europeanization in Central and Eastern Europe: Regional policy performance and administrative capacity, *European Planning Studies*, doi: 10.1080/09654313.2013.772744.

Balchin, P., Sykora, L. & Bull, G. (1999) *Regional Policy & Planning in Europe* (London: Routledge).

Batt, J. R. & Wolczuk, K. (1999) The political context: Building new states, in: P. Hare, J. Batt & S. Estrin (Eds) *Reconstituting the Market: The Political Economy of Microeconomic Transformation*, pp. 33–48 (Amsterdam: Harwood Academic).

Bennett, C. J. (1991) Review article: What is policy convergence and what causes it? *British Journal of Political Science*, 21(2), pp. 215–233.

Böhme, K. (2002) *Nordic Echoes of European Spatial Planning* (Stockholm: Nordregio).

Böhme, K., Richardson, T., Dabinett, G. & Jensen, O. B. (2004) Values in a vacuum? Towards an integrated multilevel analysis of the governance of European space, *European Planning Studies*, 12(8), pp. 1175–1188.

Böhme, K. & Waterhout, B. (2008) The Europeanization of planning, in: A. Faludi (Ed.) *European Spatial Research and Planning*, pp. 225–248 (Cambridge, MA: Lincoln Insitute of Land Policy).

Börzel, T. A. (2002) *States and Regions in the European Union: Institutional Adaptation in Germany and Spain* (Cambridge: Cambridge University Press).

Colomb, C. (2007) The added value of transnational cooperation: Towards a new framework for evaluating learning and policy change, *Planning Practice and Research*, 22(3), pp. 347–372.

Dabinett, G. (2006) Transnational spatial planning—Insights from practices in the European Union, *Urban Policy and Research*, 24(2), pp. 283–290.

Dabinett, G. & Richardson, T. (2005) The Europeanisation of spatial strategy: Shaping regions and spatial justice through governmental ideas, *International Planning Studies*, 10(3/4), pp. 201–218.

van Dijk, T. (2002) Export of planning knowledge needs comparative analysis: The case of applying western land consolidation experience in Central Europe, *European Planning Studies*, 10(7), pp. 911–922.

Downes, R. (1996) Regional policy development in Central and Eastern Europe, in: J. Alden & P. Boland (Eds) *Regional Development Strategies: A European Perspective*, pp. 256–272 (London: Jessica Kingsley and Regional Studies Association).

Dühr, S., Stead, D. & Zonneveld, W. (2007) The Europeanization of spatial planning through territorial cooperation, *Planning Practice and Research*, 22(3), pp. 291–307.

Fürst, D. (2009) Planning cultures en route to a better comprehension of 'planning processes'? in: J. Knieling & F. Othengrafen (Eds) *Planning Cultures in Europe: Decoding Cultural Phenomena in Urban and Regional Planning*, pp. 23–38 (Farnham: Ashgate).

Giannakourou, G. (2005) Transforming spatial planning policy in Mediterranean countries: Europeanization and domestic change, *European Planning Studies*, 13(2), pp. 319–331.

Goetz, K. H. (2006) *Territory, Temporality and Clustered Europeanization*, IHS Political Science Series, 109 (Vienna: Institute for Advanced Studies).

Grabbe, H. (2001) How does Europeanisation affect CEE governance? Conditionality, diffusion and diversity, *Journal of European Public Policy*, 8(4), pp. 1013–1031.

Hamedinger, A., Bartik, H. & Wolffhardt, A. (2008) The impact of EU area-based programmes on local governance: Towards a 'Europeanisation'? *Urban Studies*, 45(13), pp. 2669–2687.

Healey, P. & Williams, R. H. (1993) European planning systems: Diversity and convergence, *Urban Studies*, 30(3/4), pp. 701–720.

Héritier, A., Kerwer, D., Knill, C. & Lehmkuhl, D. (2001) *Differential Europe: The European Union Impact on National Policy-Making* (Lanham: Rowman & Littlefield).

Jaakson, R. (2000) Supra-national spatial planning of the Baltic Sea Region and competing narratives for tourism, *European Planning Studies*, 8(5), pp. 565–579.

Janin Rivolin, U. (2003) Shaping European spatial planning: How Italy's experience can contribute, *Town Planning Review*, 74(1), pp. 51–76.

Janin Rivolin, U. & Faludi, A. (2005) The hidden face of European spatial planning: Innovations in governance, *European Planning Studies*, 13(2), pp. 195–215.

Jauhiainen, J. (2013) New spatial patterns and territorial-administrative structures in the European Union: Reflections on Eastern Europe, *European Planning Studies*, doi: 10.1080/09654313.2013.772732.

Jensen, O. B. & Richardson, T. (2004) *Making European Space. Mobility, Power and Territorial Identity* (London: Routledge).

de Jong, M. & Edelenbos, J. (2007) An insider's look into policy transfer in transnational expert networks, *European Planning Studies*, 15(5), pp. 687–706.

Kule, L. (2013) Urban-rural interactions in Latvian changing policy and practice context, *European Planning Studies*, doi: 10.1080/09654313.2013.772785.

Lähteenmäki-Smith, K., Fuller, S. & Böhme, K. (Eds) (2005) *Integrated multi-level analysis of the governance of European space (IMAGES)*, Nordregio working paper, 2, Nordregio, Stockholm.

Leetmaa, K., Brade, I., Anniste, K. & Nuga, M. (2012) Socialist summer home settlements in post-socialist suburbanisation, *Urban Studies*, 49(1), pp. 3–21.

Maier, K. (1998) Czech planning in transition: Assets and deficiencies, *International Planning Studies*, 3(3), pp. 351–365.

Marshall, A. (2005) Europeanization at the urban level: Local actors, institutions and the dynamics of multi-level interaction, *Journal of European Public Policy*, 12(4), pp. 668–686.

Mason, D. (1995) Attitudes towards the market and political participation in the post-communist states, *Slavic Review*, 54(2), pp. 385–406.

Nedović-Budić, Z. (2001) Adjustment of planning practice to the New Eastern and Central European context, *Journal of the American Planning Association*, 67(1), pp. 38–52.

Nedović-Budić, Z., Tsenkova, S. & Marcuse, P. (2006) The urban mosaic of post-socialist Europe, in: S. Tsenkova & Z. Nedović-Budić (Eds) *The Urban Mosaic of Post-Socialist Europe*, pp. 3–20 (New York: Physica-Verlag).

O'Dwyer, C. (2006) Reforming regional governance in East Central Europe: Europeanization or domestic politics as usual? *East European Politics and Societies*, 20(2), pp. 219–253.

Pallagst, K. (2006) European spatial planning reloaded: Considering EU enlargement in theory and practice, *European Planning Studies*, 14(2), pp. 253–272.

Pedrazzini, L. (2005) Applying the ESDP through INTERREG IIIB: A Southern perspective, *European Planning Studies*, 13(2), pp. 297–317.

Pucher, J. & Buehler, R. (2005) Transport policy in post-communist Europe, in: D. A. Hensher & D. J. Button (Eds) *Handbooks in Transportation*, pp. 725–743 (London: Elsevier).

Raagmaa, G. (2009) Planning theories and development practices: Past dependencies contra new ideology: Impact of planning for sustainable housing development, in: A. Holt-Jensen & E. Pollock (Eds) *Urban Sustainability and Governance: New Challenges in Nordic-Baltic Housing Policies*, pp. 79–99 (New York: Nova Science).

Raagmaa, G., Kalvet, T. & Kasesalu, R. (2013) Europeanisation and de-Europeanisation of Estonian regional policy, *European Planning Studies*, doi: 10.1080/09654313.2013.772754.

Raagmaa, G. & Kroon, K. (2005) The future of collective farms' built social infrastructure: Choosing between central place and network theories, *Geografiska Annaler: Series B, Human Geography*, 87(3), pp. 205–224.

Stanilov, K. (2007) Political reform, economic development, and regional growth in post-socialist Europe, in: K. Stanilov (Ed.) *The Post-Socialist City: Urban Form and Space Transformations in Central and Eastern Europe after Socialism*, pp. 35–52 (Dordrecht: Springer).

Stead, D. (2013) European integration and spatial rescaling in the Baltic region: Soft spaces, soft planning and soft security, *European Planning Studies*, doi: 10.1080/09654313.2013.772731.

Stead, D. (2013) Convergence, divergence, or constancy of spatial planning? Connecting theoretical concepts with empirical evidence from Europe, *Journal of Planning Literature*, 28(1), doi: 10.1177/0885412212471562.

Sykes, O. (2008) The importance of context and comparison in the study of European spatial planning, *European Planning Studies*, 16(4), pp. 537–555.

Tafel-Viia, K., Viia, A., Terk, E. & Lassur, S. (2013) Policy patterns in creative industries: Comparison of European cities, *European Planning Studies*, doi: 10.1080/09654313.2013.772755.

Tammiksaar, E., Pae, T. & Kurs, O. (2013) A continuity of ideas? Salme Ňmmik, Edgar Kant and the development of economic geography in Soviet Estonia, *Geografiska Annaler: Series B, Human Geography*, 95(1), pp. 1–20.

Tewdwr-Jones, M. & Williams, R. H. (2001) *The European Dimension of British Planning* (London: Spon).

UNECE (2000) *ECE Strategy for Sustainable Quality of Life in Human Settlements in the 21st Century*, Report HBP/1999/4/Rev.1, Geneva: United Nations Economic Commission for Europe.

Van Ravesteyn, N. & Evers, D. (2004) *Unseen Europe: A Survey of EU Politics and Its Impacts on Spatial Development in the Netherlands* (The Hague: Netherlands Institute for Spatial Planning).

Waterhout, B. (2007) Episodes of Europeanization of Dutch national spatial planning, *Planning Practice and Research*, 22(3), pp. 309–327.

Waterhout, B. & Stead, D. (2007) Mixed messages: How the ESDP's messages have been applied in INTERREG IIIB programmes, priorities and projects, *Planning, Practice & Research*, 22(3), pp. 395–415.

Zonneveld, W. (2005) The Europeanization of Dutch national spatial planning: An uphill battle, *disP—The Planning Review*, 44(163), pp. 4–15.

European Integration and Spatial Rescaling in the Baltic Region: Soft Spaces, Soft Planning and Soft Security

DOMINIC STEAD

OTB Research Institute for the Built Environment, Delft University of Technology, Delft, The Netherlands

Abstract *Spatial rescaling arguably represents one of the most significant recent changes in planning. Rescaling processes do not merely imply changes in powers across existing layers of decision-making, but also entail new scales of intervention, new actor constellations and new geometries of governance. A wide range of examples of spatial rescaling can be seen across Europe, varying from local through to regional and international. The emergence of "soft spaces"—regions in which strategy is made between or alongside formal institutions and processes—is one of the phenomena associated with contemporary spatial rescaling. These spaces are often overlapping and characterized by fuzzy geographical boundaries. The formation of soft spaces is often articulated in terms of breaking away from the rigidities associated with the practices and expectations of working within existing political or administrative boundaries but can also be viewed as providing a means of bypassing formal procedures and reducing democratic accountability. Focusing on European territorial cooperation and development strategies in the Baltic region, this paper discusses how they are contributing to spatial rescaling in soft spaces and how the strategies can be seen as a form of soft planning and as a means to promote soft security policy (which could be considered as a wider form of foreign policy).*

1. Introduction: European Integration and Spatial Rescaling

> The territoriality of the European state system helped to produce a geographical imagination that privileges the "nation-states" over river basins, vegetation zones, population concentrations, or other possible regionalizations. (Murphy, 2008, p. 9)

European integration is creating new territorial boundaries for various policy fields whereby nation-states are losing their old monopolies on some areas of policy-making. However, this does not mean that powers are simply shifting to the European level:

Europe is not so much suppressing state borders as changing their meaning and impact for different social, economic and political systems (Bartolini, 2005; Keating, 2009). European integration has not only been accompanied by changes in powers across existing layers of decision-making, but also by new scales of intervention, new actor constellations and variable geometries of governance—diversity, variation and even asymmetries in how territories are governed within nation-states (Brenner, 2004; Jessop, 2005; Lidström, 2007). These changes are all part of the general process of spatial rescaling (or territorial rescaling), which McCann defines in terms of

> the process in which policies and politics that formerly took place at one scale are shifted to others in ways that reshape the practices themselves, redefine the scales to and from which they are shifted, and reorganise interactions between scales. (McCann, 2003, p. 162)

According to Keating (2009), numerous examples of spatial rescaling can be found across Europe's continent. Rescaling processes are producing new policy spaces which vary in their configuration according to their functional or political logic. In these new spaces, there may be little coincidence between functional, political and institutional boundaries, and there may be no strict hierarchies of collective action. The result is that these new spaces are often contested, since the level at which issues are managed can, by including certain actors and excluding others, affect policy outcomes (Keating, 2009). The contested nature of these new spaces is reflected in recent geographical studies on the politics of scale, processes of rescaling and impacts on the distribution of power (see, e.g. Herod & Wright, 2002; Sheppard & McMaster, 2004; Keil & Mahon, 2008). These studies illustrate how actors gain or lose influence as a result of authority being reconfigured around new spaces and territories.

The ideal construct of the nation-state with a fixed set of policy boundaries and a perfectly hierarchical structure is being eroded by processes of rescaling and the emergence of new boundaries above and below the national level, as well as transnational spaces cutting across the state system (Keating, 2009). Some of the roles or tasks of the nation-state are being transferred to these new spaces, where different actors, agendas and resources prevail (Keating, 2009). Spatial rescaling is arguably leading to broader and more inclusive processes but is on the other hand contributing to more fragmented and differentiated approaches as different groups participate in different contexts, according to their interests and values (Meadowcroft, 2002). These different groupings of actors with common interests and values do not necessarily correspond with administrative boundaries. Processes of rescaling are by no means leading to uniform changes across different territories: substantial variations in the nature of new territorial spaces are apparent across Europe but, whatever their form, these new policy spaces and territories pose significant challenges for democratic legitimacy and social equity (Keating, 2009; Moss & Newig, 2010). Moreover, new governance arrangements, new scales of interaction and/or new actor constellations resulting from rescaling are not always more participatory or more integrated or better able to respond to complex problems involving different policy sectors (Cohen, 2012). This paper examines the consequences of European territorial cooperation initiatives for spatial rescaling, particularly in relation to the creation of "soft" policy spaces that are based on functional rather than administrative boundaries.

2. Spatial Rescaling and New Approaches to Planning: "Soft Spaces" and Fuzzy Boundaries

> Territorial cohesion policy advocates the idea of soft planning, where new soft planning spaces cross the administrative borders within the EU territory. (Luukkonen & Moilanen, 2012, p. 481)

According to Allmendinger and Haughton (2009), spatial rescaling represents one of the most significant recent changes in planning. The emergence of "soft spaces"—regions in which spatial strategy is being made between or alongside formal institutions and processes—is a phenomenon associated with contemporary processes of spatial rescaling. Haughton and Allmendinger (2007) see these soft spaces are "fluid areas... between formal processes where implementation through bargaining, flexibility, discretion and interpretation dominate" which contrast to "hard spaces" that are "formal visible arenas and processes, often statutory and open to democratic processes and local political influence" (p. 306). Also associated with recent processes of spatial rescaling is the use of "fuzzy boundaries" as a means of breaking away from "the shackles of pre-existing working patterns which might be variously held to be slow, bureaucratic, or not reflecting the real geographies of problems and opportunities" (Allmendinger & Haughton, 2009, p. 619). On the one hand, this trend can be considered to represent a more place-based approach to planning—responding to the specificities of particular places. On the other hand, it can be seen as a form of neo-liberalism—trying to shortcut democratic processes that may be slow or bureaucratic (Haughton *et al.*, 2009).

Waterhout (2010) suggests that many examples of planning in "soft spaces" can already be found across much of Europe, citing French "Projets du Territoire", German "Überregionale Partnerschaften" and Italian "Sistemi Macroregionali Funzionali" as examples at the sub-national scale, and initiatives in the Saar-Lor-Lux (Saarland, Lorraine, Luxembourg), Basel Eurodistrict, Øresund and Vienna-Bratislava-Gyor regions as cross-border examples. In many cases, governments are not the main initiator or leading actor behind the strategies. Instead, they primarily play a role in promoting and coordinating public and private initiatives that are concerned with either fostering or managing spatial development. This form of planning with less state involvement represents a break from traditional government-led planning approaches and an attempt to establish cooperative arrangements and delivery mechanisms for promoting and/or managing spatial development via the public and private sector.[1] The implementation of European strategies for territorial cooperation can also be seen as another scale of planning in "soft spaces" (Metzger & Schmitt, 2012; Faludi, 2012), which is the main focus of this paper.

The emergence of planning in "soft spaces" (which is generally non-statutory and non-binding) does not, however, imply that planning is no longer concerned with "hard spaces" (i.e. mandatory and regulatory planning). Spatial planning is increasingly dealing with both hard and soft spaces. According to Haughton and Allmendinger (2007, p. 307), the softer side of planning is a complement to its harder side by "providing a form of lubrication to the development process, acting outside some of the frictions of formalised processes, engrained expectations, and institutional and professional histories". More generally, it is argued that these new areas of soft spaces often better reflect the geographies of problems or potentials than areas defined by "hard" administrative boundaries.

The distinction between hard and soft spaces is closely related to the two different forms of multilevel governance set out by Hooghe and Marks (2003) and the distinction between Euclidean and relational planning discussed by authors such as Friedmann (1993) and Healey (2006). Planning in hard spaces often closely resembles Euclidean planning or Type I governance as defined by Hooghe and Marks (2003), where decision-making takes place in uniform, general-purpose, nested administrative units. Planning in soft spaces on the other hand more closely resembles relational planning or Type II governance as defined by Hooghe and Marks (2003), where decision-making occurs in flexible, functionally defined, overlapping decision spaces (which may also be more temporary in nature than "hard" spaces). While soft spaces offer a more functional or relational approach to planning, they pose significant problems of accountability and responsibility (Keating, 2009; Faludi, 2012) and may exacerbate problems of sectoral integration (Cohen, 2012).

The fuzziness of borders and the existence of new action spaces in Europe has also been recognized outside the spatial planning and geography literature for some time although this has not generally featured in the planning literature. In the political science literature, for example, Christiansen *et al.* (2000) refer to the existence of fuzzy or permeable borders of the European Union (EU) as a consequence of different EU initiatives and policies (not just limited to spatial planning) which purposely extend beyond external borders to "intermediate spaces" comprising both EU and non-EU territories. These initiatives and policies cover a range of policy issues (e.g. environment, economic and social development, and safety) and can be multilateral or bilateral: some of them provide incentives or inducements for policy changes beyond the EU's borders (e.g. EU assistance and funding opportunities), while others impose penalties or sanctions to stimulate policy change (e.g. regulatory requirements for accession to the EU). In other words, both the manifestation of fuzzy (or fuzzier) borders and the emergence of new policy action spaces are being driven by EU initiatives and policies in the form of "carrots" and "sticks" (incentives and disincentives) to "Europeanize" policy outside the EU.

According to Filtenborg *et al.* (2002, p. 389), the modification of policy boundaries (i.e. the creation of the "intermediate spaces" to which Christiansen *et al.* refer) "can furnish the Union with the possibility to impose a degree of governance beyond its territorial borders". Influencing policy beyond the EU's borders can be seen in terms of global projections (or "export") of European norms, procedures or modes of operation (Clark & Jones, 2008) and/or an attempt to promote "soft security" goals in the so-called intermediate spaces (as defined above).[2] In these "intermediate spaces", where the EU does not have the responsibility or competence for the whole territory, actions and interventions are generally based around cooperative arrangements with external actors. The consequences of these actions and interventions can result in the redrawing (or rescaling) of boundaries defined in terms of geopolitics, institutional/legal systems, transactions (e.g. trade) and/or cultural values or beliefs (Filtenborg *et al.*, 2002). European initiatives can promote "soft security" goals via a number of possible mechanisms, such as bridging political divides (e.g. overcoming historical divisions and/or mitigating the emergence of new divisions), promoting accession processes (e.g. EU or NATO membership), addressing cross-border problems or challenges (e.g. environmental pollution) and facilitating reform processes (e.g. political, economic or military).

3. European Territorial Cooperation as "Soft Planning"

The EU offers the possibility of overcoming some of the territorial rigidities of the modern state system. (Murphy, 2008, p. 16)

Since there are no formal competences for spatial planning at the EU level, European initiatives to promote or manage spatial development frequently rely on "soft processes" of coordination, negotiation and learning (Faludi, 2001, 2008a, 2008b) which are evident in initiatives such as the European Spatial Development Perspective (ESDP) (Benz, 2002; Faludi & Waterhout, 2002), the European territorial cooperation programmes such as the INTERREG Initiative (Colomb, 2007; Waterhout & Stead, 2007; Faludi, 2008b; Stead & Waterhout, 2008) and, more recently, the European macro-regional strategies. These three European spatial planning initiatives are of course very much related: the development of the ESDP influenced the direction and content of INTERREG Initiatives (Waterhout & Stead, 2007) and INTERREG programming has in turn influenced the content and structure of European macro-regional strategies (discussed below).

European territorial cooperation programmes have, in the words of the European Commission (2008) (from where these programmes originated), focused on "soft actions such as studies, experience exchanges, best practice exchanges, joint territorial strategies and seminars" since their inception (p. 1). Although the boundaries of European territorial cooperation spaces (for cross-border, transnational and interregional cooperation) are territorially defined in some senses (e.g. delineated areas of cooperation), the visions and strategies developed under European territorial cooperation programmes often have fuzzier boundaries (Zonneveld, 2005; Dühr, 2006). In addition, new rules under the current European territorial cooperation objective (2007–2013) allow for participation beyond the boundaries of the cooperation areas,[3] which means that territorial cooperation boundaries are by no means sharp or impermeable and that these boundaries have become fuzzier over time with the creation of new programming periods. Moreover, cooperation boundaries have shifted over time—areas of intervention have been expanded across European territory, including the Baltic region where the boundaries of transnational cooperation have undergone changes between the INTERREG II and III programming periods, and again between the INTERREG III and IV periods (Figure 1), and extended the "intermediate spaces" (comprising both EU and non-EU territories) of policy influence or intervention. The redrawing of territorial cooperation boundaries has taken place in most other INTERREG programming areas (see, e.g. Dühr *et al.*, 2007).

The overlapping nature of European territorial cooperation spaces is illustrated by Deas and Lord (2006, p. 1850), who describe a "bewildering array of collaborative initiatives that have emerged in line with the European Commission's efforts to stimulate new interregional, intercity and transnational collaborative initiatives in economic development and spatial planning" (Figure 2). The non-alignment of territorial cooperation boundaries with nation-state borders is in their view a deliberate attempt to promote new institutions and policy initiatives that transcend national borders, to contribute to the "frictionless mobility" of labour and capital across the EU and to promote the international competitiveness of metropolitan regions within the cooperation areas (Deas & Lord, 2006).

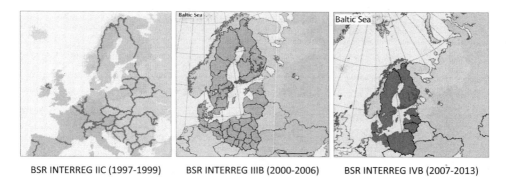

BSR INTERREG IIC (1997-1999)　　BSR INTERREG IIIB (2000-2006)　　BSR INTERREG IVB (2007-2013)

Figure 1. The widening territorial coverage of the Baltic Sea Programme under the INTERREG II, III and IV Initiatives.
Source: CSD (1999) and European Commission (2011a, 2012).

4. European Macro-regions as "Soft Spaces"

> Today's complex challenges do not respect rigid boundaries; we need new types of cooperation to tackle pressing issues such as intensifying global competition, shifting population dynamics and climate change. (European Commissioner Paweł Samecki—European Commission, 2009b)

Like the other examples of "soft spaces" (outlined above), the emergence of European macro-regions is relatively new but have been considered and discussed for more than a decade. The ideas and foundations of these strategies can often be traced back to European territorial cooperation programmes and related activities (Dubois *et al.*, 2009). Two examples of European macro-regional strategies exist to date: the EU Strategy for the Baltic Sea Region (launched in 2009) and the EU Strategy for the Danube Region (launched in 2011). In addition, strategies for the Mediterranean, Alpine and North Sea regions are under various stages of discussion/consideration.

These macro-regional strategies have been formulated in an attempt to achieve a more efficient resource use and greater policy coordination and integration, primarily between European, national and sub-national policy, but without recourse to new funds or instruments. Their primary role is to create dialogue and action plans for areas with common features (e.g. geographical, cultural or economic), either in terms of common challenges or opportunities. The emphasis of the process is on consensus across administrations and pragmatism (common action). The development of these macro-regional strategies forms part of a wider reflection on the future of European regional policy. In 2009, discussions had already begun to consider whether a specific EU budget line could be allocated to macro-regions in the programming period beginning in 2014 (Dubois *et al.*, 2009).

Despite their recent emergence, the rationale of European macro-regional strategies fits with long-standing European policies and activities in the area of spatial planning. Dubois *et al.* (2009, p. 21), for example, suggest that European macro-regional strategies do not represent a new cooperation or governance paradigm in Europe but instead represent "continuity with, and a strengthening of, previous [European] initiatives" and are consistent with a range of European policy statements over the last decade or so, such as the 2001

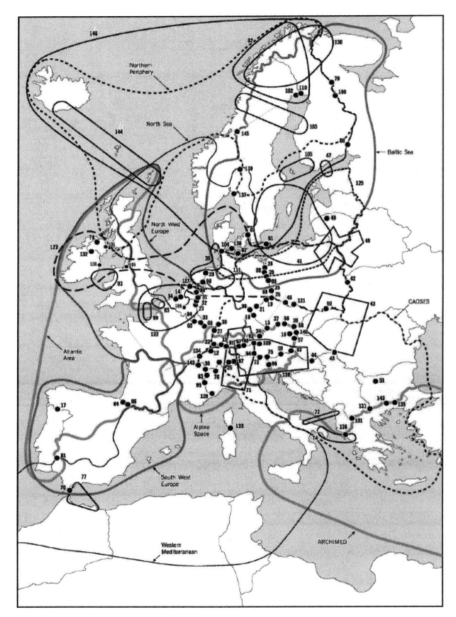

Figure 2. The overlapping nature of European territorial cooperation activities.
Source: Deas & Lord (2006). Copyright © 2006. Reprinted with the permission of SAGE.

White Paper on European Governance (Commission of the European Communities, 2001), the 2005 Territorial State and Perspectives of the European Union document (Luxembourg Ministry of the Interior and Spatial Planning, 2005) and the 2008 European Green Paper on Territorial Cohesion (Commission of the European Communities, 2008). The fuzzy nature of the boundaries of macro-regions is depicted in Figure 3 and highlighted

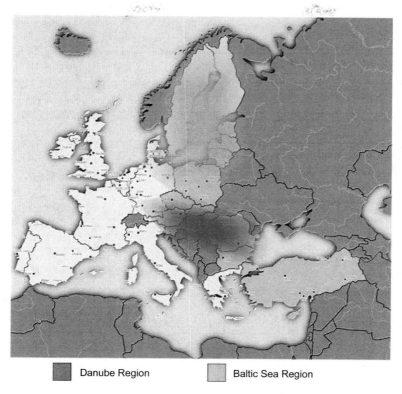

Figure 3. The coverage of the two EU macro-regional strategies.
Source: Austrian Conference on Spatial Planning (2012). Reproduced with the kind permission of Kathrin Gruber, Department of Geography and Regional Research, University of Vienna, Austria.

by a Commission discussion paper, which concludes that "regions should be defined so as to maximise the efficacy of the strategy ..., [which] ... may well mean flexible, even vague, definitions of the boundaries" (European Commission, 2009a, p. 8). An emphasis on pragmatism and "getting things done" is quite apparent here. Soft spaces in the macro-regional strategies are generally justified in terms of resource efficiency and policy coordination and integration, whereas their use as mechanisms for promoting Europeanization, both inside and outside the EU's external borders, is made much less explicit.

Some academic literature on macro-regional strategies predates the policy statements outlined above. Christiansen (1997, p. 263), for example, refers to meso-regions (macro-regions in all but name) as "intermediate structures between the state- and the European level", and Cappellin (1998) refers to "macro-regions" in terms of a set of overlapping transnational regions such as the Baltic and Mediterranean Basin, and the Alpine, Atlantic Arc and "Mitteleuropa" regions. Clearly, many of these examples closely correspond to the INTERREG IIC and IIB programming areas in operation or under development at that time. Cappellin's view is that these regions represent a political space or forum for joint political action and indicate a trend whereby borders are being replaced by spaces that are not entirely inside the EU (corresponding to the idea of "intermediate spaces" presented above).

In the case of the macro-regional strategy for the Baltic Sea Region, eight EU member states (Sweden, Denmark, Estonia, Finland, Germany, Latvia, Lithuania and Poland) and two non-member states (Norway and the Russian Federation) were involved in the strategy's development. Joint challenges were developed under the four headings of environmental sustainability, regional prosperity, accessibility and attractiveness, and safety and security. Alongside the strategy, a detailed action plan was developed, comprising 76 actions and various flagship projects across the 4 thematic "pillars" (plus another 10 horizontal actions). While the macro-regional strategy covered the whole region around the Baltic Sea, the spatial coverage of individual actions and projects varied significantly. According to the strategy, the coverage "depends on the topic" (European Commission, 2009a, p. 5) and the responsibility for coordinating each of the actions and projects was spread widely between different member states. As a result, different constellations of actors are involved in each of the actions and projects, creating a complex, spatially overlapping patchwork of policy spaces, actors and actions. Evidence to date suggests that the level of ambition across national actors, both political and administrative, has been uneven (Fritsch, 2011). There are also considerable differences in the working arrangements for the 15 priority areas, depending on existing networks and the maturity of cooperation arrangements on which implementation can be drawn (European Commission, 2011b).

It is little coincidence that the content and geographical space covered by the macro-regional strategy for the Baltic Sea Region shares some similar features with the Baltic Sea INTERREG IVC programme. After all, the INTERREG IVC programme and the macro-regional strategy for the Baltic Sea Region are both European initiatives originating from the same European Directorate (DG-REGIO), both have involved a number of the same actors in their development and implementation (especially representatives of European and national governments) and both are seen by the European Commission as important instruments for promoting the same goal of territorial cohesion (see, e.g. Piskorz, 2009). In addition, national (and regional) governments, as well as the European Commission, have been closely involved in both the INTERREG IVC programme and the macro-regional strategy for the Baltic Sea Region with differing degrees of commitment (Fritsch, 2011). The Baltic States were, for example, less involved in the development of the strategy than countries such as Germany, Sweden, Denmark and Finland (Fritsch, 2011).

The EU Strategy for the Baltic Sea Region not only includes "old" and "new" EU member states, it also extends beyond existing EU territory, forming an "intermediate space" that offers the potential to project or export European norms, procedures or modes of operation (to which Clark & Jones, 2008, refer). The importance of "exporting" the ideas and initiatives contained in the macro-regional strategies beyond EU borders (and extending the EU's influence beyond its external borders and promoting soft security) is highlighted in a recent commentary by Friis (2012), the Danish national contact person for the EU Strategy for the Baltic Sea Region, who states that "it is crucial to ensure the participation and involvement of third countries, in particular Russia, with regard to the work linked to the EUSBSR" as "many of the challenges in the Baltic Sea Region are directly related to Russia" (p. 13). To date, however, Russia has only been involved to a rather limited extent in the development of the strategy and in its implementation, either through specific projects or via existing regional frameworks such as the Northern Dimension.

5. Discussion and Conclusions

While clearly not representing a fundamental reorganization of state territoriality, the policy spaces occupied by European territorial cooperation initiatives such as the INTERREG programmes and the macro-regional strategies indicate some spatial rescaling. More generally, European cohesion policy has led to various governance shifts within nation-states in order to administer regional funding from Europe (see, e.g. Hooghe & Marks, 1996). This has in some cases led to the weakening or fragmentation of national powers and capacity for policy coordination. Because of their cooperative nature, it cannot realistically be expected that European macro-regional strategies are replacing other scales of intervention. After all, the actions set out in the macro-regional strategies are based on non-statutory cooperation, and member states are pretty much free to choose whether or not to participate in different actions. Nevertheless, these strategies are supplementing and perhaps even supplanting other existing policy spaces (Metzger & Schmitt, 2012). As Luukkonen and Moilanen (2012, p. 497) recognize, regional actors often feel obliged to operate in these new policy spaces in order to extend their networks, secure resources and "stay on the map of European spatial policies" but are on the other hand "still mostly bound to the territorial realities of the nationally determined administrative units and their functions". The appeal of the actions and soft spaces in macro-regional strategies is undoubtedly related to the ability to suit a range of political agendas across different EU member states, whether policy integration and synergy, austerity (i.e. no additional funding), economic growth, private-sector involvement or development assistance (i.e. providing support for poorer neighbours).

The space occupied by the EU Strategy for the Baltic Sea Region is closely (but not always exactly) related to other territorial cooperation areas in the region that have existed for some time, albeit in different forms and with shifting (and fuzzy) boundaries. In terms of the "texture" of territorial cooperation in the Baltic region over the past two decades (i.e. since the end of the Cold War), there has been a remarkable shift from primarily intergovernmental to new forms of transnational cooperation (Gänzle, 2011) and new soft forms of planning (Luukkonen & Moilanen, 2012). The macro-regional strategy for the Baltic Sea Region provides new arenas for European, national and sub-national actors to shape policy and action. However, this does not necessarily imply that these new arenas (and new constellations of actors) have had significant impacts on policy development to date—there is a substantial amount of resistance to policy change due to system inertia (e.g. path dependence). The creation of these new policy spaces can be interpreted as a deliberate approach to extend EU policy influence (into "intermediate spaces") as well as identifying "regionalized" policy agendas (i.e. at a lower level than the EU) and implementing practical projects between EU member states. Similarly, the macro-regional strategy for the Danube region extends well beyond EU territory. So too does the proposed Adriatic–Ionian macro-regional strategy.

Recent European initiatives for territorial cooperation in the Baltic, such as the INTERREG programmes, the Northern Dimension initiative and the EU Strategy for the Baltic Sea Region, can be considered as mechanisms for delivering "soft security" to the region (i.e. reducing serious cross-border disparities, conflicts or tensions that could affect the stability of the region or even the EU), particularly to the north-east of the Baltic States (i.e. Russia). After all, developments immediately outside the EU are highly important for both the Baltic region, especially in the Kaliningrad and

St. Petersburg regions. The former is surrounded by EU territory and has the potential to "skew the development of the Baltic region" (European Commission, undated, p. 8). The latter forms the largest metropolitan conurbation in the Baltic Sea macro-region (it has a similarly sized population to the Baltic States as a whole) and is one of the economically most advanced regions in the Russian Federation (Razumeyko, 2011), giving it in an important potential economic position for the Baltic region as a whole. To date, however, Russia has not played a very active role in the development and implementation of the macro-regional strategy for the Baltic and has not taken on the responsibility for coordinating any of the actions. In the Danube region, on the other hand, various non-EU countries have been actively involved in the development of the strategy and have taken on similar levels of responsibility as EU member states in the implementation of the strategy. Time will tell whether Russia chooses to play a fuller part in future European territorial cooperation initiatives for the Baltic region, and whether this will lead to the Europeanization of Russian territory. While some regions in north-west Russia are quite open to cooperation with their Baltic neighbours (e.g. the Novgorod and Pskov regions, where trade relations with the Baltic States have existed for centuries), the national view from Moscow on cooperation with the Baltic States is currently rather different.

Acknowledgements

The author is grateful to two reviewers for their comments on an earlier (less detailed) version of this paper and also to Garri Raagmaa for his detailed suggestions for improving the manuscript. This paper partly builds on a Policy and Planning Brief that was published in *Planning Theory and Practice* in 2011 (Stead, 2011).

Notes

1. An underlying rationale for many of these new cooperative arrangements is to provide development with lower direct costs for the state. The extent to which planning with less state involvement is really new is debateable. More than two decades ago, Brindley *et al.* (1989) were discussing shifts in planning styles to more market-led approaches with less state involvement.
2. Smith and Timmins (2000) contend that achieving security in Europe is not just related to "hard security" measures such as military and defence policy but also related to "soft security" measures that tackle serious cross-border disparities, conflicts or tensions that could affect the stability of the region or even the Union (e.g. large socio-economic disparities, environmental threats, political disputes and ethnic rivalries).
3. Article 21–2 of European Regional Development Fund (ERDF) Regulation 1080/2006 allows for up to 20% of expenditure to be incurred by partners located in the EU but outside the programme cooperation areas, and up to 10% of expenditure to be incurred by partners located outside the EU.

References

Allmendinger, P. & Haughton, G. (2009) Soft spaces, fuzzy boundaries and metagovernance: The new spatial planning in the Thames Gateway, *Environment and Planning A*, 41(3), pp. 617–633.
Austrian Conference on Spatial Planning/Österreichische Raumordnungskonferenz (ÖROK) (2012) *Makroregionale Strategien der EU* [EU macro-regional strategies]. Available at www.oerok.gv.at/?id=846 (accessed 20 November 2012).
Bartolini, S. (2005) *Restructuring Europe* (Oxford: Oxford University Press).
Benz, A. (2002) How to reduce the Burden for spatial coordination, in: A. Faludi (Ed.) *European Spatial Planning, Lessons for North America*, pp. 119–135 (Boston, MA: The Lincoln Institute for Land Policy).

Brenner, N. (2004) *News State Spaces: Urban Governance and the Rescaling of Statehood* (Oxford: University Press).
Brindley, T., Rydin, Y. & Stoker, G. (1989) *Remaking Planning: The Politics of Urban Change in the Thatcher Years* (London: Unwin Hyman).
Cappellin, R. (1998) Transborder co-operation along the EU's external borders and the turnabout of regional development policies: A Mediterranean perspective, in: L. Hedegaard, B. Lindström, P. Joenniemi, A. Östhol, K. Peschel & C. E. Stalvant (Eds) *The NEBI Yearbook 1998. North European and Baltic Sea Integration*, pp. 323–335 (Berlin: Springer Verlag).
Christiansen, T. (1997) A European meso-region? European perspectives on the Baltic Sea Region, in: P. Joenniemi (Ed.) *Neo-nationalism or Regionality. The Restructuring of Political Space Around the Baltic Rim*, pp. 254–292 (Stockholm: NordREFO).
Christiansen, T., Petito, F. & Tonra, B. (2000) Fuzzy politics around fuzzy borders: The European Union's "Near abroad", *Cooperation and Conflict*, 35(4), pp. 389–415.
Clark, J. & Jones, A. (2008) The spatialities of Europeanisation: Territory, government and power on "Europe", *Transactions of the Institute of British Geographers*, 33(3), pp. 300–318.
Cohen, A. (2012) Rescaling environmental governance: Watersheds as boundary objects at the intersection of science, neoliberalism, and participation, *Environment and Planning A*, 44(9), pp. 2207–2224.
Colomb, C. (2007) The added value of transnational cooperation: Towards a new framework for evaluating learning and policy change, *Planning Practice and Research*, 22(3), pp. 347–372.
Commission of the European Communities (CEC) (2001) *European Governance. A White Paper. COM(2001)428 Final* (Luxembourg: Office for Official Publications of the European Communities).
Commission of the European Communities (CEC) (2008) *Green Paper on Territorial Cohesion. Turning Territorial Diversity into Strength. COM(2008)616 Final* (Luxembourg: Office for Official Publications of the European Communities).
Committee on Spatial Development (CSD) (1999) *European Spatial Development Perspective. Towards Balanced and Sustainable Development of the Territory of the EU* (Luxembourg: Office for Official Publications of the European Community).
Deas, I. & Lord, A. (2006) From a new regionalism to an unusual regionalism? The emergence of non-standard regional spaces and lessons for the territorial reorganisation of the state, *Urban Studies*, 43(10), pp. 1847–1877.
Dubois, A., Hedin, S., Schmitt, P. & Sterling, J. (2009) *EU macro-regions and macro-regional strategies—a scoping study*. Nordregio Working Paper 2009/4, Stockholm: Nordregio.
Dühr, S. (2006) *The Visual Language of Spatial Planning. Exploring Cartographic Representations for Spatial Planning in Europe* (London: Routledge).
Dühr, S., Stead, D. & Zonneveld, W. (2007) The Europeanization of spatial planning through territorial cooperation. Introduction to the Special Issue, *Planning Practice and Research*, 22(3), pp. 291–307.
European Commission (2008) *Transnational Territorial Cooperation: Belgium—Germany—Ireland—France—Luxembourg—the Netherlands—United Kingdom—Switzerland*. European Commission MEMO/08/76, 7 February, DG-REGIO, Brussels: European Commission. Available at www.europa.eu/rapid/pressReleases Action.do?reference=MEMO/08/76 (accessed 20 November 2012).
European Commission (2009a) Macro-regional strategies in the EU. A Discussion Paper presented by Commissioner Pawel Samecki, 16 September. DG Regional Policy European Commission, Brussels. Available at www.ec.europa.eu/regional_policy/archive/cooperation/baltic/press_en.htm (accessed 20 November 2012).
European Commission (2009b) *Commissioner Samecki Addresses Major Conference on Cohesion Policy and Territorial Development in Kiruna, Sweden (10–11 December)*. European Commission Press Release IP/09/1894, 16 September, DG-REGIO, Brussels: European Commission. Available at www.europa.eu/rapid/pressReleasesAction.do?reference=IP/09/1894 (accessed 20 November 2012).
European Commission (2011a) *INTERREG IIIB: Transnational Cooperation*. Available at www.ec.europa.eu/regional_policy/archive/interreg3/abc/voletb_en.htm (accessed 20 November 2012).
European Commission (2011b) *Report from the Commission to the European Parliament, the Council, the European Economic and Social Committee and the Committee of the Regions on the Implementation of the EU Strategy for the Baltic Sea Region (EUSBSR). COM(2011) 381 Final*. Brussels: European Commission. Available at www.ec.europa.eu/regional_policy/cooperate/baltic/documents_en.cfm (accessed 20 November 2012).
European Commission (2012) *Cohesion Policy 2007–2013: Transnational programmes under the European Territorial Cooperation Objective*. Available at www.ec.europa.eu/regional_policy/atlas2007/transnational/index_en.htm (accessed 20 November 2012).

European Commission (undated) *Country Strategy Paper 2007–2013. Russian Federation* (Brussels: DG-RELEX, European Commission). Available at www.ec.europa.eu/external_relations/russia/docs (accessed 20 November 2012).

Faludi, A. (2001) The performance of spatial planning, in: A. Koresawa & J. Konvitz (Eds) *Towards a New Role for Spatial Planning*, pp. 105–132 (Paris: OECD).

Faludi, A. (2008a) European territorial cooperation and learning. Reflections by the guest editor on the wider implications, *disP—The Planning Review*, 172(1), pp. 3–8.

Faludi, A. (2008b) The learning machine: European integration in the planning mirror, *Environment and Planning A*, 40(6), pp. 1470–1484.

Faludi, A. (2012) Multi-level (territorial) governance: Three criticisms, *Planning Theory and Practice*, 13(2), pp. 197–211.

Faludi, A. & Waterhout, B. (2002) *The Making of the European Spatial Development Perspective* (London: Routledge).

Filtenborg, M. S., Gänzle, S. & Johansson, E. (2002) An alternative theoretical approach to EU foreign policy: "Network governance" and the case of the northern dimension initiative, *Cooperation and Conflict*, 37(4), pp. 387–407.

Friedmann, J. (1993) Toward a non-Euclidian mode of planning, *Journal of the American Planning Association*, 59(4), pp. 482–485.

Friis, J. (2012) Danish Presidency of the Council: The European priorities, *Newsletter INTERACT*, winter 2011/2012, pp. 12–13. Available at www.interact-eu.net/interact_newsletter/250

Fritsch, M. (2011) Interfaces of European Union internal and external territorial governance: The Baltic Sea Region, in: N. Adams, G. Cotella & R. Nunes (Eds) *Territorial Development, Cohesion and Spatial Planning. Building on EU Enlargement*, pp. 382–401 (London: Routledge).

Gänzle, S. (2011) Introduction: Transnational governance and policy-making in the Baltic Sea Region, *Journal of Baltic Studies*, 42(1), pp. 1–7.

Haughton, G. & Allmendinger, P. (2007) Soft spaces in planning, *Town and Country Planning*, 76(9), pp. 306–308.

Haughton, G., Allmendinger, P., Counsell, D. & Vigar, G. (2009) *The New Spatial Planning: Territorial Management with Soft Spaces and Fuzzy Boundaries* (London: Routledge).

Healey, P. (2006) Relational complexity and the imaginative power of strategic spatial planning, *European Planning Studies*, 14(4), pp. 525–546.

Herod, A. & Wright, M. (Eds) (2002) *Geographies of Power: Placing Scale* (Oxford: Oxford University Press).

Hooghe, L. & Marks, G. (1996) "Europe with the regions": Channels of regional representation in the European Union, *Publius—The Journal of Federalism*, 26(1), pp. 73–92.

Hooghe, L. & Marks, G. (2003) Unraveling the central state, but how? Types of multi-level governance, *American Political Science Review*, 97(2), pp. 233–243.

Jessop, B. (2005) Multi-level governance and multi-level meta-governance, in: F. Kratochwil & E. Mansfield (Eds) *International Organisation and Global Governance: A Reader*, pp. 355–367 (London: Pearson Longman).

Keating, M. (2009) Rescaling Europe, *Perspectives on European Politics and Society*, 10(1), pp. 34–50.

Keil, R. & Mahon, R. (Eds) (2008) *Leviathan Undone? The Political Economy of Scale* (Vancouver: University of British Columbia Press).

Lidström, A. (2007) Territorial governance in transition, *Regional & Federal Studies*, 17(4), pp. 499–508.

Luxembourg Ministry of the Interior and Spatial Planning (2005) *Scoping Document and Summary of Political Messages for an Assessment of the Territorial State and Perspectives of the European Union: Towards a Stronger European Territorial Cohesion in the Light of the Lisbon and Gothenburg Ambitions* (Luxembourg: Ministry of the Interior and Spatial Planning). Available at www.eu-territorial-agenda.eu/PresidencyConclusions/Min%20DOC%201_finlux505.pdf (accessed 20 November 2012).

Luukkonen, J. & Moilanen, H. (2012) Territoriality in the strategies and practices of the territorial cohesion policy of the European Union: Territorial challenges in implementing "soft planning". *European Planning Studies*, 20(3), pp. 481–500.

McCann, E. (2003) Framing space and time in the city: Urban policy and the politics of spatial and temporal scale, *Journal of Urban Affairs*, 25(2), pp. 159–178.

Meadowcroft, J. (2002) Politics and scale: Some implications for environmental governance, *Landscape and Urban Planning*, 61(2/4), pp. 169–179.

Metzger, J. & Schmitt, P. (2012) When soft spaces harden: The EU strategy for the Baltic Sea Region, *Environment and Planning A*, 44(2), pp. 263–280.

Moss, T. & Newig, J. (2010) Multilevel water governance and problems of scale: Setting the stage for a broader debate, *Environmental Management*, 46(1), pp. 1–6.

Murphy, A. B. (2008) Rethinking multi-level governance in a changing European Union: Why metageography and territoriality matter, *GeoJournal*, 72(1/2), pp. 7–18.

Piskorz, W. (2009) *What is the policy context, why is territorial cooperation important for territorial cohesion? The view from the European Commission*. Introductory statement at the Territorial Cooperation and Territorial Cohesion Seminar, Brussels, 25 September. Available at www.ec.europa.eu/regional_policy/archive/conferences/territorial/25092009/programme_en.cfm (accessed 20 November 2012).

Razumeyko, N. (2011) Strategic planning practices in North-west Russia: European influences, challenges and future perspectives, in: N. Adams, G. Cotella & R. Nunes (Eds) *Territorial Development, Cohesion and Spatial Planning. Building on EU Enlargement*, pp. 402–421 (London: Routledge).

Sheppard, E. & McMaster, R. B. (Eds) (2004) *Scale and Geographic Inquiry. Nature, Society, and Method* (Oxford: Oxford University Press).

Smith, M. A. & Timmins, G. (2000) The EU, NATO, and the extension of institutional order in Europe, *World Affairs*, 163(2), pp. 80–89.

Stead, D. (2011) Policy & planning brief. European macro-regional strategies: Indications of spatial rescaling? *Planning Theory and Practice*, 12(1), pp. 163–167.

Stead, D. & Waterhout, B. (2008) Learning from the application of the ESDP: Influences on European territorial governance, *disP—The Planning Review*, 172(1), pp. 21–34.

Waterhout, B. (2010) Soft spaces and governance: The transformation of planning. Paper presented at the 24th AESOP Annual Conference, Helsinki, 7–10 July.

Waterhout, B. & Stead, D. (2007) Mixed messages: How the ESDP's concepts have been applied in INTERREG IIIB programmes, priorities and projects, *Planning Practice and Research*, 22(3), pp. 395–415.

Zonneveld, W. (2005) Expansive spatial planning: The new European transnational spatial visions, *European Planning Studies*, 13(1), pp. 137–155.

New Spatial Patterns and Territorial–Administrative Structures in the European Union: Reflections on Eastern Europe

JUSSI SAKARI JAUHIAINEN*,**

*Department of Geography and Geology, University of Turku, Turku, Finland, **Institute of Ecology and Earth Sciences, University of Tartu, Tartu, Estonia

ABSTRACT *Spatial patterns and territorial–administrative structures in Eastern Europe are a mix of historical–territorial path-dependencies influenced by the current path-creating policies. Since the early 2000s, the European Union (EU) policies, practices and challenges have concerned also Eastern Europe. This article discusses spatial patterns and territorial–administrative structures in theory, illustrates their practices and presents scenarios for their future in the EU contexts. The Europeanization of spatial policy and planning and the territorial–administrative structure harmonization are the key current trends. The transposition and implementation of the EU spatial policy mechanisms and practices in Eastern Europe are influenced by contextual path-dependent legacies and the uncertain long-term future of the EU. Conditionality as governmentality and relational regions open new perspectives to territorial dynamics in the EU and Eastern Europe.*

1. Introduction

Europe has been integrating politically and economically for the past 60 years. In the European Union (EU), this process has resulted in economic convergence between the Member States fostered by economic and social cohesion policies and more recently by territorial cohesion policies. However, divergence between regions has increased. The GDP *per capita* and employment differences between the metropolitan areas and the less-favoured regions are growing (Puga, 2002). Economic activities and growth concentrate highly in and around the capital cities (CEC, 2006). There has been a faster income conditional convergence in relative income levels in the regions supported by the EU Cohesion Fund, at least before the EU eastern enlargement (Ramajo *et al.*, 2008). In the Central Eastern

Europe (CEE), in the transition years before the EU accession, regional inequality decreased between countries but increased within countries. The fastest growth took place in the capital cities and in areas close to the EU15 border (Ezcurra *et al.*, 2007). Since the early 2000s, the EU policies, practices and challenges regarding cohesion have concerned also Eastern Europe.

This article discusses the theory and practice of spatial patterns and territorial–administrative structures, their changes and future in the EU and in Eastern Europe. The first issue is the viewpoint of theory and practice. Spatial patterns and territorial–administrative structures in Eastern Europe are a mix of historical–territorial path-dependencies influenced by the current policies. Since the fundamental political changes in the early 1990s, regions have been on the political and developmental agenda in Eastern Europe. Behind are broader issues of economic globalization, partnerships between supranational, national and regional authorities, efficiency reforms of neoliberalizing state governments and ethno-political initiatives from regions and localities. The traditional administrative bounded regions are facing alternatives such as networked regions and fluid regions. The fluid regions challenge governance based on hierarchically nested territorial entities (Jauhiainen & Moilanen, 2011). Spatial and territorial modes of governing need to be addressed.

The second issue discusses the role of the EU in the spatial patterns and territorial–administrative structures in Eastern Europe. Formally, spatial planning and territorial management are not a field of EU activity. In this article, the EU-related conditionality offers a contextualized interpretation for contemporary trends in Eastern Europe. One aspect is the Europeanization of planning (see Hughes *et al.*, 2004; Böhme & Waterhout, 2008; Dühr *et al.*, 2010, pp. 159–176, 359–373). This framework consists of the emergence of planning for Europe; the influence of planning for Europe on planning in Europe and on EU policies; and the influence of EU sectoral policies and European integration on planning in Europe. "Planning for Europe" refers to the idea of spatial planning at the broad European scale, fostered through spatial policies and informal and interregional cooperation. "Planning in Europe" refers to the spatial planning systems, policies and practices in the EU Member States at the national and regional levels (Böhme & Waterhout, 2008, pp. 227–228).

In the article, the interest is in how planning for Europe connects to Eastern Europe through the Europeanization of spatial planning. Attempts to govern spatial development in Europe have been debated since the 1980s through the European Spatial Development Perspective (ESDP) up to the Territorial Agenda (CEC, 1999, 2008). Such policies signify an aim towards spatial order in the EU. The Europeanization of spatial planning has been approached as a process of governance, institutional transformation, a policy transfer and lesson-drawing, and discourse that generates meanings, material practices and power–legitimacy relations through the common participation and interaction of national planning communities in the EU-based policies (Giannakourou, 2012, p. 118). The current EU context signifies an increasing Europeanization and harmonization of spatial policies under the broader realm of competitiveness in the global economy and the related EU instruments. In this article, Europeanization is addressed from the governmentality perspective, in which security, territory and population are connected through spatial policy and planning to the economic and political organization of the state (Foucault, 2004) using persuasive and/or coercive strategies and practices.

The third issue regards the future of spatial patterns and their administrative organization in Eastern Europe. Theories suggest that agglomeration benefits are necessary for the economic growth in the EU. Farole *et al.* (2010, p. 10) claim that if Europe wants to remain competitive in the more integrated world and an innovative first mover in the global economy, agglomerations may be the geographical underpinning for that. Successful regions are competitive metropolitan areas. This fosters the spatial concentration of economic growth in Eastern Europe. Despite this, territorial diversity and specificity and cooperation between the European regions are strongly emphasized. The current EU spatial policy on polycentrism suggests that economic growth must take place in the core agglomerations but also in connection to the remaining EU territory (CEC, 2008). Spatial patterns change slowly; therefore, one should look decades ahead for path-dependent, resilient and path creation trajectories in Eastern Europe. The futures studies methods were applied to trace weak signals and megatrends for these three development scenarios.

2. Emergence of Spatial Patterns, Territorial–Administrative Structures and Regions

Spatial patterns and territorial–administrative structures are interrelated, conditioned and made by social and natural environment. Spatial pattern refers to a geographically repetitive, perceived phenomenon on the Earth's surface. The physical unbuilt environment facilitates and frictions the clustering of people and economic activities in various ways. Spatial policy and planning influence patterns of spatial development. Spatial policy indicates here the broader values, visions and strategies for development in and across regions and places. It is manifested through concrete development programmes and projects but it has also discursive dimensions. Spatial planning refers to an ensemble of territorial governing arrangements to shape patterns of spatial development and their material outcomes in particular places. The result of this complex economic and political development is a territorial–administrative structure that concretizes in the formation of regions.

Human-made spatial patterns are rather regular as specific locations of activities instead of randomly located human activities over space. The activity points and clusters are connected to each other, forming larger areas and spatial systems. The arrangement of a spatial pattern into a functional system in Europe—the Europe of regions—has been the dream, task and challenge of geographers and policy-makers for decades (Christaller, 1933; Haggett, 1965; CEC, 1999, 2008; see Dühr *et al.*, 2010, pp. 39–68). The spatial pattern of an administrative structure in the EU context means the organization of the continuously changing territory into regular, internally coherent and intertwined territorial units, regions. According to Nadin and Stead (2008), spatial planning systems are deeply embedded in their socioeconomic, political and cultural contexts. This makes their harmonious achievement more challenging in a supranational context, such as the EU. Moreover, planning systems have a path-dependency and the persistence of institutions and cultures.

Below is developed a framework for the article's analysis on the emergence of regions, the Europeanization of spatial planning and the future of spatial patterns in the EU. Here, spatial governing refers to the systematic organization of territorial–administrative structures and related practices to influence spatial development through policy and planning.

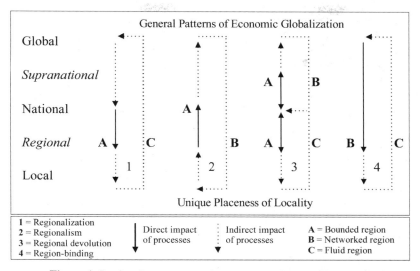

Figure 1. Regional processes and emergence of regions in the EU.

Table 1. Spatial governing in the EU

Region	Governing mode	Spatial tools	Power
Bounded	Government	Plan, rules and norms	Hierarchical
Networked	Governmentality	Strategy, agreement and learning	Networked
Fluid	(Meta)governance	Project, management and brand	Interactive

This government, governmentality and (meta)governance of regions and territories is a broader arena for power relations manifested, constituted and framed in and through discursive and material contexts. As a result, three types of regions—bounded, networked and fluid—are connected to spatial governing and the emergence of regions (Figure 1 and Table 1).

A "bounded region" is the territorial framework for material and social resources and events. The geography of bounded regions is simplified. Their spatial governing is arranged as a series of spatially nested territorial tiers encompassing exponentially increasing populations. Examples are municipality, region (subnational entity), state and macroregion (supranational entity) organized through legal administrative functions and governed hierarchically through representative democracy. An example of this, though not uniformly, is the EU with its Member States and their respective regions, cities and villages. In advanced societies, the spatial governing of bounded regions through formal plans, rules and norms is the most typical mode of organizing regions.

The territorial–administrative reforms of such regions deal mostly with equity aiming to provide as equal as possible access to goods and services. The issues and their solutions are seen to reside inside these fixed bounded regions. The reforms lean on existing spatial patterns and administrative structures. Therefore, the traditional top-down government is often caught in the path-dependent development. Power to conduct such reforms is possessed by selected legal hierarchic public and political stakeholders in these spatially nested tiers. The issue is how these stakeholders come together and have the ultimate say on development. However, spatial governing becomes much more complex when it is recognized that economic, political and environmental issues trespass simultaneously and with different speeds through all above-mentioned bounded regions. Instead of fixed hierarchical spatial tiers, there are continuously changing spatial entities.

The principal reason for the "networked region" is orientation towards economic development and business in the current globalizing economy and competitiveness. The aim is to foster path creation development with private–public agreements and strategies enhancing learning to tackle economic challenges. These regions network diverse actors in various places at varied geographical distances to support the economic competitive advantage of the urban agglomerations, of which these regions are consisted (Jauhiainen & Moilanen, 2011, pp. 732–733). Geography of the networked regions is complex. These interactively connected thematic clusters that form the networked region do not have to locate geographically close to each other and may partly overlap each other. However, the networked region can be conceived as a region due to its spatial embedding of interactive economic processes that fosters the benefits of local clustering.

In these networked regions, the relationships between stakeholders become less hierarchical, more strategic and variable. Therefore, the networked regions are partly constituted outside the formal administrative realms and their public accountability. The complexity of a networked region increases when non-human actors such as material, virtual and symbolic infrastructure, are included following the actor-network theory (Murdoch, 1998; Farías & Bender, 2009). Spatial governing of these regions can be approached through governmentality, a strategic field of interactive power relations within which the modes of development guiding are defined and exercised with persuasion and coercion techniques as a regime of practices (Foucault, 2004). Techniques are used to manage the spatial dimension in an increasingly complex connected world. Territoriality appears as a choice of how to exercise spatial development, and a region becomes an outcome to support the governing strategy. The persuading and coercive aspects of governmentality support networked regions on the basis of global economic competitiveness but these regions could become mobilized also for social and environmental motives. The management and reforms of networked regions are complex because these regions do not obey place-based representative democracy but are strategic business-oriented partnerships that change very rapidly.

Spatial governing becomes even more complex when regions are considered as relational entities. A "fluid region" is an always open process without fixed territorial boundaries. It represents a contingent coming togetherness or assemblage of proximate and distant social, economic and political relationships. The connectivity and its potentiality to exercise nodal power and aligning networks define a fluid region (see Amin, 2004; Jonas, 2012, p. 263). These regions connect people, spaces and times together through changing scalar and other processes and relationships, such as projects and brands holding momentarily together. The concept of relational regions has also received critique. Bureaucrats and planners cannot fit these relational regions into fixed plans.

The governing of relational, changing and seldom institutionalized fluid regions is challenging. No single person, institution or actor possesses power comprehensively. Instead of top-down government or beyond-all governmentality, the notion of (meta)governance is applied. Governance is the capacity of governments together with other public, private and civic societal actors and institutions to tackle the challenges of modern societies (Kooiman & Jentoft, 2009). However, in governance, the relationship and power between these stakeholders is seen as simplistic and linked to strategy-building processes.

The multi-level governance enforces participation and hybrid arrangements of partners at interdependent territorial levels (Jessop, 2009). Functional and territorial stakeholders negotiate the wanted future through strategic spatial planning (Albrechts, 2011). Multi-level governance has been seen as the most feasible solution to a legal consensus over development priorities within a given territory. However, it often bases on bounded regions.

In the governing of fluid regions come together fixed plans for bounded territories, strategies for economic networked regions and changing interests of formal and non-formal stakeholders connected to each other by interactive power mechanisms. Metagovernance deals with multiplies levels, arenas and regimes of spatial politics (Jauhiainen & Moilanen, 2011, pp. 732–734; see Kooiman & Jentoft, 2009, p. 823; also Jessop, 2009, for metagovernance). There the ensemble of territorial governance arrangements shapes patterns of spatial development in particular places (Nadin & Stead, 2008). It transforms into soft management of simultaneously existing spaces, balancing between multiple interests and actors, temporal and scalar dimensions, and diverse vertical sectors of society (Hillier, 2007). This requires participatory methods and stakeholders beyond traditional legally defined development actors (Haughton & Allmendinge, 2010).

To indicate how regions and their governing through spatial tools come together in the EU and Eastern Europe, the above-mentioned regions are discussed through emergence of regions (see Jauhiainen, 2000, pp. 26–27). Figure 1 and Table 1 illustrate how regions change from territorial to relational and vice versa.

"Regionalization" is a top-down approach originated by the state. The administrative structure is modernized to meet the challenges of a post-Keynesian and post-Fordist global economy and the welfare crisis. The state divides space into administrative and planning regions. In Eastern Europe, the complex economic and social situation resulting from globalization and past socialist legacies influence on the administrative structure. National governments decentralize responsibilities to territorially bounded subnational authorities, but not the fiscal autonomy. The decisions that have the most impact on local land, labour and capital are removed and kept at a distance from the regions (Harvey, 2005). Regions and localities are forced to deal with social exclusion and deprivation, from which national welfare systems once protected them. Bounded regions have increasingly characteristics of fluid regions (Figure 1).

In the reform of these territorial–administrative structures, the technical and interjurisdictional efficiency claims prevail. The technical efficiency aims to produce effects of policy, e.g. development at the territorial level with the lowest cost. It exploits economies of scale and internalizes externalities of a policy. The interjurisdictional efficiency aims to limit the number of government levels and overlapping functions. It minimizes the fixed costs of government and negotiation and transaction costs arising from the need to coordinate jurisdictions (Hooghe & Marks, 2009). Some power is shifted to the regional units of state administration, but the subnational authorities do not become economically autonomous and efficient. Such reforms have been implemented in Eastern Europe, for example, in Poland in the 1990s. The failures indicate problems arising from the narrow understanding of power in spatial policy.

"Regionalism" is based on a bottom-up territorial integration. This progressive regionalism is grounded on identity and collective uprising against the culturally and politically oppressing central state. These regional movements form ethnic bounded regions. Some bottom-up rising regions become networked regions connected to similar regions across the national border or elsewhere. These have seldom turned into official political administrative regions. In Eastern Europe, the bottom-up regionalism has been challenging, since the state became strong during the independence re-establishment in the 1980s and 1990s. The strength of regional interest representation and regionalism depends on the societal embeddedness, coalition-building and governmental role of pro-regional actors. At the sub-state level, the political mobilization has been generally weak, as in Bulgaria, and up to moderate strength, as in the Czech Republic (Brusis, 2010, pp. 71–72). In a reactionary top-down regionalism, legal and political decision-making power concentrates into the hands of the few (Morgan, 2007, p. 1248). The collective identity is based on an imagined and affective community. Regional history is selectively appreciated and often invented to promote regionalism and language fetishes space and region (Paasi, 2004). Understanding of regions as competitors in a global race for economic growth has promoted stereotypification, commodification and stratification of categories such as "regional culture" and "regional identity" (Syssner, 2009).

The bottom-up demands aim at autonomy or even separation, and the state has to give up at least allocative efficiency exploiting economies of scale, internalizing externalities of a policy and minimizing heterogeneity of preferences within jurisdictions. It aims to be responsive to heterogeneous preferences (Hooghe & Marks, 2009). Often the wealthier parts of countries are more willing for such separation instead of the subsidized peripheral areas.

"Regional devolution" means the devolution of power and partial redistribution of the national-level tasks to lower and upper territorial units and other non-jurisdictional entities. This has resulted in various modes of multi-level governance in Eastern Europe (Bruszt, 2008). The major reason for this is the implementation of the EU concepts of partnership and subsidiarity (see Gualini, 2008). The decision-making takes place in cooperation between appropriate administrative units at different territorial levels utilizing the interjurisdictional efficiency. The devolution leads into partnerships between bounded regions (i.e. formal administrative regions territories at different spatial scales).

In Eastern Europe, such emergence of regions at subnational level is related to the pre-accession period and the pressure exerted by the EU conditionality regime (Pitschel & Bauer, 2009). The Commission and the pre-accession framework catalyzed processes in which most CEE regions enhanced their political salience; however, not uniformly in all countries. In fact, the EU expectations regarding regions and regional self-government were ambiguous, approximate and inconsistent over time (Brusis, 2010, p. 74). The Commission supported the hierarchical and centralized governance regime in Eastern European Member States through the EU structural policies (Bruszt, 2008). The Commission recentralized the management of the Structural Funds when it realized the persistent weakness of regional administrative capacities and absorption in Eastern Europe (Brusis, 2010, p. 74). Sometimes the growth coalitions break the consistency of bounded regions, particularly in the cross-border areas. Supported by supranational and global processes and actors, bounded regions diverge into networked and fluid regions (Figure 1). The regional contracts in Poland are an example of such networked framework in regional development policy.

"Region-binding" links mostly to economic globalization to organize space and economy more efficiently: the faster the investments are, the faster the surplus is. This fosters economic development and reinvestment of the profits and opens up global networks as tools for the neoliberal agenda (Leitner & Sheppard, 2002). The global production and consumption networks access flexible specialized suppliers and labour in selected lower-cost regions (Henderson et al., 2002). Without the state intervention, the negotiations between global companies needing a location with low-cost labour and a region providing them can be concluded faster. Global companies make the regions to compete between each other for the investments. This process is not linked to any of the efficiency claim discourses.

Such development has been evident and common up to recent years in Eastern Europe, particularly when the state has remained passive in economic development and not implemented any devolution. However, the state can still be significant in the global era. The complexity of economy and politics is seen in the feedback from the regions into the global economic system. The open networked regions have elements of fluid regions leaking out from the top-down constrains of the global economy and transnational companies (Figure 1).

3. Europeanization of Spatial Policies in Eastern Europe

Important trends in territorial governance in Eastern Europe until the EU accession period were, following Lidström (2007), redefining and enhancing the role of the nation state; strengthening the role of lower levels of self-government; accepting increasing diversity within the country; variation and asymmetry between governance within the state; and increasing privatization of the public domain (Maier, 2012, p. 140). Obviously, not all trends went through the newly liberated states at equal speed and strength or had a similar impact on the organization of planning for spatial development.

In the economy, after a short period of low-cost production, there has been a move towards information economy in consumption society in which innovations emerge in austere conditions with low resources. The early years after the EU integration led to substantial narrowing of the manifold economic − material gap between the West and the East. Convergence at the Member State level took place despite that within the new EU Member States also divergence was witnessed. Economically, the capital cities progressed the fastest and, in some cases, so did the regions adjacent to older Member States. According to Farole et al. (2010, p. 5), specific geographical agglomeration continues. The income divergence grows between the largest core economic agglomerations with geographical concentration of innovation and the peripheries lacking agglomerations and potential to generate economies of scale. Accordingly, the progress was the slowest in peripheral agricultural areas and those remote border areas, particularly eastern parts of Estonia, Latvia, Poland, Romania and Bulgaria, near non-EU Member States (see Gorzelak & Smetkowski, 2010).

In Eastern Europe, the spatial pattern is influenced by earlier material realities and more recent policies and planning. These bind values, visions and strategies into territorial governing arrangements for shaping development. In the turn of the 1980s/1990s, many collective social uprisings in Eastern Europe presented novel enthusiastic governing ideas. The regions entered on the agenda following a long period of central planning. Already before the formal EU integration, significant territorial−administrative reforms took place, for example, in Poland, Hungary, the Czech Republic and Slovakia. The regional dimension increased its importance in society. Varied trajectories and outcomes of regional-level reforms in the CEE countries combined domestic institutional legacies, policy approaches of reformers and their adversaries, and the influence of ethnic/historical regionalism. The European Commission's interest in regional self-government created a rationale and an incentive for substantial fiscal and legal autonomy at the regional level (Brusis, 2002). However, the emergence of politically, economically and culturally strong regions has so far mostly failed in Eastern Europe.

For broader spatial, political and economic analysis, it is useful to utilize the Europeanization of spatial planning and link it as conditionality to governmentality. There, spatial policy and planning are softer persuasive and/or harder coercive strategies and practices to bind population (people), territory (regions) and security (development) together (see Foucault, 2004) in the economic and political (re)organization of the Eastern European states. Lagendijk et al. (2009, p. 8) argue that each policy domain, such as the EU spatial policy, develop their own structure of governance, spatiality, territoriality and governmentality. The spatial policies and informal and interregional cooperation influence the spatial planning systems, policies and practices in the EU Member States at the national and regional levels (Böhme & Waterhout, 2008, pp. 227–228). In the current context of the EU facing challenging economic credibility, governmentality signifies the task of competitiveness in the global economy. Therefore, the related EU instruments must accomplish that, including the Europeanization of spatial planning and harmonization of spatial policies.

In practice, the Europeanization of spatial planning is a process with harder (coercive and binding) and softer (persuasive and voluntary) elements. The core "acquis" is formally a legal hard element. Its implementation varies in Eastern Europe, thus bringing in softer elements in the less-binding development realms such as European spatial policy and planning. This harder–softer continuum fits into the definition of the EU governing through Europeanization by Bulmer and Radaelli (2004). There, at the two ends of governing are positive integration (hierarchic compliance with fitting into the EU politics) and negative integration (competitive regulatory economic competition). In between is facilitated coordination as communicative horizontal learning-based policies, such as open method of coordination.

Despite the differences in Eastern Europe, a summarizing trajectory can be provided. Europeanization was formally initiated and applied through softer institutional mechanisms before the achievement of the full membership by the forthcoming Member States. These included, for example, the application of the pre-accession support instruments Phare, ISPA and SAPARD. There were also practices related to the European Agreements and the formal application procedure since the mid-1990s.

Conditionality became an instrument of spatial governing in Eastern Europe, including specific initiatives, programmes and instruments for the planning of the EU territory. A harder approach towards harmonization at the policy level took place through a complete set of abstract rules and principles in advance of decision-making related to spatially oriented programmes and projects in the EU. The continental European legal system influenced the development in Europe, including Eastern Europe, which has followed more intensively the EU context only since the early 2000s. The idea is to make plans, regulate things in advance and draw up and systematize rules (Zweigert & Kötz, 1998). The acquisition of the "acquis" took place in some countries faster and in others slower but nevertheless necessarily during the membership negotiation process in the late 1990s.

IMPACTS OF EUROPEAN TERRITORIAL POLICIES IN THE BALTIC STATES

The short period of integration in the EU, since 2004 and 2007 for Eastern European countries, has shaped spatial patterns and administrative rhythms and structures in Eastern Europe. It has resulted in the obligatory application of the EU conditionality by legal transposition. Europeanization has impacted on the territorial–administrative structures through the harmonization of the roles of national and subnational entities for regional policies (Benz & Eberlein, 1999; Hughes et al., 2004).

Another direct, but a harder, approach towards the Europeanization of spatial planning has been conducted through financial means (Schimmelfennig & Sedelmeier, 2004). Already in the early 1990s, it was noticed that the Europeanization of spatial planning derives from the orientation to competition by cities and regions (Healey & Williams, 1993). However, competition is also enhanced through interregional cooperation for investment, tourism flows and other benefits from the single market. Since the full membership, the EU funding, particularly through the Structural Policy and Cohesion Policy, has become central for the Europeanization of planning. Their impact on national planning has been studied extensively in older Member States (Dühr et al., 2010, pp. 363–369). Conditionality has been implemented through the structural policies and Structural Fund and Cohesion Fund projects. Accordingly, the development strategies have related to the EU programming periods, i.e. 2007–2013 and 2014–2020. An impact of Europeanization is the request for transparency and coherence among national administrations and planning procedures connected to fund management (Maier, 2012, p. 143). The Cohesion Policy-related funding has been important to Eastern Europe. However, this Europeanization process has not been without weaknesses and paradoxes. For Eastern Europe, for example, the necessity to comply with formal requirements related to the Structural Funds has resulted in ad hoc instruments solely for the purpose of EU funding (Maier, 2012, p. 149). As recent examples from Romania, Bulgaria and Greece indicate, the differences in administrative rhythms remain.

One aspect is the devolution of power in the EU spatial policy. The structural policies have proved to link partnership, programming and administrative capacity together. Part of the process is the implementation of subsidiarity, the devolution of decision-making to the appropriate territorial level, often the regional public authorities. However, despite subsidiarity, spatial and related policies have not moved from being under the control of the Member States' central public authorities to being under the control of the Community institutions (Estella, 2002, pp. 1–11). In addition, Gualini (2008, pp. 12–13) argues that subsidiarity increasingly takes into account also the non-jurisdictional arenas in the transnational policy transfer in the EU spatial policy. Therefore, the issue is about how to govern the public–private partnership with broader civic engagement in societal transformation (Faludi, 2010a). Nevertheless, Bachtler and Mendez (2007) claim that, at least in the Cohesion Policy, the strong role of national governments relative to the European Commission in key decisions on the Cohesion Policy implementation has been exaggerated in the literature.

A softer persuasive approach to the harmonization in Europe takes place through broader spatial development visions such as the ESDP and the Territorial Agenda and through policy-oriented spatial development analyses promoted, for example, by the European Observation Network for Territorial Development and Cohesion (ESPON). Economy and politics come together in the European policies for more competitive EU, as the Lisbon Agenda and the Europe 2020 indicate. The current EU spatial policies call for a stronger coordination of spatially relevant policies and actions at all spatial levels to overcome the challenges of density, distance, division and different geographical features (CEC, 2008, pp. 5–9). The Territorial Agenda and the territorial cohesion principles indicate that spatial policy and planning take form as concrete development tools. The Territorial Agenda has added also new forms of cooperation between different types of regions, acknowledging the importance of competitive innovative clusters for economic growth in Europe and including ecological, climatic and cultural objectives (Territorial Agenda of the European Union, 2007).

This softer approach is fostered by the ongoing formation of the supranational territorial cohesion policies with place-based approaches. These are seen as a prerequisite for achieving sustainable economic growth and implementing social and economic cohesion across Europe (Territorial Agenda of the European Union, 2007, p. 3; Barca, 2009). The Europe 2020 strategy emphasizes places and regions to achieve smart, sustainable and inclusive growth. Knowledge and innovation, resource efficiency and environmental issues and their place-based implementation are seen to foster sustainable economic development in the EU (CEC, 2010). However, the EU-level spatial policies are only recommendations. As Waterhout and Stead (2007) indicate, the impact of the ESDP on national and regional planning varies highly between the Member States and regions. It may also be so with the Territorial Agenda. Nevertheless, the European spatial planning agenda with its layer above and/or apart from the national planning systems has started to penetrate and influence them through the national planning policies (Maier, 2012, p. 149).

One important softer aspect in the Europeanization of spatial planning is social learning. Since the 1990s, it has been a learning process regarding working with the European Commission and later in spatial development programmes and projects. Legally, the Member States matter substantially due to the limited direct powers of the Community institutions in spatial policy and spatial planning. Faludi (2010a) states that due to the informal binding of the all-European spatial policies, it is not clear what spatial policy or spatial planning, by definition, exactly means or what it, by implementation, actually enforces. There is room for discussion, negotiation, learning and implementing. There is a feedback into this system, thus opening a cyclical Europeanization process. Giannakourou (2012, p. 125) synthesizes that the EU-level planning discourses and agendas have only been absorbed to a certain extent in the Member States, having a low impact on domestic change. The EU-level planning structures and instruments have had a modest impact and achieved mostly through accommodation. However, the EU-level planning styles and/or territorial governance modes have had high impact by transforming the Member States.

Faludi (2008) remarks that learning is arguably more important than the distant strategic goal of harmonious and balanced development in a truly integrated Europe (see also Janin Rivolin, 2010). The Europeanization of spatial planning through learning becomes a learning machine. To support mutual learning between the partners and increase the weight of the "best arguments" in the policy development process, a technique recently used has been the open method of coordination involving various experts (Faludi, 2010b). Jessop (2009), however, argues that this tool takes place in the shadow of hierarchy and the coordination of the state government interests. As Nadin and Stead (2008) point out, particular socioeconomic, political and cultural contexts are important for the spatial planning systems, and institutions and cultures have path-dependencies. This constrains the scope of mutual learning and harmonization of planning across Europe. In the end, the Europeanization of spatial planning is not a straightforward top-down process from the EU, resulting in exclusively domestic changes but more a cyclical process, influencing also the development of spatial planning in the EU through responses and practices.

4. Three Scenarios for Eastern Europe in the EU

Economy, demography and politics are the cornerstones of the megatrends for the EU. The amount of population and the volume of the economy are simple quantitative indicators related to more complex qualitative challenges, for example, aging. In 2010, there were 85 million people in the EU older than 65 years. By 2030, it is forecast that this number will have increased to 131 million, which will be more than one in four inhabitants in the EU. In the economy, the EU has progressed only slowly towards entrepreneurial knowledge-based economy. The Lisbon Strategy to become the globally leading economy by 2010 failed. According to the new strategies, by 2020 the EU has smarter and greener sustainable economy (CEC, 2010). A particular challenge for the EU is the rise of China in the global economy and the strengthening of the economic ties between China and the US, Africa, Central Asia and other areas outside the EU (see Doucet, 2010).

The future of the EU is seen also in the formation of spatial patterns and regions in the EU. The current EU spatial policies support the division of populations and resources into functional geographical areas connected into a polycentric network. Building on Meijers *et al.* (2007), polycentrism refers to the policies supporting cohesion (spatial balance and equity by diminishing regional disparities); competitiveness (strengthening the competitive position of metropolitan regions); networking (development of urban and urban–rural networks); sprawl regulation (limiting the challenges resulting from overconcentration into cities) and enhancing periphery (preventing out-migration from peripheral and rural areas). However, in the national spatial policies of the EU Member States, polycentrism refers to purposeful flattening of the urban system hierarchy in a territorially balanced way by distributing economically relevant functions. Sometimes polycentric policies are designed also for intra-metropolitan areas. Polycentrism requires connections but the territorial scale matters as well. A recognized polycentric pattern at the national level might disappear when it is observed at another geographical scale (Davoudi, 2003).

To apply the spatial policy of polycentrism to an enlarged EU means necessary networking between Eastern European metropolises and the EU core metropolises as well as the networks between the metropolises and the less-favoured regions. Looking at the early 2010s' situation in the EU, Farole *et al.* (2010, pp. 18–20) have divided the EU into five types of regions according to their strength and position vis-à-vis the global economy. Such a division is a starting point to discuss the future spatial patterns of the enlarged EU.

The strongest areas are the core metro regions. They are few, such as London, Paris, the Randstad, Milan and Berlin. These have been the key agglomerations in Europe for a long time and belong to the economic core of the EU territory. All these regions locate in the territory of the old EU Member States. These are growth-promoting regions with a strong agglomeration force at the technological frontier. This is the core of the polycentric network.

The secondary metro regions with modest growth and agglomeration potential form the next strongest category. They are located at the core of the EU and regions adjacent to the core metro regions. Their integration to the core areas and their endogenous innovation capacity are promoted. However, geographical proximity to the core is not decisive. Examples of this are important technology hubs near the technology frontier in less central areas such as Helsinki, Rhone-Alps and Tuscany. These are important nodes in the polycentric network.

The metro regions in lagging and peripheral areas as the third category are located both in the western and in the eastern EU. These include the capital areas in Eastern Europe such as Prague, Warsaw, Budapest and Bucharest. They are moderately far from the technology frontier but have moderate potential in selected technological fields. Since they are the relative core agglomerations in their areas, they can promote scale benefits with the home market. However, they need institutional modernization and support from the growth-promoting national sectoral policies. These areas are lower-level nodes in the polycentric network. With proactive cross-border cooperation, Bratislava–Vienna area has potential to rise to the category of the secondary metro regions.

The fourth category is underdeveloped or peripheral, often semi-rural regions around the EU. Eastern Europe is territorially mostly consisted of such regions. They are far from the technology frontier and have limited potential to innovative agglomeration and scale benefits. Various policy interventions are needed to improve the competitiveness of these regions and to realize local sources of comparative advantage. These include human capital and home market development through public good provision, tailored productivity enhancement, improvement of infrastructure connection to leading regions and institutional modernization. One private sector-related action in Eastern Europe has been the attraction of less-demanding branch plants and labour-intensive activities from more advanced agglomerations. These areas are challenging for the polycentric network since they can be excluded from it or they become solely the providers of less-qualified, low-cost labour force for the nodes and locations for less-demanding and more polluting industries.

The final, fifth category contains relatively sparsely populated rural and peripheral regions that have limited capacity in terms of technology frontier, agglomeration effects, home market and productivity. Again, in Eastern Europe there are many such remote and land-locked areas. These regions are excluded as proactive agents from the global economy competitiveness race and their development depends largely on public policies and interventions. Much of their potential is linked to social entrepreneurship, innovation in limited niches in peripheral contexts and improving connections to the better-off areas. These areas are mostly excluded from the polycentric network despite that urban–rural networks are discussed in recent EU policies (see Territorial Agenda of the European Union, 2007).

Building on the futures studies methods, the following three scenarios for 2030 discuss the future of spatial patterns and territorial–administrative structures in the EU. The scenarios derive from the megatrends and weak signals taking into account the strategy that the EU would enlarge (Table 2) as it has continuously done since the 1950s. The material elaborated included the demographic and economic statistics and spatial planning strategies for the EU as a whole and selected Member States, the ESPON material regarding the future territorial development of Europe (ESPON, 2007a, 2007b, 2007c) and recent analyses of the future EU spatial development (Dammers, 2010; Davoudi & Dammers, 2010; Doucet, 2010; Evers, 2010; Gorzelak *et al.*, 2010; Lennert & Robert, 2010; Smith & Dubois, 2010).

Table 2. Scenarios for spatial patterns in the enlarged EU

Scenario	EU spatial structure	EU regions	EU regional processes	EU spatial governing mode	EU spatial policy
Empty empire of rules	Core/periphery	Bounded	Regionalization/region-binding	Top-down government	Passive
Metropolitan states with periphery	Core/periphery	Networked	Regionalism/region-binding	Metropolitan government	Reactive
Emerging borderland Europe	Development zones	Fluid	Regional devolution/region-binding	Metagovernance	Proactive

"Empty Empire of Rules" is the first scenario. According to this, after the eastern enlargement, the EU has 36 Member States. This is a path-dependent trajectory with poor consideration of the spatial challenges in economy and politics. The current polycentric "status quo" between the core areas, areas adjacent to the core and peripheral areas continues. The bureaucratic EU conditionality is slowing down the initiatives. The EU has a complete set of abstract rules and principles in advance of decision-making but it is unable to create and implement visions, thus remaining passive in spatial policy. The EU-level converge is achieved due to the slow development or even decline of the core areas. Polycentrism means formal relationships between these regions. The EU resembles a matryoshka of spatially nested hierarchies of territorial–administrative bounded regions. The multi-level governance has narrowed into a bureaucratic functional regional decentralization concerning bounded regions. Administratively similar spatial patterns are promoted throughout the EU, thus slowing down the dynamism of the new border areas. The bureaucracy and the aging challenge have been recognized by vital enterprises and young entrepreneurs who have left the EU. Therefore, the innovation-based development is thin. The majority, the slow and grey EU-pensioners, have adapted to this system. With the increasing budgetary problem for social cohesion, there is a possibility of regionalism and separation by the selected old Member States or their still wealthy metropolitan regions in the traditional core of the EU.

"Metropolitan States with Periphery" is the second scenario. The EU has expanded to the east, however, not to include Turkey or Ukraine. The polycentric Europe means the functional division of labour between the key economic drivers located in different regions, thus accepting divergence across the EU. Competitiveness, sustainability or smartness in the EU is, depending on the location, very high or very low. This is a path-dependent development with some resilient strategies and practices for the selected nodes with key enterprise clusters. There are several strongly competitive and globally competing metropolitan areas, i.e. those who have held that position for decades. These possess substantial economic – political decision-making powers and implement self-governing practices accordingly. The bottom-up regionalism promotes the identity these regions. Furthermore, there are around 50–60 less significant but still competitive urban agglomerations in the EU territory. Some are geographically close to the core areas, others are specialized centres. The remaining areas are periphery-supplying labour force, young people and food for the wealthy agglomerations. The processes of region-binding exist there, i.e. the global enterprises benefit from these areas and their less-expensive labour force. In general, the EU-level spatial policy is reactive. The core metropolitan areas form between them networked regions utilized for political lobbying for changing the EU conditionality according to their needs. The EU is a general policy framework at strategic level in Europe, but not much more. Spatial pattern is polarized; hence, the EU as an integrated converging whole has collapsed.

"Emerging Borderland Europe" is the third scenario. The EU has expanded substantially to the east. The EU has a proactive spatial policy for overlapping fluid regions as the main mode to organize space. Polycentrism has turned away from the largest nodal agglomerations to development between larger and smaller centres across the EU and between urban and less-urban areas. Such development zones fit better into increased fluidity of regions. There are still more advanced and less-developed areas in the EU; hence, the connection to the traditional economic core area is important. The significance of neighbourhood programmes across the EU border areas has increased. The EU conditionality has enhanced persuasive instruments in and outside the EU. Partnership has become more important than the formal EU membership for the bordering states. Therefore, governance of regions is challenging. Metagovernance discusses about values, principles and possibilities for development choices but there is an increasing tension of governance incompatibility between fixed bounded regions based on representational democracy and continuously changing fluid regions with various interest groups. The EU convergence aim has turned into a political issue. A clash emerges between the pro-growth and de-growth development policies and regions.

5. Conclusions

This article discussed spatial patterns and territorial–administrative structures in theory, illustrated related changes in practice and presented future scenarios for the EU and Eastern Europe. Three interrelated conclusions are drawn. First, the emergence of regions occurs through coexisting trends. Some processes are top-down directed whereas others rise from below, some are connected to the EU policies and others are driven by the economic imperative. Bounded, networked and fluid regions are accordingly connected to these trends. In the emergence of regions, spatiality and governing of economic and political processes must be reflected.

Second, conditionality is implemented in regions with various techniques in varying contexts. The direct experience and policy transfers with same results from one context and region to another are impossible. Governmentality in the Europeanization of spatial planning indicates how people, regions and development are bound together in the economic and political (re)organization of the Member States and their regions. In the current EU context, governmentality signifies the task of competitiveness as regards the global economy—though vested in the inclusive smartness of polycentric sustainability—that the related EU instruments must accomplish. The Europeanization of spatial planning is a process with harder and softer elements. The core "acquis" is a formal legal hard element, but its implementation varies in Eastern Europe. Softer elements include European spatial policy and planning. These practices in between hard and soft elements, including the facilitated coordination, turn the Europeanization of spatial planning into a more cyclical rather than top-down process.

Third, the spatial patterns and territorial–administrative structures in Europe change slowly. Historical path-dependencies have a significant impact. The economic core of the EU and the key metropolitan areas remain for decades in the territory of the older Member States. This occurs even if the eastern enlargement is necessary, if the EU wants to hold its global position in terms of population and economy. Selected metropolitan areas in the east benefit from their better connectivity to the core EU and become more important nodes in the European polycentric network. The engagement of more peripheral areas to polycentric Europe is challenging. More resilient, path-creative and proactive spatial policies and governing are needed for increasingly networked and relational regions.

References

Albrechts, L. (2011) Strategic planning and regional governance in Europe: Recent trend and policy responses, in: J. Yeh, A. Yeh & J. Xu (Eds) *Governance and Planning of Mega-City Regions: An International Comparative Perspective*, pp. 75–98 (London: Routledge).

Amin, A. (2004) Regions unbound: Towards a new politics of place, *Geografiska Annaler B*, 86(1), pp. 33–44.

Bachtler, J. & Mendez, C. (2007) Who governs EU cohesion policy? Deconstructing the reforms of the structural funds, *Journal of Common Market Studies*, 45(3), pp. 535–564.

Barca, F. (2009) *An Agenda for Reformed Cohesion Policy: A Place-based Approach to Meeting European Union Challenges and Expectations*. Independent report prepared at the request of D. Hübner, Commissioner for Regional Policy. Available at http://www.eu-territorial-agenda.eu/Related%20Document/report_barca_v0605.pdf (accessed 20 August 2011).

Benz, A. & Eberlein, B. (1999) The Europeanization of regional policies: Patterns of multi-level governance, *Journal of European Public Policy*, 6(2), pp. 328–348.

Böhme, K. & Waterhout, B. (2008) The Europeanization of planning, in: A. Faludi (Ed.) *European Spatial Research and Planning*, pp. 227–250 (Cambridge, MA: Lincoln Institute of Land Policy).

Brusis, M. (2002) Between EU requirements, competitive politics, and national traditions: Re-creating regions in the accession countries of Central and Eastern Europe, *Governance*, 15(4), pp. 531–559.

Brusis, M. (2010) European Union incentives and regional interest representation in Central and Eastern European countries, *Acta Politica*, 45(1–2), pp. 70–89.

Bruszt, L. (2008) Multi-level governance—the eastern versions: Emerging patterns of regional developmental governance in the new member states, *Regional & Federal Studies*, 18(5), pp. 607–627.

Bulmer, S. & Radaelli, C. (2004) The Europeanization of national policy? *Queen's Papers on Europeanization* 1/2004.

CEC (Commission of the European Communities) (1999) *European Spatial Development Perspective: Towards Balanced and Sustainable Development of the Territory of the EU* (Luxembourg: Office for Official Publications of the European Communities).

CEC (Commission of the European Communities) (2006) *Growing Regions, Growing Europe. Fourth Report on Economic and Social Cohesion* (Luxembourg: Office for Official Publications of the European Communities).

CEC (Commission of the European Communities) (2008) *Green Paper of Territorial Cohesion. Turning Territorial Diversity into Strength*. Communication from the Commission to the Council, the European Parliament, the Committee of the Regions and the European Economic and Social Committee, {SEC(2008) 2550}.

CEC (Commission of the European Communities) (2010) *Europe 2020. A Strategy for Smart, Sustainable and Inclusive Growth*. Communication from the Commission, Brussels 3.3.2010, COM (2010) 2020.

Christaller, W. (1933) *Die Zentralen Orte in Süddeutschland* (Jena: Carl Fischer).

Dammers, E. (2010) Making territorial scenarios for Europe, *Futures*, 42(2), pp. 785–793.

Davoudi, S. (2003) Polycentricity in European spatial planning: From an analytical tool to a normative agenda, *European Planning Studies*, 11(8), pp. 979–999.

Davoudi, S. & Dammers, E. (2010) The territorial futures of Europe: Introduction to the special issue, *Futures*, 42(8), pp. 779–784.

Doucet, P. (2010) 1950–2050: Sunset and sunrise over the Eurasian continent, in: K. Kunzmann, W. Schmid & M. Kroll-Schretzenmayr (Eds) *Europe and China: The Implications of the Rise of China for European Space*, pp. 256–270 (London: Routledge).

Dühr, S., Colomb, C. & Nadin, V. (2010) *European Spatial Planning and Territorial Cooperation* (London: Routledge).
ESPON (2007a) *ESPON 3.4.1. Europe in the World. Final Report* (Luxembourg: ESPON).
ESPON (2007b) *ESPON 3.2. Scenarios on the Territorial Future of Europe* (Luxembourg: ESPON).
ESPON (2007c) *Territorial Futures. Spatial Scenarios for Europe* (Luxembourg: ESPON).
Estella, A. (2002) *The EU Principle of Subsidiarity and Its Critique* (Oxford: Oxford University Press).
Evers, D. (2010) Scenarios on the spatial and economic development of Europe, *Futures*, 42(8), pp. 804–816.
Ezcurra, R., Pascual, P. & Rapún, M. (2007) The dynamics of regional disparities in Central Eastern Europe during transition, *European Planning Studies*, 15(10), pp. 1397–1421.
Faludi, A. (2008) European territorial cooperation and learning: Reflections by the guest editor on the wider implications, *disP*, 172(1/2008), pp. 3–10.
Faludi, A. (2010a) Centenary paper: European spatial planning: Past, present and future, *Town Planning Review*, 81(1), pp. 1–22.
Faludi, A. (2010b) The process architecture of the EU territorial cohesion policy, *European Journal of Spatial Policy*, 39, August 2010. Available at http://www.nordregio.se/Global/EJSD/Refereed%20articles/refereed39.pdf (accessed 20 August 2011).
Farías, I. & Bender, T. (Eds) (2009) *Urban Assemblages: How Actor-Network Theory Changes Urban Studies* (London: Routledge).
Farole, T., Rodríguez-Pose, A. & Storper, M. (2010) *Cohesion Policy in the European Union: Growth, Geography, Institutions*. IMDEA Working Paper Series in Economics and Social Sciences, 14/2010. Available at http://repec.imdea.org/pdf/imdea-wp2010-14.pdf (accessed 20 August 2011).
Foucault, M. (2004) *Sécurité, Territoire, Population. Cours au Collége de France 1977–1978* (Paris: Seuil/Gallimard).
Giannakourou, G. (2012) The Europeanization of national planning: Explaining the causes and the potentials of change, *Planning Practice and Research*, 27(1), pp. 117–135.
Gorzelak, G. & Smetkowski, M. (2010) Regional development dynamics in Central Eastern European countries, in: G. Gorzelak, J. Bachtler & M. Smetkowski (Eds) *Regional Development in Central and Eastern Europe: Development Processes and Policy Challenges*, pp. 34–58 (London: Routledge).
Gorzelak, G., Bachtler, J. & Smetkowski, M. (2010) *Regional Development in Central and Eastern Europe: Development Processes and Policy Challenges* (London: Routledge).
Gualini, E. (2008) "Territorial cohesion" as a category of agency: The missing dimension in the EU spatial policy debate, *European Journal of Spatial Development*, no. 28, pp. 1–22.
Haggett, P. (1965) *Locational Analysis in Human Geography* (London: Arnold).
Harvey, D. (2005) *A Brief History of Neoliberalism* (Oxford: Oxford University Press).
Haughton, G. & Allmendinger, P. (2010) Spatial planning, devolution and new planning spaces, *Environment and Planning C: Government and Policy*, 28(5), pp. 803–818.
Healey, P. & Williams, R. (1993) European urban planning system: Convergence and divergence, *Urban Studies*, 30(4/5), pp. 701–720.
Henderson, J., Dicken, P., Hess, M., Coe, N. & Yeung, H. (2002) Global production networks and the analysis of economic development, *Review of International Political Economy*, 9(3), pp. 436–464.
Hillier, J. (2007) *Stretching beyond the Horizon: A Multi-Planar Theory of Spatial Planning and Governance* (Aldershot: Ashgate).
Hooghe, L. & Marks, G. (2009) Does efficiency shape the territorial structure of government? *Annual Review of Political Science*, 12(1), pp. 225–241.
Hughes, J., Sasse, G. & Gordon, C. (2004) *Europeanization and Regionalization in the EU's Enlargement to Central and Eastern Europe* (Paris: Lavoisier).
Janin Rivolin, U. (2010) EU territorial governance: Learning from institutional progress, *European Journal of Spatial Development*, 38, April 2010. Available at http://www.nordregio.se/Global/EJSD/Refereed%20articles/refereed38.pdf (accessed 20 August 2011).
Jauhiainen, J. (2000) *Regional Development and Regional Policy. European Union and the Baltic Sea Region* (Turku: University of Turku).
Jauhiainen, J. & Moilanen, H. (2011) Towards fluid territories in European spatial development. Regional development zones in Finland, *Environment and Planning C: Government and Policy*, 29(4), pp. 728–744.
Jessop, B. (2009) From governance to governance failure and from multi-level governance to multi-scalar metagovernance, in: B. Arts, A. Lagendijk & H. van Houtum (Eds) *The Disoriented State. Shifts in Governmentality, Territoriality and Governance*, pp. 79–100 (Dordrecht: Springer).

Jonas, A. (2012) Region and place. Regionalism in question, *Progress in Human Geography*, 36(2), pp. 263–272.
Kooiman, J. & Jentoft, S. (2009) Meta-governance: Values, norms and principles and the making of hard choices, *Public Administration*, 87(4), pp. 818–836.
Lagendijk, A., Arts, B. & van Houtum, H. (2009) Shifts in governmentality, territoriality and governance: An introduction, in: B. Arts, A. Lagendijk & H. van Houtum (Eds) *The Disoriented State. Shifts in Governmentality, Territoriality and Governance*, pp. 3–12 (Dordrecht: Springer).
Leitner, H. & Sheppard, E. (2002) The city is dead, long live the network: Harnessing networks for a neoliberal era, in: N. Brenner & N. Theodore (Eds) *Spaces of Neoliberalism: Urban Restructuring in North America and Europe*, pp. 148–171 (Oxford: Blackwell).
Lennert, M. & Robert, J. (2010) The territorial futures of Europe: "Trends", "Competition" or "Cohesion", *Futures*, 42(8), pp. 833–845.
Lidström, A. (2007) Territorial governance in transition, *Regional & Federal Studies*, 17(4), pp. 499–508.
Maier, K. (2012) Europeanization and changing planning in East-Central Europe: An easterner's view, *Planning Practice and Research*, 27(1), pp. 137–154.
Meijers, E., Waterhout, B. & Zonneveld, D. (2007) Closing the gap: Territorial cohesion through polycentric development, *European Journal of Spatial Development*, 24, October 2007. Available at http://www.nordregio.se/Global/EJSD/Refereed%20articles/refereed24.pdf (accessed 15 February 2013).
Morgan, K. (2007) The polycentric state: New spaces of empowerment and engagement? *Regional Studies*, 41(9), pp. 1237–1252.
Murdoch, J. (1998) The space of actor-network theory, *Geoforum*, 29(4), pp. 357–374.
Nadin, V. & Stead, D. (2008) European spatial planning systems. Social models and learning, *disP*, 172(1), pp. 35–47.
Paasi, A. (2004) Bounded spaces in the mobile world. Deconstructing "regional identity", *Tijdschrift voor Economische en Sociale Geografie*, 93(2), pp. 137–148.
Pitschel, D. & Bauer, M. (2009) Subnational governance approaches on the rise: Reviewing a decade of eastern European regionalization research, *Regional & Federal Studies*, 19(3), pp. 327–347.
Puga, D. (2002) European regional policies in the light of recent location theories, *Journal of Economic Geography*, 2(4), pp. 373–406.
Ramajo, J., Märguez, M., Hewings, G. & Salinas, M. (2008) Spatial heterogeneity and interregional spillovers in the European Union: Do cohesion policies encourage convergence across regions? *European Economic Review*, 52(3), pp. 551–567.
Schimmelfennig, F. & Sedelmeier, U. (2004) Governance by conditionality: EU rule transfer to the candidate countries of Central and Eastern Europe, *Journal of European Public Policy*, 11(4), pp. 669–687.
Smith, C. & Dubois, A. (2010) The "wild cards" of European futures: Planning for discontinuities? *Futures*, 42(8), pp. 846–855.
Syssner, J. (2009) Conceptualizations of culture and identity in regional policy, *Regional & Federal Studies*, 19(3), pp. 437–459.
Territorial Agenda of the European Union (2007) *Towards a More Competitive and Sustainable Europe of Diverse Regions*. Agreed on the occasion of the informal ministerial meeting on urban development and territorial cohesion in Leipzig on 24/25 May 2007.
Waterhout, B. & Stead, D. (2007) Mixed messages: How the ESDP's concepts have been applied in INTERREG IIIB programmes, priorities and projects, *Planning Practice and Research*, 22(3), pp. 395–415.
Zweigert, K. & Kötz, H. (1998) *An Introduction of Comparative Law* (Oxford: Oxford University Press).

The Engagement of Territorial Knowledge Communities with European Spatial Planning and the Territorial Cohesion Debate: A Baltic Perspective

NEIL ADAMS*, GIANCARLO COTELLA** & RICHARD NUNES[†]

*Department of Urban, Environment and Leisure Studies, London South Bank University, London, UK, **IPS—Department of International Planning Systems, University of Kaiserslautern, Kaiserslautern, Germany, [†]School of Real Estate and Planning, University of Reading, Reading, UK

ABSTRACT *Recent, dramatic spatial development trends have contributed to the consolidation of a unique territorial governance landscape in the Baltic States. The paper examines the transformation of this evolving institutional landscape for planning practice and knowledge, which has been marked by the disintegration of Soviet institutions and networks, the transition to a market-based economy and the process of accession to the EU. It explores the evolution of territorial knowledge channels in the Baltic States, and the extent and nature of the engagement of actors' communities with the main knowledge arenas and resources of European spatial planning (ESP). The paper concludes that recent shifts in the evolution of these channels suggest the engagement of ESP has concentrated among epistemic communities at State and trans-national levels of territorial governance. The limited policy coordination across a broader spectrum of diverse actors is compounded by institutionally weak and fragmented professional communities of practice, fragmented government structures and marginalized advocacy coalitions.*

Introduction

The nature of European spatial planning (ESP), as it has evolved in recent years, has seen it characterized as a "learning machine" (Faludi, 2008) and this increases the appropriateness of applying a knowledge perspective to the analysis of this evolution. The paper explores the evolution of territorial knowledge communities (Adams *et al.*, 2011) in the Baltic States of Estonia, Latvia and Lithuania, and the extent and nature of the engagement of these communities with some key knowledge arenas of ESP, particularly the territorial cohesion debate. This underlying knowledge perspective focuses on the role of knowledge in the policy process (Radaelli, 1995) and more specifically on the interplay of knowledge and policy development. The role of diverse actors and networks as epistemic communities (Haas, 1990, 1992, 2004; Pallagst, 2006, 2011), communities of practice (Lave & Wenger, 1991) and advocacy coalitions (Sabatier & Jenkins-Smith, 1993; Sabatier, 1998) is emphasized. The paper explores the way these territorial knowledge communities engage with different "knowledge arenas" to advance, inform or legitimize policy agendas and approaches through the strategic use of "knowledge resources" (Adams et al., 2011). Selected multi-scalar institutional arrangements ("territorial knowledge channels") in the Baltic States are examined to explore how diverse actors and networks may potentially influence the policy development process after having acquired the power to shape or "frame" new "policy images" (Kingdon, 1995).

Despite their linguistic and cultural diversity (Lieven, 1993; Smith et al., 2002), the Baltic States possess similar characteristics in terms of location, size and collective memories shaped by shared recent histories. The disintegration of Soviet structures, networks and institutions combined with the complexities of transition to a market economy and the process of accession to the EU contributed to new spatial development trends and challenges and a rapidly evolving territorial governance landscape. Their planning systems have been continually readjusted to new realities whereby the absorption of EU structural funds and the promotion of economic development have been prioritized.

The evidence suggests that the engagement of Baltic actors in the key arenas of ESP has been marginal in comparison to other Central and Eastern European (CEE) countries (Cotella et al., 2012) and that detailed discussion over shared competencies and actor engagement appears to be limited. Though there is evidence that high-level epistemic communities in the Baltic States are engaging in trans-national and State-level discussions over strategic spatial planning of the Baltic Sea Region (BSR), the pragmatic attitude behind this engagement has often resulted in mutually exclusive contributions to shared knowledge arenas. The evolving institutional landscape for planning practice has also been subject to Europeanization and internationalization pressures, facilitating processes of policy mobility (Larner & Laurie, 2010), which are derived from the increasing confrontation with planning practices and approaches from elsewhere as well as the incremental consolidation of an EU territorial governance framework (Böhme & Waterhout, 2008; Waterhout et al., 2009; Cotella & Janin Rivolin, 2010; Janin Rivolin, 2010; Cotella et al., 2011; Stead & Cotella, 2011). The recently published *Fifth Report on Economic, Social and Territorial Cohesion* (CEC, 2011) emphasizes that these processes may reveal competing knowledge claims and associated power and competence struggles, together with the importance of an EU role in better co-ordination and co-operation. The Report underlines how emphasis should be placed on the newly shared competences between the EU and Member States over territorial cohesion matters, as well as the increasing importance of engaging broad coalitions of actors.

This paper argues that recent shifts in the evolution of territorial governance arrangements in the Baltic States suggest that engagement with ESP is concentrated among epistemic communities at State and trans-national levels. The limited policy coordination across a broader spectrum of actors at sub-national levels is compounded by the institutionally weak and fragmented nature of professional communities of practice (Maier, 2011), fragmented local government structures and the marginalization of advocacy coalitions. These shifts have been consistent with a neo-liberal reassertion of economic priorities, the climate of public austerity, uncertainty over institutional reforms and the dissolution of knowledge networks.

The paper sets out to determine the extent and nature of engagement of some of these actor coalitions or territorial knowledge communities in the Baltic States with some of the key arenas of ESP, including the Vision and Strategies around the Baltic Sea (VASAB), Interreg and the European Observation Network for Territorial Development and Cohesion (ESPON). However, the main focus of the paper is based on an analysis of the State-level responses from the Baltic States and the responses of selected interest groups with a Baltic focus, to the *Green Paper on Territorial Cohesion* (CEC, 2008). The documentary analysis was supplemented by a series of face-to-face and telephone interviews with selected key stakeholders in the field of regional development and spatial planning in each of the three countries.[1]

The first section of the paper introduces the evolving institutional landscape for planning practice in the Baltic States. Section two brings a knowledge perspective to the transformation of this unique governance landscape together with a brief summary of the engagement of Baltic actors in diverse knowledge arenas of ESP. Section three constitutes the core of the contribution, providing an analysis of the extent and nature of their responses to the *European Commission Green Paper on Territorial Cohesion* (CEC, 2008). The paper concludes with some reflections on prospects and future challenges for an effective engagement of territorial knowledge communities of the Baltic States with the ESP discourse.

EU Enlargement and Territorial Development in the Baltic States

The location of the Baltic States at the crossroads between Eastern and Western Europe has ensured a complex and often volatile history during the twentieth century when each country obtained independence in the inter-war period before being integrated into the Soviet Union, invaded by Germany and then reintegrated into the Soviet Union at the end of World War II. As Soviet Socialist Republics, they were more deeply integrated into the Soviet space in political, socio-economic and spatial terms than other former members of the socialist block. They were consequently also more isolated from Western Europe and less able to interact and exchange knowledge and ideas. Since the collapse of the Soviet Union, the Baltic States have re-established independence and become full members of both the EU and NATO, though the transition and transformation to democracy and a market economy have been highly complex (Williams, 1996). The Baltic States were among the poorest countries to join the EU in 2004 with levels of prosperity well below the EU average (see Table 1). A period of rapid economic

Table 1. GDP per capita as percentage of EU-27 average

Country	GDP as % of EU-27 average	
	2004	2008
Estonia	57	68
Latvia	46	56
Lithuania	50	61

Source: Eurostat (2011).

growth between 1997 and 2008 saw GDP growth rates approaching or surpassing double figures in percentage points before the severe economic downturn when GDP in the Baltic States plummeted, far more than any other Member State.

Development has been driven overwhelmingly by the capital cities, strengthening their already dominant role. Socio-economic disparities and environmental impacts have been exacerbated by the contrasting demands of rapid economic growth followed by recession. Equally dramatic changes to institutional structures have also been necessary to make them more appropriate to new market-based realities. The transition period and the evolving landscape for planning practice have been strongly influenced by a culture of pragmatism and political expedience linked to national efforts to satisfy accession requirements and absorb EU funding, as well as by increasing processes of internationalization that have stimulated policy mobility. These two distinct perspectives on the evolving institutional landscape for planning practice and knowledge are now introduced in detail.

An Evolving Institutional Landscape for Planning Practice: Pragmatism and Political Expedience

The EU exerted considerable top-down influence over the dramatic reforms undertaken by the recent CEE entrants through the offer of funding, the transposition of the *acquis communautaire* and formal and informal internalization of EU concepts and priorities (Adams, 2008). Europeanization pressures notwithstanding, the strong individual cultural identities are reflected in the diversity of approaches to spatial planning inspired by diverse sources (Adams & Harris, 2005; Adams *et al.*, 2006; COMMIN, undated). Regular institutional reforms have resulted in the spatial planning portfolio being passed between ministries once in Estonia and twice in Latvia. The Ministry of the Environment in Lithuania has retained responsibility for territorial planning during this time.

Latvia has been in an almost constant state of institutional reform since regaining independence in 1991 when the 1922 Constitution was reinstated, resulting in a highly fragmented local government structure with over 550 municipalities (Pabriks & Purs, 2002). Despite a new constitution in Estonia, a similarly fragmented local government structure emerged (Smith, 2002) with approximately 250 municipalities. Incentives to amalgamate and reduce the number of local governments had limited success due to resistance from local populations eager to retain their recently acquired independence. Significant institutional reform in Latvia took place in 2009 when the 26 administrative districts were abolished and the number of municipalities reduced to 118 including nine cities. Recent austerity measures in Estonia have seen financial incentives for local governments to amalgamate removed and it is unclear whether further reductions from the current 226 municipalities are likely. In Lithuania the ten county administrations were abolished in July 2010 with powers passed down to the local level and up to the territorial subdivisions of the Ministry of Interior. Discussions regarding the future of the five planning regions persist in Latvia. Several interviewees suggested that the motivation for the (potential) dissolution of regional structures was predominantly political and financial.

Such instability is reflected by numerous reforms to planning legislation in each country. National spatial planning documents have been adopted in Estonia (Ministry of the Environment, 2001), Lithuania (Ministry of the Environment, 2002) and Latvia

(Saeima, 2010). The Latvian and Estonian documents are highly strategic compared to the much more detailed Lithuanian Comprehensive Plan (Adams, 2006). The Estonia 2010 document is currently under revision under the banner of Estonia 2030 Strategy. These processes have tended to be expert driven, implying that strategic and abstract national planning debates tend to be dominated by expert communities. The need to satisfy accession requirements and subsequently to absorb EU funding has resulted in the emergence of a culture of pragmatism and political expedience. The situation has been exacerbated by the limited institutional capacity and resources at sub-national levels and by the extremely high turnover of staff in public sector agencies. One interviewee identified a reduction in staff turnover and resulting stability as the only positive impact of the global economic crisis. Under such circumstances it has been difficult to foster collaborative vertical links between scales, which appear to be at best fragmented and at worst absent in the Baltic States.

An Evolving Institutional Landscape for Planning Practice: Internationalization and Europeanization of Planning Knowledge

The wider context for the evolution of the domestic planning communities in the Baltic States including the collapse of the Soviet Union and EU enlargement is highly relevant. Domestic territorial knowledge communities, whose contact with international actors had been severely restricted, started to enjoy more freedom from Moscow hegemony in the final years of the Soviet period. The resulting internationalization of ideas such as those of Arnolds Lamze[2] started to generate debate among the Baltics' planning communities from the 1980s onwards (Kule *et al.*, 2011). The early post-Soviet period was characterized by the increasing dominance of neo-liberal ideologies, ensuring that reforms necessary to adapt to the new market-based system took priority over the production and cultivation of knowledge. The respective national academies of science, which were not only viewed as expensive but also as a symbol of former Soviet control, were dismantled. These academies were responsible for extensive research in Soviet times and played a key role in informing policy development and their dissolution particularly weakened planning communities and knowledge networks.

A dramatic renewal of the membership and philosophy of the planning communities was therefore required in order for them to adapt to the post-Soviet realities and to gain wider public acceptance. The EU exerted increasing influence on domestic actors from the mid-1990s onwards through top-down processes of Europeanization, which involved the setting of rules and the provision of external incentives (Schimmelfennig & Sedelmeier, 2005; Dagliene, 2006). Planning remains a contested professional domain and the planning community in each Baltic State is characterized by a diversity of professions including architects, geographers, economists, surveyors and political scientists. The battle for professional legitimacy is exacerbated by limited planning higher education opportunities[3] and recent severe cuts to higher education budgets (EUA, 2011). The resulting vicious circle means that the fragmented nature of spatial planning higher education does little to consolidate the respective planning communities and the fragmented planning communities have insufficient influence to consolidate planning education. This fragmentation is also reflected in professional practice. National associations representing the interests of spatial planners in Estonia and Latvia have memberships of approximately 70 and 50, respectively. Many planners are also active in other networks and communities such as the Association of Architects and the Association of Local and Regional Government in Latvia and the Union of Architects in Lithuania. The associations provide a platform for debate, to raise planning capacity, to disseminate information and to provide advice to local and national governments. Despite focusing primarily on domestic issues, both Estonian and Latvian associations are increasingly engaged with similar associations in other countries[4] and have a limited but increasing influence on the policy-development process.

Extensive Baltic diasporas included numerous individuals practicing planning in various countries, and contacts with these groups and individuals were extremely important in the early post-Soviet phase as mechanisms for knowledge transfer (Kule *et al.*, 2011). Larner and Laurie (2010) reflect on the ways different types of knowledge are transferred and transformed by different individuals, networks and communities with different agendas and in different contexts. The role of individual actors can also change as " ... technocrats may become politicians, scientists may become development experts, academics may become activists, engineers may set up NGOs ... " (Larner & Laurie 2010, p. 219). The fluidity of the Baltic States' political and institutional context during transition facilitated such changes. Members of these exile communities returned to their respective countries to become involved in politics, advocacy groups, academia, public administration and the private sector whereas others played a more indirect role by undertaking initiatives from their new host countries.

Independence also led to the resumption of other historical contacts, exemplified by the significant Finnish and Swedish influence on the initial planning legislation in Estonia in 1995. Internationalization processes were also facilitated by numerous bilateral co-operation agreements with governments including Canada, Finland, Denmark, Sweden, Germany, the Netherlands and Flanders. In combination with initiatives such as VASAB, these contacts were highly influential on the evolution of spatial planning in each country, introducing members of the domestic planning communities to ideas and approaches from abroad. The vast majority of these links tended to be horizontal between agents operating at the same level in different countries and generally did little to strengthen vertical links between actors in the individual Baltic States. The evolution of territorial knowledge communities in the Baltic States will be considered in more depth in the next section.

Territorial Knowledge Communities and the Engagement of Baltic Actors in ESP

Claims that policy and practice should be informed by evidence are not new but have enjoyed something of a revival in the last decade (Clarence, 2002; Faludi & Waterhout, 2006; Krizek *et al.*, 2009; Adams *et al.*, 2011). There is therefore a need to advance these debates over evidence, argument and persuasion in spatial planning, of which the potential for "common understanding" and "epistemic distance" between actors remains an intrinsic part (Cotella *et al.*, 2012). While agent interactivity may lead to the development and consolidation of new policy ideas, discourses or preferences, and new institutional arrangements (Jensen & Richardson, 2004), it can often be subject to the vested interests of political alliances and the traditional silo-mentality of sectorally organized institutions (Allmendinger & Tewdwr-Jones, 2000; Benz, 2000). The instability surrounding regional tiers of governance in the Baltic States and the fragmented nature of sub-national territorial knowledge communities increase the importance of understanding the role of agent interactivity in producing path-shaping policy change. Such change can occur either through the framing of new "policy images" (Kingdon, 1995) or the addition of new dimensions that "punctuate" (Baumgartner & Jones, 2002) path-dependent processes of policy stability.

The following discussion charts the evolution of diverse territorial knowledge communities consisting of professional "communities of practice" (Wenger, 1998), "epistemic communities" (Haas, 1992) and "advocacy coalitions" (Sabatier & Jenkins-Smith, 1993) in the Baltic States and the extent of their engagement with ESP knowledge arenas (cf. Adams *et al.*, 2011, p. 45). The analysis is rooted in a knowledge perspective that focuses on the role of territorial knowledge communities and the evolution of specific territorial governance arrangements or territorial knowledge channels (Adams *et al.*, 2011). The evolution of these knowledge channels is strongly linked to the evolution of the institutional landscape of planning referred to in the previous sections. Such a knowledge perspective implies that engagement of ESP must be broadened beyond its traditional narrow expert audience (Waterhout, 2008, 2011; Faludi, 2009). Multi-actor networks, engaging in diverse territorial knowledge communities, will have diverse skills and experiences and possess different types of knowledge (Larner & Laurie, 2010). The spectrum of knowledge will range from "hard" scientific knowledge, often in the form of quantitative statistics, to more qualitative, intangible, tacit and "soft" types, which are more commonplace among non-expert communities and can be more difficult to access, articulate and quantify (Rydin, 2007; PURR, 2011). The combination of these different types of knowledge is important and it is unlikely that accurate and comprehensive insights can be obtained without accessing this broad spectrum of knowledge.

The most influential ESP knowledge arena for Baltic actors in the last two decades has been VASAB (Fritsch, 2011). Set up in 1992, VASAB aimed to share knowledge and ideas about spatial development through joint spatial planning activities and for many participants provided their first exposure to a diverse range of international ideas, concepts and approaches. VASAB achievements listed in the workshop report from the seventh VASAB Ministerial Conference (VASAB, 2009)[5] clearly demonstrate the characteristics of a knowledge arena where knowledge is debated.

The influence of Baltic States' actors in VASAB has increased over the years due to the role of individual personalities, the influence of the alternating chairpersonship of VASAB and the presidencies of the Council of the Baltic Sea States and the location of the VASAB Secretariat in Riga since 2007. Despite the emergence of the potentially competing and more politically popular EU Strategy for the BSR (EC, 2009), there appears to be a general consensus among key stakeholders that VASAB remains relevant and influential. It continues to provide a platform for the promotion of supra-national issues and for uploading national interests into the international arena, as well as for informing national and sub-national planning discourses and documents.[6]

The emphasis on the role of knowledge arenas such as VASAB rests on a knowledge resources-based interpretation of policy-relevant events. These knowledge resources are channelled into certain arenas where they are tested and validated via specific territorial governance mechanisms. These multi-agent, cross-scalar governance arrangements manifesting across and within different territorial knowledge communities are the territorial knowledge channels, which potentially influence policy development as a result of having acquired the powers to shape or frame alternatives for future policy change or safeguard existing policy approaches. That is to say "knowledge has less to do with specific actors than with the structure in which actors act" (Radaelli, 1999, p. 769). The key knowledge arenas of ESP include the former Community Initiative Interreg, recently evolved into the mainstream objective of European Territorial Cooperation, and ESPON. Actors from Estonia, Latvia or Lithuania appear to have been particularly active within the context of the Interreg IIIB BSR Programme—partly evolving from and overlapping with the above-mentioned VASAB (Fritsch, 2011). In contrast, they appear to have been significantly less active in the inter-regional cooperation initiatives promoted under Interreg IIIC. The limited engagement of Baltic actors in the inter-regional strand appears to have continued into the current programming period. The evidence suggests that actors from the Baltic States are engaging primarily with issues of a geographical focus on the BSR or that they prefer to explore themes with partners from neighbouring countries. Once again, this may reflect a culture of pragmatism whereby more concrete and specific issues take priority over more abstract and ambiguous ones.

Whereas Interreg focuses on a broad spectrum of knowledge, ESPON is traditionally more focused on quantitative scientific knowledge. ESPON is an arena within which epistemic communities within research institutions throughout the EU look "to support policy development and to build a European scientific community in the field of territorial development" (ESPON, no date). The Baltic States were initially reluctant to engage with ESPON and they did not participate in the 2006 Programme due to a lack of national resources and scepticism regarding the scientific relevance of ESPON data for informing national policy development.[7] Despite all three Baltic States participating in the ESPON 2013 programme at the time of writing, Baltic actors are still not participating in any of the trans-national project groups responsible for Applied Research Projects and are currently active in only two Targeted Analysis Projects.[8] The dominance of large Scandinavian research institutes with sufficient expertise, resources and capacity to provide high-quality analysis of the Baltic States forms one barrier to participation. Other potential reasons include different priorities and a lack of human and other resources for research, particularly at sub-national levels. The next section of the paper examines the extent and nature of the responses of Baltic actors to the consultation process launched by the European Commission *Green Paper on Territorial Cohesion* (CEC, 2008).[9]

Territorial Knowledge Communities and Engagement of Actors from the Baltic States in the Territorial Cohesion Debate

The concept of territorial cohesion was introduced in the Treaty of Amsterdam (1997) and gained increasing relevance initially with the Treaty of Nice (2001) and, subsequently, with the Laeken European Council (2001) as fears about post enlargement disparities grew (Cotella, 2009; Cotella *et al.*, 2012). The territorial cohesion objective was ultimately ratified under the Treaty of Lisbon (2007) and subsequently the publication of the *Fifth Report on Economic, Social and Territorial Cohesion* (CEC, 2011) and the Territorial Agenda 2020 (HU Presidency, 2011) formally advanced the objective across EU policy agendas.

The Green Paper was a response from the Commission to the uncertainty about the implications of territorial cohesion (cf. Evers, 2007) and represented a clear attempt to broaden the debate beyond the narrow expert community that has traditionally been engaged in ESP. Despite having been subject to considerable apprehension and confusion (Evers *et al.*, 2009), territorial cohesion remains a "generative metaphor" through which long-standing issues continue to be re-examined and debated (Schön, 1978). The question therefore emerges as to whether planners are simply "talking the talk" rather than "walking the walk" when bringing together evidence-informed arguments to advance policy interests behind the veil of territorial cohesion.

The results of the consultation process, accounting for almost 400 reactions submitted from bodies located in both Member and non-Member States, provide a valuable resource in relation to current interpretations of the principle as well as significant clues as to the extent and nature of the engagement of diverse territorial knowledge communities in this debate (see Cotella et al., 2012 for a more detailed quantitative analysis).

A preliminary mapping of the institutional geography of the Green Paper consultation process reveals significant differentiation in the levels of engagement. National institutions from all 27 EU Member States except Ireland responded to the consultation. However, the geographical distribution of other respondents is dominated by actors in north-west Europe where 43% of regional and local respondents are located. Among CEE countries, actors from the Visegrád countries appear to have been most active, particularly those from Poland. Engagement of actors from the Baltic States appears to be concentrated at national and trans-national levels. No responses were received from any regional or local institutions, universities, research institutes or consultancies in the Baltic States and interest groups involving Baltic actors also appear to have been less active. Excluding those interest groups with a clear pan-European focus, Estonian actors participated in eight responding interest groups, Lithuanian actors in six groups and Latvian actors in only three groups. The responses to the Green Paper from state institutions in the three countries and responses from selected interest groups will now be considered in more detail.

Responses from State Institutions

The evidence from the responses to the Green Paper and from the stakeholder interviews suggests that the territorial cohesion discourse in the Baltic States is primarily restricted to expert communities concentrated in national-level institutions. The ministries responsible for spatial planning and regional development submitted responses on behalf of the Estonian and Latvian governments (MRDLG 2009 and Estonian Ministry of Interior 2009) and the Ministry of Finance submitted the Lithuanian response (Lithuanian Ministry of Finance 2009). No submissions were made by sub-national state institutions. The strategic level and abstract nature of territorial cohesion mean such discourse is far removed from every day work of many regional and local actors possibly reducing the perceived relevance of the debate. To address this issue a National Co-ordination Group has been established in Latvia to disseminate information and translate debates into a form to which actors at lower territorial levels can relate. The culture of pragmatism is also demonstrated by the fact that the Latvian and Estonian associations for spatial planners, who focus primarily on domestic issues, have yet to formally discuss territorial cohesion and did not respond to the Green Paper.

An analysis of the three national responses reveals commonalities and differences in relation to interpretations and perceived implications of territorial cohesion (see Table 2 for summary). The Latvian and Lithuanian responses adopt a structured approach addressing the questions in turn though the Estonian response follows a broader structure. All three demonstrate a positive attitude to the concept, which might be expected from

Table 2. Commonalities and differences in the Estonian, Latvian and Lithuanian national responses to the Green Paper on territorial cohesion

Theme	Commonalities between all national responses	Country-specific recommendations and practical measures
Definition and overall attitude to territorial cohesion	Identification of similar range of themes encapsulated in the concept Positive attitude to the concept Strong link to quality of life and access to services of general interest	*Latvia*: equal access *Estonia*: fair access.
Scale and scope of territorial action	Importance of subsidiarity	*Lithuania*: stronger role for the EU in setting objectives, co-ordination implementation and monitoring *Estonia*: importance of territorial cohesion offering European added value *Latvia and Lithuania*: importance of retaining socio-economic characteristics as the basis for allocating EU funding
Better co-operation and co-ordination	Emphasizing policy integration and the importance of horizontal and vertical co-operation Advocating strategic role for the EU level with the Member States having flexibility in application of territorial cohesion to allow for context-sensitive policy responses and interventions	*Estonia and Lithuania*: EU Strategy for the BSR as a good example of integrated action *Estonia*: integration of cohesion and rural policy with integrated community strategic guidelines *Latvia*: stronger role of Informal Council of Ministers responsible for Regional Development, EU Guidelines followed by national strategies promoting territorial cohesion and territorial impact assessment of sector policies
	Promoting more efficient and effective use of existing mechanisms rather than introduction of new mechanisms Promoting co-operation over external EU borders Emphasizing importance of addressing regional disparities Sectors where it is important to consider the territorial impacts: transport, energy, environment and rural development	*Estonia*: stronger role for territorial cooperation, trans-national spatial planning and increased support for administrative reform *Estonia and Latvia*: science policy and research *Latvia and Lithuania*: innovation, competitiveness, ITC and the knowledge society *Estonia*: neighbourhood policy *Latvia*: maritime policy *Lithuania*: social policy including health and education

(Continued)

Table 2. Continued

Theme	Commonalities between all national responses	Country-specific recommendations and practical measures
New territorial partnerships	Engaging a broad coalition of actors in the territorial cohesion debate	*Estonia*: reallocating part of structural funds through focused macro-regional strategies and using such strategies as a means of pursuing territorial cohesion *Lithuania*: raising awareness and knowledge about territorial cohesion and more specifically its practical application
Improving the understanding of territorial cohesion	Developing effective and meaningful territorial cohesion goals and indicators	

Source: Authors' own elaboration.

major beneficiaries of EU cohesion policy. The general tone of the responses reflects some of the key challenges facing the Baltic nations, including low levels of prosperity, negative demographic trends and concerns over access to services and employment. All three responses identify a range of themes encapsulated by the concept rather than putting forward a specific detailed definition. Territorial co-operation, the co-ordination of sector policies, the integration of the territorial dimensions of national and EU policies, and the harnessing of specific territorial characteristics are recurring themes. Such similarities may also imply interaction between actors and knowledge communities debating the issue.

There is a strong affinity with the equity-based focus of territorial cohesion that has its roots in the French *amenagement du territoire* and an emphasis on reduction of social and economic disparities. The Latvian discussion of an appropriate definition is the broadest of the three and demonstrates familiarity with the relevant EU discourses and terminology. It refers to territorial cohesion as

> horizontal guidelines for sustainable and coordinated development of all EU regions oriented towards provision of equal standards of quality of life and access to basic services for citizens by paying special attention to the less developed regions to enhance their competitiveness. (MRDLG, 2009, p. 1)

The Estonian response refers to the need to ensure "fair opportunities in terms of living conditions and quality of life" compared to the Latvian emphasis on equality. This may imply recognition by the Estonians of the conflict between much spatial planning rhetoric on the importance of localizing service provision and the reality of increasing centralization.

In relation to the scale and scope of territorial action, all three responses emphasize the importance of multi-level governance, effective vertical and horizontal integration and the principle of subsidiarity. Though this implies a degree of common interests, there is also some suggestion of competing agendas. The responses envisage a strategic role for the EU with the Estonian and Lithuanian responses emphasizing the setting of objectives and priorities, the co-ordination of implementation, evaluation and the identification of policy gaps. The Latvian response defines the EU's primary role as the promotion of territorial cohesion leaving individual Member States to apply the principle and identify the Latvian territorial development index as an example of how territorial cohesion is integrated into national policy. The Estonian response emphasizes the creation of European added value through a focus on the specific territorial potential of each region. None of the responses support the idea that areas with specific geographical features require special policy measures, though this conflicts with the agendas of some of the interest groups discussed in the next section. The responses examined here reflect the challenges facing the nation as a whole and demonstrate pragmatic motivations for identifying social and economic characteristics as the crucial factor when considering national policy and funding.

Much attention is given to governance issues particularly in relation to horizontal and vertical co-operation and policy co-ordination, though recent reforms and ongoing uncertainty about the sub-national levels of governance are not conducive to the consolidation of governance networks. All responses (including those from interest groups discussed in the next section) emphasize the importance of greater flexibility in the designation of areas for planned intervention as a means of allowing creative and context-sensitive solutions to be developed. The Estonian and Lithuanian responses cite the EU Strategy for the BSR as a good example of integrated action, which was echoed by a number of the stakeholders during interviews. The Estonian response calls for partial reallocation of the structural funds via macro-regional strategies on condition that they focus on a limited number of agreed priorities. However, the general emphasis appears to be on the optimization of existing territorial co-operation mechanisms rather than the creation of new ones.

Improved co-ordination is a strong recurring theme and a wide variety of sector policies are identified where more consideration needs to be given to territorial impacts. All three responses identify the transport, energy, environment and rural development sectors and there is also a strong emphasis on science, research, innovation and competitiveness. The reassertion of economic priorities, in combination with an intensive engagement with international economic development networks (Capik, 2011), reflects the policy pragmatism and political expedience that has become increasingly apparent in the current economic climate. Such pragmatism is also revealed in other ways. The Estonian response identifies neighbourhood policy as a key area, reflecting the priority given to the external dimensions of EU territorial governance. The Lithuanian response focuses more strongly on the importance of co-ordinating social, health and education policy, stressing the impact that such services have on quality of life. Finally, the Latvian response identifies the importance of considering the territorial impacts of maritime policy which has become a key issue in Latvia in recent years.

At a practical level, the Estonian response recommends removing the distinction between cohesion policy and rural policy by preparing integrated community strategic guidelines. The Latvian response suggests strengthening the role of the Informal Council of Ministers responsible for Regional Development as well as drawing up EU guidelines on territorial cohesion as a framework for national strategies with mandatory territorial impact assessments of sector policies. The Latvian response also emphasizes the role of ESPON in developing effective monitoring instruments. The Estonian response promotes the application of territorial cohesion through an increased focus on territorial co-operation and trans-national spatial planning.

Each national response recognizes the need to engage a broad coalition of actors in the territorial cohesion debate despite the evidence suggesting that this debate is currently concentrated in expert communities operating in national-level institutions. The stakeholder interviews confirmed the view that sub-national knowledge communities are not fully engaged in this discourse, suggesting that vertical governance structures and knowledge channels appear to be highly fragmented with limited capacity and effectiveness. In contrast to the Latvian attempts to broaden engagement at the sub-national level through its National Co-ordination Group, a Lithuanian interviewee argued that the ambiguous nature of territorial cohesion means that its practical aims and potential added value first need to be clarified at the EU level before Lithuanian planners can divert their attention from more urgent domestic issues, including a new round of planning documents and new planning legislation. Once again, the focus on day-to-day domestic planning practice illustrates the pragmatic approach that characterizes the actions of many planning communities in the Baltic States.

Responses from Selected Interest Groups

A number of responses were submitted by interest groups consisting of trans-national networks. Though the extent to which the contributions have been debated and assembled as a joint product of each member of the network is unclear, six responses have been selected that were submitted by networks where the thematic and/or geographical focus was relevant to the Baltic States and within which actors from the Baltic States participated. The selected groups include VASAB and the Euroregion Baltic, the former displaying characteristics of both an epistemic community and a community of practice and the latter displaying more characteristics of a professional community of practice. The remaining four groups, Innovation Circle Network, the B7 Baltic Sea Islands Network, the Commission for the Peripheral and Maritime Regions (CPMR) and the Network of Eastern External Border Regions (NEEBOR) display characteristics of both advocacy coalitions and communities of practice.

VASAB was identified earlier in the paper as a well-established and influential actor in the field of spatial development in the BSR. Euroregion Baltic focuses on the south-east of the BSR and included eight partner regions in Denmark, Lithuania, Poland, Sweden the Kaliningrad Region of Russia. The B7 network has a long history of participation in EU debates and represents the interests of the largest seven islands in the Baltic Sea, including the two Estonian islands of Saaremaa and Hiiumaa. Innovation Circle Network is a trans-European network of municipalities, regional authorities, public institutions, enterprises and individuals that work together to promote the interests of small towns and rural areas. The response from the CPMR was submitted on behalf of the North Sea and Baltic Sea commissions, two of the six geographical commissions that have been established and currently represent 160 regions from 28 different countries. NEEBOR consists of 34 members from regional and municipal authorities in thirteen countries, representing the interests of the border regions on both sides of the eastern external border of the EU. The Baltic States are represented by respective national associations of regional and municipal governments. An overview of the responses of these groups is provided in Table 3.

Table 3. Commonalities and differences in responses of selected interest groups to the Green Paper on territorial cohesion

Theme	Commonalities between selected interest groups	Group-specific recommendations and practical measures
Definition and overall attitude to territorial cohesion	Identification of similar range of themes encapsulated in the concept Positive attitude to the concept Strong link to balanced, polycentric and sustainable development, equality and access to services and turning diversity into strength Strong focus on maritime aspects	*VASAB*: territorial cohesion as a long-term goal *B7, CPMR and NEEBOR*: areas with specific geographical challenges
Scale and scope of territorial action	Strong focus on issues relevant to geographically peripheral areas, reflecting the nature of the focus of the groups Strong emphasis on local and flexible solutions and role of local knowledge in understanding complexities of local challenges Importance of subsidiarity	*Innovation Circle*: innovative actions and investments in modern infrastructure as means of making periphery more attractive to high-quality human resources
Better co-operation and co-ordination	Emphasizing policy integration and the importance of horizontal and vertical co-operation Advocating strong role for sub-national levels	*Innovation Circle and CPMR*: bottom-up approach *Euroregion Baltic and B7 Islands*: better use of existing co-operation structures such as the Euroregions and cross-border co-operation structures. *Euroregion Baltic and B7 Islands*: increased co-operation through more efficient use of European Groupings of Territorial Co-operation and Territorial Pacts to promote more effective territorial governance between actors from local to EU level
	Promoting facilitation of co-operation over external EU borders	*Euroregion Baltic and NEEBOR*: macro-regional strategies such as the EU Strategy for the BSR as good practice in terms of governance and co-operation
	Sectors where it is important to consider the territorial impacts: rural development, transport, energy, environment and culture	*Euroregion Baltic and B7 Islands*: importance of an integrated maritime policy

(*Continued*)

Table 3. Continued

Theme	Commonalities between selected interest groups	Group-specific recommendations and practical measures
		Euroregion Baltic and CPMR: state aid
		Euroregion Baltic: access to services and climate change
		CPMR: ICT infrastructure
New territorial partnerships	Key role for established territorial partnerships	
Improving the understanding of territorial cohesion	Developing more diverse effective and meaningful territorial cohesion goals and indicators	*Euroregion Baltic, CPMR and B7 Islands*: qualitative and quantitative indicators focusing on geographical peripherality and associated challenges relating to accessibility, access to services, demographic trends, quality of life and quality of the environment
		NEEBOR more diverse indicators
		Innovation Circle: local distinctiveness
		CPMR: central role for ESPON in generating knowledge resources necessary to inform decision-making but also emphasize the importance of local/regional knowledge

Source: Authors' own elaboration.

The responses from VASAB, Innovation Circle Network and Euroregion Baltic are relatively brief and general while those from B7 Islands Network, CPMR and NEEBOR respond more fully and in a more structured way to the Green Paper questions. All respondents are generally positive about the concept of territorial cohesion. They identify a similar range of themes that include balanced, polycentric and sustainable development, equality and access to services, and diversity. These themes reflect both familiarity with EU debates and terminology, as well as an emphasis on issues that are specifically relevant to more geographically peripheral areas. The strong focus on maritime issues reflects the importance of the sea in the BSR and the degree of knowledge and expertise developed on maritime issues in countries such as Latvia.

The Committee for Spatial Development submitted the response on behalf of VASAB.[10] The response is relatively superficial, but refers to the VASAB Long-Term Perspective (LTP) (VASAB, 2010) that was published soon after the consultation closed. The LTP is considered to be a means of contributing towards territorial cohesion and offers a formal definition of the concept as "a desired long-term goal of initiatives and actions resulting from both territorial development policies at national and regional level as well as from those sector policies that show a clear territorial dimension" (VASAB, 2010, p. 14). This definition shows some similarities to the Lithuanian response to the Green Paper, which also implies that territorial cohesion is some form of desired end state, though this does not appear to be a common assumption in other responses.

There is also a significant degree of consensus in relation to the scale and scope of territorial action. Innovation Circle identifies the importance of innovative actions to make geographically peripheral areas more attractive to high-quality human resources. The identification of local responses and local knowledge strengthens arguments about the importance of the spectrum of knowledge discussed earlier in the paper. The concept of subsidiarity is generally articulated as a means of strengthening the role of the sub-national levels, which the Innovation Circle and the CPMR, in particular, both advocate through bottom-up approaches to territorial cohesion policy. All groups recognize the importance of policy integration and improved vertical and horizontal co-operation. Euroregion Baltic and NEEBOR specifically promote the use of macro-regional strategies, such as the EU Strategy for the BSR, as a means of improving governance and co-operation. The responses from Euroregion Baltic and B7 Islands Network share a common equity-based perspective and both demonstrate familiarity with EU debates and instruments. Both support an EU-level Territorial Pact to promote more effective territorial governance and also strongly advocate improved co-operation via the European Groupings of Territorial Cooperation (EGTC). They complain that a number of Member States have not yet integrated the EGTCs into their respective legislative systems, while others have implemented the regulation in such a way as to make it difficult to establish territorial cooperation structures with partners from neighbouring countries. The latter points may be an example where actors are talking the talk but not necessarily walking the walk in relation to EU policy discourse.

The interest group responses also demonstrate a high degree of consensus (also compared to national responses) in relation to the sectors where it is important to consider the territorial impacts with rural development, transport, energy, environment and culture being the most common. Individual responses also identify access to services, climate change and maritime policy. The predominantly sub-national partners forming these trans-national networks do not appear to link territorial cohesion to economic development as strongly as the national governments.

All interest groups identify the importance of increasing our understanding of territorial cohesion and suggest the development of more effective and meaningful goals and indicators. Qualitative and quantitative indicators focusing on geographical peripherality, accessibility, access to services, demographic trends, quality of life and quality of the environment are given high priority. The similarities identified earlier between the responses from Euroregion Baltic and B7 Islands Network are reflected in almost identical recommendations for quantitative and qualitative indicators. These common understandings may reflect agent interaction within the same or related territorial knowledge communities and arenas (the Danish island of Bornholm is a member of both networks). The CPMR response emphasizes the importance of local and flexible solutions and the role of local knowledge on the one hand while on the other hand advocating the role of ESPON in generating the knowledge resources necessary to facilitate informed decision-making.

All of the interest groups discussed operate as knowledge arenas within which territorial knowledge communities seek to advance, inform or legitimize policy agendas and approaches through the strategic use of knowledge resources. The groups emphasize the importance of local knowledge, but in the case of CPMR they recognize the importance of more quantitative scientific knowledge—thus reflecting the full spectrum of knowledge discussed earlier. These knowledge communities display varying degrees of flexibility in terms of their membership and organization, though all are subject to institutional reforms in countries within which they have members. Recently, both Euroregion Baltic and CPMR Baltic Sea Commission have lost members due to the dissolution of institutional structures in Lithuania and Latvia[11] meaning that these two countries are no longer represented in these influential advocacy coalitions.

Innovation Circle and NEEBOR represent even more flexible structures with some members participating in projects while others are simply members of the broader network. The origins of the Innovation Circle Network can be traced back to an Interreg IIIB project, PIPE (Participation, Identity, Planning and Entrepreneurship), which has been further followed by the projects "Innovation Circle" and "Trans-in-form". The fluidity of the partnership also reflects institutional reforms and changing priorities in different countries and the emergence or disappearance of particular personalities within the partner organizations. The wider network currently has approximately thirty partners in eight countries: the three Baltic States plus Norway, Poland, Sweden, Finland and Russia. NEEBOR is similar to the Innovation Circle Network in that some members co-operate in projects including an ongoing Interreg IVC project focusing on SME development and innovation policies in external border areas. The fluidity of these arrangements and networks creates conditions conducive to the types of internationalization of knowledge and policy mobility discussed earlier in the paper.

Conclusions

This paper has sought to explore the evolution of the institutional landscape for planning practice and knowledge in the Baltic States. It examines the extent and nature of engagement of territorial knowledge communities with key knowledge arenas of ESP and identifies the drivers of institutional change following a neo-liberal reassertion of economic priorities, State funding cuts, the dissolution of territorial governance structures and the dismantling of State research institutions or knowledge networks. These factors may potentially affect future policy coordination across a broader spectrum of diverse actors at sub-national levels, which are already marked by the institutionally weak and fragmented nature of professional communities of practice, fragmented local government structures and the marginalization of advocacy coalitions.

Territorial knowledge communities in the Baltic States far exceed the membership of planning associations and include politicians, academics and researchers operating within different networks at different spatial scales within diverse institutions. However, these communities are weak and fragmented in character. The strong pro-development lobby in many CEE countries, including the Baltic States, exacerbates this fragmentation as different interests pursue their own agendas "to catch up with the West both economically and conceptually" (Maier, 2011, p. 267). Institutional reforms across the Baltic States and the dismantling and dissolution of knowledge networks have hampered the evolution and consolidation of knowledge among policy communities. The abolition or weakening of regional tiers of territorial governance has compounded the effects of State funding cuts and has left a planning practice vacuum and inhibited the potential to reinforce the weak and fragmented state of professional communities of practice. These communities have been restricted at a time when their capacity to package funds together with the evidence of good practice may have offered a resurgence of new "cultures of practice" (Stead & Meijers, 2009). Within this scenario, territorial knowledge communities battle for identity and legitimacy in a context exacerbated by the fluid and uncertain nature of territorial knowledge channels making the consolidation of these communities extremely difficult. Analysis of the nation-state and trans-national interest group responses to the *Green Paper on Territorial Cohesion* and the stakeholder interviews suggest that engagement of these territorial knowledge communities with ESP is concentrated among epistemic communities at the State and trans-national level.

The Green Paper has succeeded in extending the territorial cohesion debate to a broader coalition of groups that compete for influence over policy development, though there is an evident possibility of territorial governance gaps or epistemic distance between the EU and Member States and sub-national territorial governance activity. In other words, there is a danger that broader common interests in territorial development will be forgotten because of the increased pressures from these competing agendas within knowledge arenas such as VASAB and Interreg. Even so, there are sufficient grounds for examining the potential for co-ordination and common understanding among these knowledge communities. Indeed, all national and selected interest group responses to the Green Paper identified the EU BSR Strategy as a good example of co-operation, co-ordination and territorial governance, implying that macro-regions have potential in future policy development. Nevertheless, these stakeholder contributions constitute a growing supra-national concentration of epistemic communities. They are increasingly directed by the policy pragmatism and political expedience that has become evident in a reassertion of economic priorities and a much stronger engagement with actors of international economic development networks (Capik, 2011). Furthermore, the emergence of new multi-level cross-scalar arrangements is limited. Rather, it appears that varied policy responses have placed an emphasis on existing co-operation mechanisms and arrangements.

Despite the Green Paper's achievement in engaging a broad range of actors in the debate over territorial cohesion, wider interests appear to be losing out to competing agendas from epistemic communities of extra-regional/trans-national influence. The ESPON knowledge arena is associated primarily with high-level epistemic communities and aggregated data at national and regional scales, which in turn restricts sub-national contributions from local knowledge communities. Thus, it remains to be seen whether planners are simply "talking the talk" rather than "walking the walk" when bringing together evidence-informed arguments to advance policy interests for a broader coalition of actors. There thus remains a need to closely examine the ability of sub-national actors to access and articulate an appropriate spectrum of knowledge and this consideration would need to examine the State financing of participation in collaborative projects (cf. Razumeyko, 2011) as well as the effects of State cuts in education and research funding. The importance of continued investigation in this regard remains pertinent to studies of the powers that shape or "frame" new strategic visions and policy alternatives. Further investigations of the interplay of knowledge and policy development will be especially relevant to this future research. Finally, there is a need to separate the rhetoric of EU spatial development concepts and precepts like territorial cohesion from the reality of territorial development impacts on local communities. Efforts to reconcile "competitiveness with local authority, sustainability with growth, market forces with quality of life—may take place only in the field of abstract rhetoric" (Vanolo, 2010). The challenge for expert communities operating particularly at national and trans-national levels is to translate the abstract notion of territorial cohesion into forms that are meaningful and relevant to sub-national actors and to facilitate the development of effective knowledge channels to strengthen vertical cooperation.

Acknowledgements

Giancarlo Cotella would like to thank the Alexander von Humboldt foundation (http://www.humboldt-foundation.de) for the financial support of his research activity. The authors also would like to thank the anonymous reviewers for providing us with constructive comments and suggestions.

Notes

1. The methodology for this paper involved a series of semi-structured interviews undertaken in late 2010 and early 2011 with some of the key spatial planning and regional development actors in the Baltic States, including academics, civil servants and practitioners active at the national and sub-national levels in both the public and private sectors. Identities have been concealed upon request of the interviewees. The data generated during this process have supplemented desktop analysis of relevant documents and databases, with a particular focus on the responses to the Green Paper on Territorial Cohesion and the relevant websites for Interreg and ESPON programmes and projects.
2. Chief Planner for Riga City in the inter-war period, whose ideas were influenced by the English Garden City movement and resulted in proposals for low density suburban development.
3. There is only one dedicated postgraduate programme in spatial planning available in the Baltic States (started at the University of Latvia in 2007).
4. The Estonian Association, for example, is a full member of the European Council of Spatial Planners, which provides opportunities for exposure to and engagement in European debates.
5. List of VASAB achievements identified at the 2009 Vilnius conference: (1) defined common vision and principles for sustainable spatial development in the BSR; (2) inspired transnational spatial planning policy documents within the framework of CEMAT and the EU; (3) provided a forum for discussion on spatial policy issues within the BSR; (4) improved basic knowledge on spatial development processes and challenges in the BSR; (5) initiated integrate coastal zone management and maritime spatial planning processes in BSR; (6) strengthened spatial planning at national and regional level (with the emphasis on new EU countries); (7) generated transnational co-operation projects and (8) contributed to InterreegIIC and Interreg IIIB operational programmes for BSR ad to overcoming incompatibilities among Interreg, PHARE and TACIS programmes.
6. Estonian stakeholders confirmed during interviews that the Estonia 2030 process has been informed and influenced by the VASAB LTP and that the influence of the latter could be seen clearly in many local and county-level planning documents.
7. Much ESPON data are presented at NUTS2 or NUTS3 levels and therefore provide only limited insights in terms of sub-national issues for the individual Baltic States, which in the ESPON space constitute as many NUTS2 regions.
8. EUROSILANDS project focusing on the sustainable development of the European islands included Saarema County in Estonia and the PURR: Potential of Rural Regions has stakeholder regions in the UK, Norway and Latvia.
9. All responses to the consultation are available at http://ec.europa.eu/regional_policy/archive/consultation/terco/consultation_en.htm
10. The Committee of Spatial Development is the coordinating organ of VASAB and may be closely associated with an epistemic community composed of experts from the different countries, whose expertise focuses on spatial planning and development in BSR.
11. Klaipeda County in Lithuania was a member of both Euroregion Baltic and the Baltic Sea Commission and Riga Region in Latvia was a member of the Baltic Sea Commission.

References

Adams, N. (2006) National spatial strategies in the Baltic States, in: N. Adams, J. Alden & N. Harris (Eds) *Regional Development and Spatial Planning in an Enlarged EU*, pp. 155–181 (Aldershot: Ashgate).

Adams, N. (2008) Convergence and policy transfer: An examination of the extent to which approaches to spatial planning have converged within the context of an enlarged EU, *International Planning Studies*, 13(1), pp. 31–50.

Adams, N. & Harris, N. (2005) *Best Practice Guidelines for Regional Development Strategies* (Cardiff: Cardiff University Press).

Adams, N., Alden, J. & Harris, N. (2006) *Regional Development and Spatial Planning in an Enlarged EU* (Aldershot: Ashgate).

Adams, N., Cotella, G. & Nunes, R. (2011) *Territorial Development, Cohesion and Spatial Planning: Knowledge and Policy Development in an Enlarged EU* (London: Routledge).

Allmendinger, P. & Tewdwr-Jones, M. (2000) Spatial dimensions and institutional uncertainties of planning and the new regionalism, *Environment and Planning C*, 18, pp. 711–726.

Baumgartner, F. R. & Jones, B. D. (Eds) (2002) *Policy Dynamics* (Chicago: University of Chicago Press).

Benz, A. (2000) Two types of multi-level governance: Inter-governmental relations in Germany and European regional policy, *Regional and Federal Studies*, 10(3), pp. 21–44.

Böhme, K. & Waterhout, B. (2008) The Europeanisation of planning, in: A. Faludi (Ed), *European Spatial Research and Planning*, pp. 225–248. (Cambridge, MA: Lincoln Institute of Land Policy).

Capik, P. (2011) Regional promotion and competition: An examination of approaches to FDI attraction in the Czech Republic, Poland and Slovakia, in: N. Adams, G. Cotella & R. Nunes (Eds) *Territorial Development, Cohesion and Spatial Planning: Knowledge and Policy Development in an Enlarged EU*, pp. 320–344 (London: Routledge).

CEC (2008) *Green Paper on Territorial Cohesion—Turning Territorial Diversity into Strength* (Brussels: Commission of the European Communities).

CEC (2011) *Fifth Report on Economic, Social and Territorial Cohesion: Investing in Europe's Future* (Luxembourg: Office for Official Publications of the European Communities).

Clarence, E. (2002) Technocracy reinvented: The new evidence based policy movement, *Public Policy and Administration*, 17(1), pp. 1–11.

COMMIN (undated) *Baltic Sea Conceptshare National Spatial Planning Systems*. Available at http://commin.org/en/planning-systems/national-planning-systems/nations.html (accessed March 2011).

Cotella, G. (2009) Governance territoriale comunitaria e sistemi di pianificazione: Riflessioni sull'allargamento ad est dell'Unione europea, PhD dissertation, Inter-university department of territorial studies and planning, Politecnico di Torino, Torino, Italy.

Cotella, G. & Janin Rivolin, U. (2010) *Institutions, Discourse and Practices: Towards a Multi-dimensional Understanding of EU Territorial Governance*, Paper Presented at the 24th AESOP Congress, Helsinki (Finland), 7–10 July 2010.

Cotella, G., Janin Rivolin, U. & Reimer, M. (2011) Structure, tools, discourse and practices: A multi-dimensional comparative approach to EU territorial governance. Paper Presented at the 3rd World Planning Schools Congress, Perth, Western Australia, 4–8 July 2011.

Cotella, G., Adams, N. & Nunes, R. (2012) Engaging in European spatial planning: A central and Eastern European perspective on the territorial cohesion debate, *European Planning Studies*, 20(7), pp. 1197–1220.

Dagliene, G. (2006) The response to regional disparities in Lithuania, in: N. Adams, J. Alden & N. Harris (Eds) *Regional Development and Spatial Planning in an Enlarged EU*, pp. 221–240 (Aldershot: Ashgate).

EC (2009) *Communication from the Commission to the European Parliament, the Council, the European Economic and Social Committee and the Committee of the Regions concerning the European Union Strategy for the Baltic Sea Region*. Available at http://ec.europa.eu/regional_policy/sources/docoffic/official/communic/baltic/com_baltic_en.pdf (accessed March 2011).

Estonian Ministry of Interior (2009) *Estonia's contribution regarding Commission communication, Green Paper on Territorial Cohesion—Turning territorial diversity into strength*. Available at http://ec.europa.eu/regional_policy/consultation/terco/contrib_en.htm (accessed February 2011).

Estonian Ministry of the Environment (2001) *Estonia 2010 National Spatial Plan* (Tallinn: Ministry of the Environment).

EUA (2011) *Impact of the economic crisis on European universities*. Available at http://www.eua.be/news/09-11-13/EUA_delegation_visit_to_Latvia_focuses_on_higher_education_funding_and_reforms.aspx (accessed January 2011).

Eurostat (2011) Available at http://epp.eurostat.ec.europa.eu/portal/page/portal/eurostat/home/ (accessed February 2011).

Evers, D. (2007) Reflections on territorial cohesion and European spatial planning, *Tijdschrift voor Economische en Sociale Geografie*, 99(3), pp. 303–315.

Evers, D., Tennekes, J., Borsboom, J., Heiligenberg, H. & Van Den, Thissen, M. (2009) *A Territorial Impact Assessment of Territorial Cohesion for the Netherlands*, Netherlands Environmental Assessment Agency (PBL). Available at http://www.eukn.org/binaries/eukn/netherlands/research/2009/07/tia_tc_webversie.pdf (accessed March 2010).

Faludi, A. (2008) The learning machine: European integration in the planning mirror, *Environment and Planning A*, 40(6), pp. 1470–1484.

Faludi, A. (2009) *Territorial Cohesion under the Looking Glass*, Synthesis paper about the history of the concept and policy background to territorial cohesion. Available at http://ec.europa.eu/regional_policy/consultation/terco/pdf/lookingglass.pdf (accessed February 2011).

Faludi, A. & Waterhout, B. (2006) Introducing evidence-based planning, *disP*, 165(2), pp. 4–13.

Fritsch, M. (2011) Interfaces of European union internal and external territorial governance: The Baltic Sea region, in: N. Adams, G. Cotella & R. Nunes (Eds) *Territorial Development, Cohesion and Spatial Planning: Knowledge and Policy Development in an Enlarged EU*, pp. 382–401 (London: Routledge).

Haas, E. B. (1990) *When Knowledge is Power* (Berkley CA: University of California Press).

Haas, P. (1992) Introduction: epistemic communities and international policy coordination, *International Organization*, 46(1), pp. 1–35.

Haas, P. (2004) When does power listen to truth? A constructivist approach to the policy process, *Journal of European Public Policy*, 11(4), pp. 569–592.

HU Presidency (2011) *Territorial Agenda of the European Union 2020: Towards an Inclusive, Smart and Sustainable Europe of Diverse Regions*. Available at http://www.eu2011.hu/files/bveu/documents/TA2020.pdf (accessed July 2012).

Janin Rivolin, U. (2010) EU territorial governance, learning from institutional progress, *European Journal of Spatial Development*, 38, pp. 1–28.

Jensen, O. B. & Richardson, T. (2004) *Making European Space* (London: Routledge).

Kingdon, J. W. (1995) *Agendas, Alternatives and Public Policies* (New York: Harper Collins).

Krizek, K., Forysth, A. & Slotterback, C. S. (2009) Is there a role for evidence-based practice in Urban planning and policy? *Planning Theory and Practice*, 10(4), pp. 459–478.

Kule, L., Krisjane, Z. & Berzins, M. (2011) The rhetoric and reality of pursuing territorial cohesion in Latvia, in: N. Adams, G. Cotella & R. Nunes (Eds) *Territorial Development, Cohesion and Spatial Planning: Knowledge and Policy Development in an Enlarged EU*, pp. 291–319 (London: Routledge).

Laeken European Council (2001) *Presidency Conclusions: European Council meeting in Laeken*, 14 and 15 December. Available at http://ec.europa.eu/governance/impact/background/docs/laeken_concl_en.pdf (accessed March 2011).

Larner, W. & Laurie, N. (2010) Travelling technocrats, embodied knowledges: Globalising privatisation in telecoms and water, *Geoforum*, 41, pp. 218–216.

Lave, J. & Wenger, E. (1991) *Situated Learning: Legitimate Peripheral Participation* (Cambridge: Cambridge University Press).

Lieven, A. (1993) *The Baltic Revolution: Estonia, Latvia and Lithuania and the Path to Independence* (New Haven, CT: Yale University Press).

Lithuanian Ministry of Finance (2009) *Conclusions of Lithuania's Public Discussions on Issues Raised in the Green Paper on Territorial Cohesion*. Available at http://ec.europa.eu/regional_policy/consultation/terco/contrib_en.htm (accessed February 2011).

Lithuanian Ministry of the Environment (2002) *Comprehensive Plan of the Territory of the Republic of Lithuania* (Vilnius: Ministry of the Environment).

Maier, K. (2011) The pursuit of balanced territorial development: The realities and complexities of the cohesion agenda, in: N. Adams, G. Cotella & R. Nunes (Eds) *Territorial Development, Cohesion and Spatial Planning: Knowledge and Policy Development in an Enlarged EU*, pp. 266–290 (London: Routledge).

IMPACTS OF EUROPEAN TERRITORIAL POLICIES IN THE BALTIC STATES

MRDLG—Latvian Ministry of Regional Development and Local Government (2009) *Latvia's Position on the European Commission's Green Paper on Territorial Cohesion Turning Diversity into Strength.* Available at http://ec.europa.eu/regional_policy/consultation/terco/contrib_en.htm (accessed February 2011).

Pabriks, A. & Purs, A. (2002) Latvia's democracy examined: 1991–1999, in: D. Smith, A. Pabriks, A. Purs & T. Lane (Eds) *The Baltic States: Estonia, Latvia and Lithuania*, pp. 1–169 (London: Routledge).

Pallagst, K. (2006) European spatial planning reloaded: considering EU enlargement in theory and practice, *European Planning Studies*, 14(2), pp. 253–272.

Pallagst, K. (2011) The emergence of "Epistemic communities" in the New European landscape: some theoretical implications for territorial development and the spatial agenda of the EU, in: N. Adams, G. Cotella & R. Nunes (Eds) *Territorial Development, Cohesion and Spatial Planning: Knowledge and Policy Development in an Enlarged EU*, pp. 124–142 (London: Routledge).

PURR (2011) *Draft Final Report, Potential of Rural regions*, ESPON 2013 Programme. Available at http://www.espon.eu/export/sites/default/Documents/Projects/TargetedAnalyses/PURR/PURR_DFR.pdf (accessed July 2012).

Radaelli, C. M. (1995) The role of knowledge in the policy process, *Journal of European Public Policy*, 2(2), pp. 159–183.

Radaelli, C. M. (1999) The public policy of the European Union: whither politics of expertise? *Journal of European Public Policy*, 6(5), pp. 757–774.

Razumeyko, N. (2011) Strategic planning practices in North-West Russia: European influences, challenges and future perspectives, in: N. Adams, G. Cotella & R. Nunes (Eds) *Territorial Development, Cohesion and Spatial Planning: Knowledge and Policy Development in an Enlarged EU*, pp. 402–421 (London: Routledge).

Rydin, Y. (2007) Re-examining the role of knowledge within planning theory, *Planning Theory*, 6(1), pp. 52–68.

Sabatier, P. A. (1998) The advocacy coalition framework: revisions and relevance for Europe, *Journal of European Public Policy*, 5(1), pp. 98–130.

Sabatier, P. A. & Jenkins-Smith, H. C. (Eds) (1993) *Policy Change and Learning: An Advocacy Coalition Approach* (Boulder, CO: Westview Press).

Saeima (2010) *Latvia 2030: Sustainable Development Strategy of Latvia until 2030, Spatial Development Perspective.*

Schimmelfennig, F. & Sedelmeier, U. (2005) *The Europeanization of Central and Eastern Europe* (Ithaca, NY: Cornell University Press).

Schön, D. (1978) Generative metaphor: A perspective in policy setting in social policy, in: A. Ortony (Ed) *Metaphor and Thought*, pp. 137–164 (Cambridge: Cambridge University Press).

Smith, D. J. (2002) Old wine in new bottles: the politics of independence, in: D. Smith, A. Pabriks, A. Purs & T. Lane (Eds) *The Baltic States: Estonia, Latvia and Lithuania*, pp. 65–110 (London: Routledge).

Smith, D. J., Pabriks, A., Purs, A. & Lane, T. (2002) *The Baltic States: Estonia, Latvia and Lithuania* (London: Routledge).

Stead, D. & Cotella, G. (Eds), (2011) Differential Europe: Domestic Actors and their Role in Shaping Spatial Planning Systems, *Special issue of DISP—The Planning Review*, 186(3).

Stead, D. & Meijers, E. (2009) Spatial planning and policy integration: concepts, facilitators and inhibitors, *Planning Theory & Practice*, 10(3), pp. 317–332.

Treaty of Amsterdam (1997) Treaty of Amsterdam, *Official Journal of the European Union*, C 340/10. Available at http://eur-lex.europa.eu/en/treaties/index.htm (accessed March 2011).

Treaty of Lisbon (2007) Treaty of Lisbon, *Official Journal of the European Union*, C 306/01. Available at http://eur-lex.europa.eu/en/treaties/index.htm (accessed March 2011).

Treaty of Nice (2001) Treaty of Nice, *Official Journal of the European Union*, C 80/01. Available at http://eur-lex.europa.eu/en/treaties/index.htm (accessed March 2011).

Vanolo, A. (2010) European spatial planning between competitiveness and territorial cohesion: shadows of neo-liberalism, *European Planning Studies*, 18(8), pp. 1301–1315.

VASAB (2009) *VASAB 15: From Tallinn to Vilnius, workshop working document.* Available at http://www.vasab.org/conference/upload/dokumenti/vasab_15.jpg (accessed January 2011).

VASAB (2010) *VASAB Long Term Perspective for the Territorial Development of the Baltic Sea Region: Towards better territorial integration of the Baltic Sea Region and its integration with other areas of Europe.* Available at http://www.vasab.org/conference/page/67 (accessed January 2011).

Waterhout, B. (2008) *The Institutionalisation of European Spatial Planning* (Amsterdam: IOS Press).

Waterhout, B. (2011) European spatial planning: current state and future challenges, in: N. Adams, G. Cotella & R. Nunes (Eds) *Territorial Development, Cohesion and Spatial Planning: Knowledge and Policy Development in an Enlarged EU*, pp. 84–102 (London: Routledge).

Waterhout, B., Mourato, J. & Böhme, K. (2009) The impact of europeanization on planning cultures, in: J. Knieling & F. Othengrafen (Eds) *Planning Cultures In Europe: Decoding Cultural Phenomena in Urban and Regional Planning*, pp. 239–254 (Aldershot: Ashgate).

Wenger, E. (1998) *Communities of Practice: Learning, Meaning, and Identity* (Cambridge: Cambridge University Press).

Williams, R. H. (1996) *European Union, Spatial Policy and Planning* (London: Paul Chapman).

From Conditionality to Europeanization in Central and Eastern Europe: Administrative Performance and Capacity in Cohesion Policy

JOHN BACHTLER*, CARLOS MENDEZ* & HILDEGARD ORAŽE**

*European Policies Research Centre, School of Government and Public Policy, University of Strathclyde, Glasgow, UK, **Metis GmbH, Vienna, Austria

ABSTRACT *This article assesses the role of administrative capacity in explaining the performance of eight Central and Eastern European countries in managing Cohesion policy over the 2004–2008 period. Drawing on a conceptual framework from the Europeanization literature, it explores whether pre-accession administrative adjustment to comply with the "acquis" continued in the post-accession period, against a backdrop of critical assessments about the state of administrative capacity for managing Cohesion policy. We conclude that administrative capacity was developed faster and more substantially than commentators predicted. The findings have implications for our understanding of the post-accession compliance record of the EU8, challenging the contention that they fall within a "world of dead letters". Administrative capacity has been underestimated and insufficient attention has been given to the dynamics of capacity evolution and learning.*

1. Introduction

In recent years, administrative capacity has been identified as an explanation of the variable performance of European Union (EU) Cohesion policy. Studies have concluded that the contribution of the policy to economic development is conditional on the capacity of national and regional institutions to design robust strategies, allocate resources effectively and administer EU funding efficiently (Ederveen *et al.*, 2002, 2006; Cappelen *et al.*, 2003; Horvat, 2005; Bachtler & Gorzelak, 2007; Milio, 2007). These findings are echoed in policy-maker criticisms of Cohesion policy (Barca, 2009; EC, 2009) and underpin the European Commission's proposals for improving the policy's performance in the 2014–2020 period (EC, 2011).

The Member States of Central and Eastern Europe (CEE) have been subjected to particular scrutiny, reflecting policy-maker concern about their ability to spend Structural and Cohesion Funds. In the run-up to EU enlargement in 2004, commentators questioned the administrative capacity of the CEE accession countries to manage EU funding (Bollen *et al.*, 2000; Kalman, 2002; Hughes *et al.*, 2004; Šumpíková *et al.*, 2004). Adoption of the EU's "acquis communautaire" required wide-ranging reforms of economic, political and social structures, especially public administration, but many reforms were slow and incomplete (SIGMA, 1998; Bossaert *et al.*, 2001; Bossaert & Demmke, 2003; Demmke *et al.*, 2006).

The implementation of Cohesion policy is complex, yet the lack of formal conditionality in the "acquis" meant that most CEE countries did not prioritise regional policy in preparing for accession (Hughes *et al.*, 2003). Despite pre-accession funding, most CEE countries had perceived weaknesses in their legal frameworks, administrative structures and management systems. Initial assessments after accession showed a mixed picture. While some structures were in place, the planning and implementation of Structural Funds was affected by weak coordination, high turnover of staff, lack of skills and frequent institutional change (OECD, 2001; McMaster & Novotný, 2006; Bachtler & McMaster, 2008).

After completion of the 2004–2008 cycle[1] and much of the 2007–2013 programme period, the question is whether these concerns were warranted. With new data and information for 2004–2008, it is timely to undertake a new assessment of the performance of CEE countries and what it says about administrative capacity.

In doing so, the paper contributes to the limited in-depth research on the "post-accession" institutional and administrative record of the CEE countries. This is salient given concerns about a possible "reversal" of pre-accession progress as a result of changes in EU incentive structures (Epstein & Sedelmeier, 2008; Dimitrova & Toshkov, 2009; Meyer-Sahling, 2009; Dimitrova, 2010). Meyer-Sahling argues that only three of the 2004 accession countries continued to make progress with public administration reforms, the others demonstrating "reform reversals", while Cerami (2008) found signs of "accession fatigue". This paper directly addresses the question posed by Schimmelfennig and Sedelmeier (2004) of whether short-term effectiveness in pre-accession compliance was achieved at the expense of long-term inefficiency, and responds to the plea of Sedelmeier (2011) for more research on the application of the "acquis" in the new members.

This article assesses the role of administrative capacity in explaining the performance of eight CEE countries (EU8[2]) in managing and implementing Cohesion policy over the 2004–2008 period following their accession to the EU. Employing a Europeanization conceptual framework, the main question is whether and how the diffusion and institutionalization of European policy rules influenced the administrative performance of Cohesion policy in the EU8, especially the role of administrative capacity.

The article initially sets out the conceptual framework and methodology. It then empirically assesses administrative performance in the EU8 during 2004–2008 and investigates the role of administrative capacity. The final section presents conclusions, highlights the contribution to the state-of-the-art and identifies policy implications.

2. Conceptual Framework

The conceptual basis for this investigation of EU policy performance in CEE is derived from the literature on Europeanization and EU conditionality. We begin with Radaelli's (2000) well-known definition of Europeanization, comprising processes of:

(a) construction (b) diffusion and (c) institutionalization of formal and informal rules, procedures, policy paradigms, styles, "ways of doing things" and shared beliefs and norms which are defined and consolidated in the EU policy process and then incorporated in the logic of domestic discourse, identities, political structures and public policies.

This article focuses on the post-decisional stage of diffusion and institutionalization of policy rules. That said, the nature of the EU-level pressure (the independent variable) requires clarification. Although expressed in various ways in the literature (Knill 2001; Bulmer & Radaelli, 2004; Knill & Lenschow, 2005), the key issue is whether Cohesion policy conforms to a "hard" or "soft" adaptational pressure/policy regime. Grabbe (2006) places EU aid programmes, such as pre-accession assistance, at the harder end of this policy influence continuum since they set out concrete policy models for adoption in exchange for funding and other benefits. Indeed, the regulatory prescriptiveness of Cohesion policy (Mendez & Bachtler, 2011) suggests Cohesion policy to be a highly coercive domain (Schmidt, 2002). However, the intensity of pressure varies across the policy's different functional domains; the regulatory provisions are often open-ended—characterized by McAleavey (1995) as "incomplete contracts" allowing considerable discretion to Member States.

With respect to the dependent variable, this enquiry focuses on "policy" rather than "politics" or "polity", and specifically the EU impact on policy "processes", as opposed to final "outcomes" (i.e. economic development impacts). As such, the assessment of Cohesion policy (administrative) performance is concerned with the functions of programme design, project selection, financial management, reporting, monitoring and evaluation.

Conventional conceptualizations of Europeanization usually distinguish between no, minimal and radical change, employing labels such as inertia, accommodation and transformation (Héritier et al., 1996; Börzel & Risse, 2000; Schmidt, 2002). The emphasis of this study is on reform trajectories and capacities (Featherstone & Papadimitriou, 2008), rather than spillover effects on domestic frameworks. Of course, evidence of reform could be interpreted as spillover (or policy transfer) given the rudimentary nature of regional policies in CEE before accession (Hughes et al., 2004), in line with the "tabula rasa" conception of the CEE-receiving environment in the Europeanization literature (Goetz, 2001).

The baseline definition of effective performance is the extent to which systems are "fit for purpose" in fulfilling the regulatory, strategic and financial requirements of policy programme management and implementation. The terms "weak", "moderate", "significant" and "strong" are preferred to categorize variations in administrative performance.

The methodological challenges of measuring differential outcomes in Europeanization research are taken seriously (Radaelli, 2003). Instead of the rather formal, structural indicators employed in other studies of administrative performance (NEI, 2002; Horvat, 2005) or quantitative analyses used by Hille and Knill (2006) and Dimitrova and Toshkov (2007), we adopt an explorative, bottom-up approach based on qualitative indicators sensitive to key features of Cohesion policy implementation (Table 1).

Regarding the mechanisms of influence and mediating factors between (EU) cause and (domestic) effect, a key distinction is between rationalist mechanisms of adaptation (based on power and interests) and sociological mechanisms of adaptation (driven by norms of

Table 1. Operationalization of administrative performance in the EU8

Administrative performance	Specific indicators	Assessment of administrative performance			
		Strong (A)	Significant (B)	Moderate (C)	Weak (D)
(1) Programming	Organization of programming	Processes clearly defined and implemented well	Processes clearly defined, and implemented adequately	Processes defined, but implemented inadequately	Processes poorly defined and implemented inadequately
	Programme documents	Well-structured documents. Clear strategic focus	Programme documents with some deficiencies in strategy	Programme documents without a clear strategic focus	Programme documents with major deficiencies in strategy
	Negotiation and approval	Efficient and speedy negotiation and timely approval	Minor delays in negotiation/approval	Major problems with negotiations but minor delays in approval	Major problems with negotiations. Significant delays in approval
(2) Project preparation and selection	Project generation	Sufficient demand, high quality of project applications	Sufficient demand, quality of project applications needing improvements	Mostly sufficient demand with some delays, project applications of low quality	Low demand
	Project appraisal and selection	Defined criteria, including well-developed and applied quality criteria, short decision times	Defined criteria with deficiencies in quality criteria, partly long decision times	Mostly defined criteria, lengthy procedures with focus on formal criteria	Lack of defined criteria for appraisal and selection
	Commitment of funds	Most or all funds committed, no decommitment	Above-average commitment of funds, below-average decommitment	Below-average commitment of funds, above-average decommitment	Significantly below-average commitment of funds, and/or significantly above-average decommitment

Category	Criterion	(Best)			(Worst)
(3) Financial management	Processing of payment claims	Clearly defined and quick processing of payment claims, efficient checks	Clearly defined processing of payment claims, partly multiple checks and delays	Defined processing of payment claims. Frequent delays. Multiple checks	Processes not clearly defined. Major processing problems
	Financial (de)commitment	Strategic approach to programme management to avoid decommitment	Measures in place to manage financial flows to avoid de-commitment	Passive approach, case-by-case response to decommitment	No management mechanisms for decommitment
	Financial management and control	All systems effective	Some systems partially effective	Some systems ineffective	All systems ineffective
(4) Monitoring and reporting	System of indicators and monitoring procedures	System and procedures fully operational, with coherent indicator system	System operational, procedures established, but not fully operational; some indicator weaknesses	System exists but is only partly operational; indicator and procedural weaknesses	No monitoring system
	Availability of financial, physical and procedural data	High-quality and comprehensive data, easily available and used for programme management	Good quality data, with some gaps, and/or imperfect procedures	Partial data available, mostly cumbersome procedures	No data available
(5) Evaluation	Evaluation reports	Developed evaluation system with regular reports	Ex ante, interim and/or thematic reports produced	Only ex ante report(s) produced	No reports produced
	Evaluation methods and culture	Evaluation embedded. High level of capacity and utilization	Evaluation system established, good capacity but utilization is mixed	Evaluation undertaken but capacity constraints or limited utilization	Evaluation is not considered useful. Limited or no capacity

appropriate behaviour and learning) (Börzel & Risse, 2000). Rationalist mechanisms have been used to explain policy outcomes in the process before and after CEE accession by Schimmelfennig and Sedelmeier (2005). Sedelmeier (2011) has also highlighted the key mediating factors that are rationalist (domestic political costs of adopting rules; societal mobilization; supportive formal institutions and administrative capacities); or sociological/constructivist (identification with the EU; positive normative resonance with domestic rules and transnational (epistemic) networks).

Administrative capacity is the key factor motivating this study, given assumptions of its importance in accounting for Cohesion policy performance outcomes. The survey by Sedelmeier (2011) only briefly touches on this issue, and it is absent from classic conceptualizations and analyses of Europeanization (Risse *et al.*, 2001; Featherstone & Radaelli, 2003), arguably because of the EU15 bias and presumptions of adequate administrative standards to meet EU policy demands. Where CEE administrative capacity has been recognized as an important factor, its treatment has not been entirely satisfactory. Quantitative studies on the transposition of EU directives have included an administrative capacity variable, but usually measured indirectly through proxies relating to transposition timing, previous experiences (Steunenberg & Kaeding, 2009) or by using indicators on the quality of governance in CEE rather than capacity in policy areas of interest (Toshkov, 2008). Moreover, statistical regression techniques are blind to the contextualized understanding of policy processes. Finally, most studies of administrative capacity for Cohesion policy in CEE relate to the pre-accession period and were often partial, in some cases ignoring key programme management tasks (NEI, 2002; Horvat, 2005).

Our approach builds on this earlier work but takes a broader and deeper approach. In analysing administrative performance, we assess the complete programme management cycle for implementing Cohesion policy, measured using 13 indicators. Further, in assessing the role of administrative capacity (using six indicators), we examine not just whether structures, human resources and procedures and tools were put in place, but also how they functioned over the 2004–2008 period (see Table 2).

Our framework is also sensitive to other explanatory factors of policy performance, such as actor preferences and veto points. It has been argued that CEE Member States might behave according to their own logic, reducing their compliance efforts once pre-accession conditionality is lifted. The EU10 has been characterized as a "world of dead letters" with politicized implementation and systematic enforcement problems (Falkner *et al.*, 2008). Change is presumed to be formalistic adaptation, responding opportunistically to incentives (Schimmelfennig & Sedelmeier, 2005; Bruszt & Verdes, 2011).

A rival rationalist hypothesis is that CEE policy processes may be radically transformed due to the shock therapy of EU policy treatment (Meyer-Sahling & Yesilkagit, 2011, p. 319). Moreover, sociological perspectives on Europeanization point to the role of learning as a domestic facilitating factor, with the CEE countries being particularly receptive to EU Cohesion policy norms (Scherpereel, 2010). Administrative adaptation may be easier because CEE countries can go policy-shopping in Western Europe to draw lessons (Meyer-Sahling, 2009), although assimilating EU Cohesion policy may require learning through experience for at least one complete programme period (Bachtler *et al.*, 2002).

The empirical research for this article is based on data from European Commission and European Court of Auditor reports, national programme documents, evaluation studies and academic research. Fieldwork research involved over 120 interviews carried out during 2008–2010 with government officials, senior personnel in implementing bodies

Table 2. Operationalization of administrative capacity in the EU8

Administrative capacity	Specific indicators	Assessment of administrative capacity			
		Consolidated/strong (A)	Developing (B)	Basic (C)	Absent/rudimentary (D)
(1) Organizational structures	Allocation of competencies and responsibilities	Clear allocation of competencies and effective operation	Clear, formalized allocation of competencies and responsibilities but operational weaknesses	Partially formalized allocation of competencies and responsibilities. Significant operational weaknesses	Unclear or largely informal allocation of competencies and responsibilities. Major operational weaknesses
	Coordination/ cooperation among ministries and implementing bodies	Strong, open intra-department communication, with good use of formal and informal channels and periodic review	Good intra-departmental communication but limited openess. Use of formal and informal channels	Modes of intra-departmental communication. Emerging formal channels for dialogue and decision-making	Poor intra-departmental communication. Lack of formal and informal channels for coordination
	Organizational stability	Stable structures and responsibilities throughout the programme period	Largely stable structures. Minor internal reorganization	Some instability, with episodic reallocation among ministries or implementing bodies	Unstable structures with frequent/substantial reorganization of responsibilities among ministries or implementing bodies
(2) Human resources	Availability of suitably qualified staff	Sufficiently qualified and experienced staff available. Low turnover	Staff available with some constraints in qualification, experience or turnover	Staff available, but major constraints in qualification or experience, or turnover	Severe lack of sufficient and qualified staff
	Human resource management	Well-developed HR management system. Effective performance assessment and staff development	Developed HR management system. Operational weaknesses in performance assessment and staff development	HR management system with limited performance assessment and staff development functions	No HR management system
(3) Administrative adaptability	Establishment and adaptability of procedures and tools	Flexible mechanisms for on-going adaptation and use of staff experience	Some mechanisms for adaptation, partly using staff experience	Cumbersome, inflexible mechanisms for adaptation	No mechanisms for adaptation established

and external observers. For each administrative function examined, qualitative interview-based assessment is complemented by data relating to commitment, expenditure, decommitment, errors and system effectiveness.[3]

3. Cohesion Policy Performance in CEE

The assessment of administrative performance involved research on six stages of the programme cycle for Cohesion policy: programming; project generation, appraisal and selection; financial management; reporting; monitoring; and evaluation. These account for c. 80% of the workload and costs incurred in the administration of Cohesion policy (SWECO, 2010).

3.1 Programming of Resources

The administrative cycle starts with the programming of resources. EU regulations for 2000–2006 required an analysis of development challenges, a strategy setting out objectives and priorities, a justification for financial allocations, targets and implementation arrangements.

The programming process was demanding for the EU8, all of which lacked experience with the strategic planning and coordination required for EU funds, despite capacity-building under PHARE and ISPA (Instrument for Structural Policies for Pre-Accession). In each country, national development plans were drawn up by central government ministries as a basis for strategies, and regional/local and non-governmental organizations were consulted to a limited extent. The structure of EU8 programmes was simpler than in the EU15, concentrating resources on a limited number of priorities and focusing on basic infrastructure (transport and telecoms), education and training and the agricultural sector (Applica *et al.,* 2009).

Ex ante evaluations of the strategies were conducted, mostly by foreign experts, but were sometimes "quasi-appraisals", providing officials with specialist expertise on particular topics rather than formal evaluations of expenditure plans and intended outcomes. These studies commonly found that programmes lacked a clear national development strategy, especially in Estonia, Hungary, Lithuania and Slovakia.

Despite the difficulties involved, all countries finalized their negotiations with the Commission by Spring 2004, and all programming documents were adopted on time by the Commission in June/July 2004.

3.2 Project Generation, Appraisal and Selection

The generation, appraisal and selection of EU-funded projects involve a series of steps from informing potential applicants to the final approval of selected projects. This required the preparation of relevant documents for calls, transparent and objective appraisals, the definition of selection criteria and the preparation of templates for applications and contracts.

Implementing bodies made considerable efforts, in advance of programme launch, to inform potential applicants about the application requirements of EU funding. Calls for projects were issued and applications submitted quickly after programmes were approved. A combination of automatic (first-come-first-served) and competitive selection systems were used in most countries. Larger infrastructure projects were usually pre-selected.

Table 3. Financial absorption of Cohesion policy funds

	Allocations		Percentage of allocations paid out, 2004–2008				
	€ mill	% of EU8	ERDF	ESF	EAGGF	FIFG	Total SF
Czech Rep.	1584.35	10.5	92.95	83.49	95.00	95.00	90.64
Estonia	371.36	2.5	95.00	94.75	95.00	95.00	94.95
Hungary	1995.72	13.2	95.00	91.02	95.00	86.19	94.11
Latvia	625.75	4.1	95.00	95.00	95.00	95.00	95.00
Lithuania	895.17	5.9	95.00	95.00	95.00	95.00	95.00
Poland	8275.81	54.8	93.96	91.34	95.00	75.19	93.05
Slovakia	1115.19	7.4	94.52	90.06	95.00	95.00	93.31
Slovenia	237.51	1.6	95.00	85.06	95.00	92.85	91.82
EU8	**15,100.86**	**100.0**	**94.18**	**90.49**	**95.00**	**79.62**	**93.18**
EU25	**211,923.20**		**90.60**	**90.89**	**91.9**	**89.08**	**90.80**

Notes: Data are for payments made by the Commission to Member States up to 2008 for expenditure relating to 2004–2006 (2000–2006 for the EU25). 95% is the maximum amount payable by the Commission before formal closure. ERDF: European Regional Development Fund; ESF: European Social Fund; EAGGF: European Agricultural Guidance & Guarantee Fund; FIFG: Financial Instrument For Fisheries Guidance.
Source: Extracted from EC (2009).

The effectiveness of project generation is evident in the high demand for funding (see Table 3). Already after 12 months, applications exceeded the funding earmarked for some measures (EC, 2005). It took time for projects to be in a position to actually absorb (use) the funding that had been awarded, a process which accelerated towards the end of the 2004–2008 period (EC, 2008).

By 2008, the EU8 had absorbed 93% of Cohesion policy funding across the four Funds. EU8 performance was considerably better than for the EU25 as a whole, particularly under the ERDF, with the three Baltic countries having the best absorption figures. However, EU8 performance was weaker in the case of the ESF (as a result of absorption problems, mainly in the Czech Republic and Slovenia) and for the FIFG because of low absorption in Poland and to a lesser extent in Hungary.

A further measure of absorption performance is the correspondence of spending with the priorities set out in the Community Support Framework or Operational Programme (OP). The EU8 were largely able to absorb Objective 1 funding (for the productive environment, human resources and basic infrastructure) in line with programme objectives. Deviations were minimal, much lower than for the EU15. For Objective 2, there were no recorded deviations from planned expenditure in the Czech Republic (for spending in the Prague region), but the equivalent programme for the Bratislava region in Slovakia experienced a substantial reallocation of expenditure of over 10% away from the productive environment, primarily to basic infrastructure (Applica *et al.*, 2009).

Finally, absorption can be judged in terms of compliance with the "decommitment rule".[4] Overall, the pace of spending was sufficient (see Table 4), the exceptions being the Czech Republic, Estonia, Latvia and Slovakia. Decommitments for the EU8 were little more than one-tenth of the EU15 figure, as a proportion of the Structural Funds allocated (Applica *et al.*, 2009).

Although the headline absorption figures for the EU8 were relatively good, spending in some sectors was much slower than in the EU15 (Applica *et al.*, 2009). There is also evidence that the quality and geographic coverage of projects selected was uneven, and there

Table 4. Decommitments of Structural Funds (Objectives 1 and 2), 2004–2006

	Allocations (€ mill)			Decommitments (€ mill)			%
	Obj. 1	Obj. 2	Total	Obj. 1	Obj. 2	Total	
Czech Rep.	1453.3	71.3	1524.6	−3.1		−3.1	−0.21
Estonia	371.4		371.4	−6.8		−6.8	−1.84
Hungary	1995.7		1995.7				
Lithuania	895.2		895.2				
Latvia	625.6		625.6	−9.8		−9.8	−1.57
Poland	8275.8		8275.8				
Slovakia	1041.0	37.0	1078		−0.1	−0.1	−0.01
Slovenia	237.5		237.5				
EU8	**14,895.5**	**108.3**	**15,003.8**	**−19.8**	**−0.1**	**−19.9**	**−0.13**
EU15	146,241.6	24,171.5	170,413.1	1908.5	−106.3	−2014.8	−1.18
EU25	161,201.2	24,307.9	185,509.1	−1928.3	−106.5	−2034.7	−1.10

Notes: Data are for Objectives 1 and 2, accounting for 94–99% of Structural Funds allocations to the EU8. For EU15 and EU25, figures are for 2000–2006. Percentages are the proportion of total funding decommitted.
Source: Applica *et al.* (2009).

were difficulties in getting certain types of projects underway, as under Objective 3 (EC, 2005, 2007).

Fieldwork research found country-specific problems. In the Czech Republic, commitment suffered from a lack of active project development. In several countries (especially Hungary and Slovakia), poor selection procedures resulted in low project quality. There were problems with public procurement compliance (Slovakia), bureaucratic procedures (in Estonia, Hungary and Slovenia), low transparency (Estonia and Slovenia) and long processing times (Hungary and Latvia). In Poland, there were frequent changes to a complex and centralized set of procedures.

Project generation, appraisal and selection systems were adapted over time. Better management of the programme management cycle reduced workload pressures and delays. More consultation with potential project applicants improved project quality. Application forms were often standardized, and project appraisal was rationalized with common templates and revised procedures for handling appeals and complaints.

3.3 Financial Management and Control

Financial management regulations required the verification and certification of expenditure at project level, checks of documentation and preparation of payment claims to the Commission and payment transfers. In practice, the management of committed funds and payment claims by the EU8 ensured the high absorption and low decommitment rates noted above.

Commission data indicate that expenditure was verified and certified largely according to regulatory requirements, and payment claims were submitted to the Commission and payments executed. Two statistical measures of the administrative performance of financial management are financial corrections (in the form of withdrawals and recoveries) made by Member States and formal recoveries by the Commission, where irregularities in financial management are detected (see Table 5).

Table 5. Financial corrections and recoveries of Cohesion policy funds for 2004–2006 (€ mill)

Country	Member State corrections		Commission corrections
	Withdrawals	Recoveries	
Czech Rep.	0	4.12	–
Estonia	2.17	0	–
Hungary	11.45	0.02	0.04
Latvia	1.07	0.26	3.08
Lithuania	1.20	0.21	–
Poland	0	13.00	37.41
Slovakia	0.88	2.70	1.07
Slovenia	0	1.54	1.89
EU8	**16.77**	**21.85**	**43.49**
EU25	**1854.74**	**1701.70**	**3156.24**

Note: Data are cumulative for 2004–2006 (2000–2006 for the EU25).
Source: Extracted from EC (2009).

There were deficiencies in management and control systems according to the European Court of Auditors. Annual checks in 2006–2007 in four countries (see Table 6) found ERDF systems in the Czech Republic and Slovakia to be "partially effective", and EAGGF and ESF systems in Poland and Slovenia to be "ineffective" (ECA, 2008, 2009). However, this has to be seen in a context where in 2007, across the EU25, 63% of programmes had deficiencies with moderate or significant impact and 6% were ineffective (ECA, 2010). Further, in subsequent assessments, the two EU8 programmes examined by the ECA (both in Poland) were judged to be working as well as or better than other ERDF programmes examined in Italy, Spain and the UK (ECA, 2009, 2010).

Fieldwork research revealed many administrative problems. Financial management processes were complex and cumbersome in all countries apart from Lithuania; the paperwork requested from beneficiaries was initially excessive in some countries, and claim processing could take six months or more, with multiple checks of invoices. Problems included

Table 6. ECA assessment of EU8 control systems

Country	Fund/programme	Main internal control bodies				Overall assessment
		Managing authority	Paying authority	Audit body	Winding-up body	
Czech Rep	ERDF – Industry & enterprise	Not effective	Partially effective	Not effective	Partially effective	Partially effective
Czech Rep	ERDF – Infrastructure	Partially effective	Partially effective	Partially effective	Partially effective	Partially effective
Poland	EAGGF	Not effective	Not effective	Not effective	Effective	Not effective
Slovakia	ERDF – Basic infrastructure	Not effective	Partially effective	Not effective	Not effective	Partially effective
Slovenia	ESF – Obj 1 - Education	Not effective	Not effective	Not effective	Not effective	Not effective

Key: Effective / Partially effective / Not effective

Notes: Assessments of Poland and Slovenia are for 2006; and of the Czech Republic and Slovakia for 2007. In 2006, the ECA assessed the systems for Cohesion Fund projects in Poland, Czech Republic and Latvia but found no significant deficiencies.
Source: ECA (2007, 2008, 2009).

distrust (Czech Republic and Hungary), heavy controls (Czech Republic, Estonia, Hungary and Latvia), frequent changes to the implementation of controls (Slovenia) and misalignment of domestic and Cohesion policy procedures (Poland).

Financial management was adapted during 2004–2008 by simplifying procedures, a process which continued into 2007–2013 with some success (ECA, 2011). Examples included closer contact and more support for beneficiaries with payment claims, pre-financing, interim payments and reduced requirements for documentation.

3.4 *Reporting to the Commission*

Structural Funds reporting in 2004–2006 required the organization of information flows, identification of institutions responsible for data collection and input, aggregation of data and compilation of obligatory reports, such as the annual implementation report (AIR) for the Commission.

The main indicator of performance is the submission of AIRs. Containing mostly financial information, these were submitted by the EU8 countries on time and were deemed to be "admissible" by the Commission. In all countries, additional regular or ad hoc reports were produced to inform politicians or to monitor programme implementation.

The drawback of the reporting process was its compliance orientation. Interview research found that reports had limited utility for monitoring and management purposes. The process was constrained by complex and demanding procedures (Estonia and Slovenia) and the lack of reliable data (Czech Republic, Poland and Slovenia). Initial difficulties with data collection were addressed through better guidance and clarification of indicators, which reduced the administrative burden.

3.5 *Monitoring of Progress*

The monitoring process, as set out in the regulations, involved establishing a "monitoring committee" with regular meetings to decide changes to programme documents, approval of AIRs and discussion of programme implementation. Electronic monitoring systems had to be established at programme and/or national level for tracking defined indicators of financial progress (inputs) and physical progress (outputs, results and impacts)

All EU8 countries established monitoring committees for the 2004–2006 period, with the first formal meetings arranged during 2004 to agree on the rules of procedure, coordination mechanisms and formal adoption of the Programme Complement. "Shadow" monitoring committees were often in place prior to accession. The committees mostly had a compliance function; strategic discussions were rare. Monitoring systems were operational in good time in most countries, but with indicator and data weaknesses. Financial indicators predominated with limited attention to physical outcomes.

The main monitoring-related constraints were the delays in systems becoming fully operational and inadequacy of indicators. Systems were only partly functional in the Czech Republic, Poland and Slovenia; they were unreliable in Estonia and Slovakia and there was a strong emphasis on financial monitoring and little exploitation of monitoring for management purposes (Estonia, Slovakia and Slovenia).

Monitoring systems were refined in the course of 2004–2008 and especially at the start of the 2007–2013 period. Indicator weaknesses were at least partly addressed. A mid-term solution for partly-functioning systems was to run less-sophisticated parallel systems which ensured ongoing monitoring of programme implementation.

3.6 *Evaluation of Achievements*

EU regulations required ex ante evaluation reports. Mid-term evaluations were not obligatory, but the use of evaluations and capacity-building were recommended. Administrative capacity was needed to prepare calls for tender, manage contracts with external experts, define the scope of evaluation studies and supply programme-level data.

The ex ante evaluations contributed—to varying degrees—to the coherence of the programme documents and to the design of indicators. All countries undertook at least some additional evaluation studies (Oraže, 2009, p. 49), partly small-scale thematic and process evaluations and partly comprehensive programme evaluations of structures or implementation. Evaluation plans were developed in five countries. The main drawbacks were the limited use of evaluation results (Estonia and Slovenia), a lack of evaluation capacity (Hungary, Slovakia and Slovenia) and a poorly developed evaluation culture (Latvia, Lithuania and Slovakia).

3.7 *Overall Assessment of Administrative Performance*

Drawing the above research together, this analysis challenges the conventional assessments of the capability of the EU8 to implement Cohesion policy effectively. Contradicting the expectations of previous studies, the research shows that the EU8 not only met regulatory requirements and spending targets but their performance exceeded that of the EU15 in several areas. Based on country research, the grades in Table 7 show that overall EU8 performance was "moderate" in every area, and some two-fifths of processes are rated as having demonstrated "significant" administrative performance.

However, Table 7 also shows varied patterns of performance across processes and countries. There is evidence of a disjuncture between the organization and application of administrative processes. For example, programming was often well-organized but this did not follow through into the quality of programme documents; major efforts were made to generate projects but their appraisal and selection was sometimes problematic; and while evaluation reports were produced, the evaluation culture was weak.

4. Assessment of Administrative Capacity

The second task of this article is to investigate the role of administrative capacity as an explanation for performance. Studies examining EU8 administrative capacity before and after accession highlighted deficiencies in the state of public sector reform, administrative and organizational culture, corruption, transparency and public trust (Bossaert & Demmke, 2003; Fatzer, 2005; Demmke et al., 2006). Assessments of policy and human resources (HR) capabilities found poor management systems and a lack of skills and experience in the civil service (World Bank, 2006).

This picture sits uneasily with our assessment of administrative performance (Bachtler et al., 2009b) and corresponds more with the research on policy domains such as pre-accession transposition of internal market directives (Zubek, 2005; Dimitrova & Toshkov, 2007). This study has sought to identify the more detailed components of

Table 7. Overall assessment of administrative performance in the EU8

Administrative performance		CZ	EE	HU	LT	LV	PL	SI	SK	EU8
(1) Programming	Organization of programming	B	B	B	C	B	B	B	C	**B**
	Programme documents	C	C	C	C	C	C	B	C	**C**
	Negotiation and approval	B	B	B	B	B	B	B	B	**B**
(2) Project preparation and selection	Project generation	B	B	B	B	B	B	C	B	**B**
	Project appraisal and selection	B	B	B	C	C	B	C	C	**B/C**
	Commitment of funds	C	B	A	B	B	A	A	A	**A/B**
(3) Financial management	Processing of payment claims	C	B	C	B	B	B	C	C	**B/C**
	Financial (de)commitment	B	B	B	B	B	B	B	B	**B**
	Financial management and control	C	B	[a]	B	[a]	C	B	A	**B**
(4) Monitoring and reporting	System of indicators and of monitoring procedures	B	B	B	B	B	C	C	C	**B/C**
	Availability of financial and physical data	B	A/B	B	B	B	C	C	C	**B/C**
(5) Evaluation	Evaluation reports	B	A	B	B	B	A	B	C	**B**
	Evaluation methods and culture	C	B	C	C	B	B	C	C	**B/C**
Summary		**B/C**	**B**	**B**	**B/C**	**B**	**B**	**B/C**	**B/C**	**B/C**

Note: See Table 1 for definitions of performance ratings.
[a] No assessment possible.

administrative capacity—specific to Cohesion policy—that explain the above record of performance. Based on the interview research, three sets of variables were critical factors in determining performance overall and variations between countries:

- the "organizational structures" established for implementing Cohesion policy, notably the allocation of functions and responsibilities, the effectiveness and stability of coordination mechanisms;
- the "adequacy and quality of human resources" for implementing Cohesion policy, including human resources management, professional leadership and employment conditions and
- "administrative adaptability", meaning the organizational, systemic or procedural changes made to administration in line with experience, and organizational learning mechanisms (e.g. the use of quality management tools, learning from evaluations).

The interview research focused on understanding how these elements of capacity were configured, their effectiveness and sustainability.

4.1 Organizational Structures

The administrative structures for implementing Cohesion policy were established relatively quickly. All countries had a centralized approach to management and implementation, led by finance ministries (Estonia, Latvia and Lithuania), regional development ministries (Czech Republic, Poland, Slovakia and Slovenia) or central government offices (Hungary). Regional-level authorities (where they existed) were involved only in the larger countries and mostly at the stage of project implementation. Only 1.5% of the total programme resources were allocated to regional programmes in the EU8, compared to 71% in the EU15 (Applica et al., 2009).

Across the EU8, most of the Funds were allocated by government ministries, agencies or other central implementing bodies. Centralization was regarded as being the most effective approach, facilitating the implementation of the Funds according to regulatory requirements. In practice, the EU8 managing authorities did consult socio-economic partners, non-governmental organizations and (partly) regional and local authorities during the programming stage. As members of the monitoring committee, these partners were also invited to contribute to programme monitoring, but they generally did not have significant influence on the allocation of resources.

Some smaller countries implemented Cohesion policy with highly centralized systems, involving only a few ministries (Slovenia, Estonia and Slovakia), while others had more complex systems, with several ministries and implementing agencies (Latvia and Lithuania). Larger countries—Czech Republic, Hungary and Poland—also used more implementing bodies, including regional-level institutions for the regional OPs.

The complexity of administrative structures posed new challenges for allocating responsibilities and devising coordination arrangements between ministries and implementing bodies. The larger countries faced particular difficulties, a key factor being the unwillingness of sectoral ministries to accept coordination, especially where the coordinating ministry was considered "weak" (as in the Czech Republic, Hungary and Slovenia). Coordination was exceptionally difficult in Poland, where up to 130 different organizations were involved and there were periodic changes to the coordinating ministry. Institutional unwillingness to take or share responsibility led to double or triple repetition of tasks, and there were disputes about the interpretation of EU rules, for example, on public procurement.

4.2 Adequacy and Quality of Human Resources

The availability of adequate human resources initially proved to be a major challenge. Capacity limitations differed depending on the tasks and particularly affected implementing bodies and final beneficiaries. The strategic tasks of the programming phase (2003–2004) were mainly undertaken by existing civil servants from the managing authorities, supported by PHARE-funded external experts. From 2004, staff resources were increased, often by hiring young and well-qualified personnel, albeit with limited professional experience. Younger staff proved to be flexible and open to "learning by doing" which contributed to capacity-building. The situation was different with higher management positions where staff had (partly) gained experience through PHARE.

Staff mostly had clearly specified responsibilities and tasks and—according to interviewees—worked with a high level of commitment. At the outset, high staff turnover made it difficult to manage programmes on a stable basis. Over time, human resources management improved, contributing to staff retention. Salaries were often increased and career prospects improved. Through better management of the policy cycle, staff shortages and workloads were reduced. Specific training and advice were made available, and international exchanges were organized through twinning projects, study trips and secondments abroad.

4.3. *Administrative Adaptability*

During 2004–2008, administrative adaptability varied significantly between countries, but the main adaptations can be grouped into three categories, relating to coordination, absorption and systematization of administrative procedures.

First, institutional change and adaptation were undertaken to strengthen coordination. In Hungary, a reorganization brought all managing authorities into one institution, albeit only in 2006. Further changes streamlined the structures, established a "one-stop-shop" for applicants and reduced the number of implementing bodies. While this was the only case of substantial restructuring, minor adaptations contributed to stronger coordination and collaboration in all countries. Better collaboration was achieved by aligning domestic and EU administrative procedures.

Second, procedures were introduced to ensure absorption, particularly compliance with N+2, through closer monitoring of project progress and payments. Project generation was enhanced through support for beneficiaries with the preparation of payment requests (Hungary and Slovakia), additional information and training on application needs (Czech Republic and Latvia), and direct consultation with beneficiaries (Czech Republic, Hungary and Slovakia). Payment handling was accelerated. Extra certifications and applications for payments were undertaken where necessary (Czech Republic and Lithuania), larger payment claims were prioritized and document management was simplified.

Third, procedures and tools were systematized, especially for project generation, appraisal and selection, financial management, reporting and monitoring. More and better guidance was provided to implementing bodies and staff, particularly by updating the manuals of administrative procedures. IT tools and management information systems were refined to improve the processing times for applications and claims.

Some of the increases in administrative productivity were measurable. The processing time for applications was reduced: in Lithuania from six to nine months to four to five months; in Hungary from four to three months and in the Czech Republic (under the OP Industry and Enterprise) from eight to two months. The processing of payment claims and the collection of monitoring/reporting data were reportedly accelerated through more direct contact with beneficiaries and reduced administrative requirements. More generally, interviewees noted smoother cooperation and collaboration in most stages of the programme management cycle.

4.4 *Overall Assessment of Administrative Capacity*

The three components of administrative capacity—organizational structures, human resources and administrative adaptability—presented here as explanatory factors for the administrative performance of the EU8 are complex variables, which cannot be seen in isolation from the broader state of public administration. For example, the

Table 8. Assessment of administrative capacity in the EU8

Administrative capacity	Specific indicators	CZ	EE	HU	LT	LV	PL	SI	SK	EU8
(1) Organizational structures	Allocation of competencies and responsibilities	B	B	B	B	C	B	C	C	B
	Coordination/cooperation among ministries and implementing bodies	C	B	C	C	B	C	C	B	B/C
	Organizational stability	B	B	C	B	B	C	C	B	B
(2) Human resources	Availability of suitably qualified staff	C	B	B	B	C	B	C	C	B/C
	Human resource management	B	B	B	B	B	B	B	C	B
(3) Administrative adaptability	Establishment and adaptability of procedures and tools	B	B	C	B	B	C	C	C	B/C
Summary		B/C	B	B/C	B	B/C	B/C	C	B/C	B/C

Note: See Table 2 for definitions of capacity ratings.

configuration and permanence of organizational structures is a function of political stability; and the prevalence of human resource management depends on the state of civil service reform.

The analysis does, however, provide insights into how administrative capacity for Cohesion policy was established and evolved. The EU8 were largely able to put in place the requisite organizational structures and human resources, procedures and tools but it sometimes took until 2006 for the capacity to be fully available. A grading of each of the capacity indicators (see Table 8) shows that for every indicator, each country had put in place at least a basic level of capacity and in many cases it was rated as "developing", albeit with variation between countries.

5. Conclusions

This article has assessed the role of administrative capacity in explaining the performance of eight CEE countries in implementing Cohesion policy in 2004–2008. The research investigated whether pre-accession administrative adjustment to comply with the "acquis" continued in the post-accession period.

Involving a more detailed investigation of post-accession administrative performance and capacity than hitherto conducted on Cohesion policy, the distinctive aspects of the analysis involved: disaggregating policy management into a series of six administrative functions as a basis for analysing administrative performance; decomposing administrative capacity into three sets of indicators (and sub-indicators) covering organizational structures, human resources and administrative adaptability that are sensitive to the key features of Cohesion policy management and developing a refined categorization for ranking variations in administrative performance and capacity across administrative functions and countries.

The empirical research found that EU8 administrative capacity for implementing Cohesion policy developed faster and better than policy-makers and academic commentators predicted. Administrative performance appears to have been superior to the capacity of the government service more generally (as assessed by the World Bank and others) and compared favourably with the EU15. There is some evidence for a possible association between administrative performance and administrative capacity—evidenced by both higher capacity and performance scores in the case of Estonia, and conversely lower scores on both scales for Slovakia and Slovenia—that would be worth exploring further.

The building of a relatively advanced degree of administrative capacity suggests specific Europeanization factors at work. First, as noted earlier, Cohesion policy can be regarded as one of the policy domains with harder EU influence based on a coercive regulatory framework, and for which the EU8 had been "prepared" through intensive pre-accession aid programmes to build administrative capacity. Other studies have come to similar conclusions, noting that the EU8 were "socialized" during the pre-accession process (Sedelmeier, 2011).

Second, although Member States have discretion for implementing rules, the contractualization of EU spending—and the associated administrative capacity requirements—has steadily increased since the 1990s, in particular during 2000–2006 when EU financial management and control was intensified (Mendez & Bachtler, 2011).

Third, the EU8 were under pressure to overcome a certain expectation of administrative failure, with predictions that they would have difficulty in absorbing funding and complying with EU regulations. An important political sub-text to this debate was the planning underway for the 2007–2013 EU budget, where concerns about administrative capacity were used to justify an "absorption cap" on budgetary allocations to the new Member States. For the EU8, demonstrating good management of Cohesion policy in 2004–2006 was important to buttress EU8 arguments for substantial funding in 2007–2013.

Thus, it could be argued that, in the domain of Cohesion policy, the three to four years following accession was an "interim period" that does not accord with the characteristics of "pre-accession" or "post-accession" period discussed in other studies. In this interim period, the EU8 were no longer subject to the conditionality of accession, but there was an implicit conditionality associated with the negotiations underway on the post-2006 financial perspective.

These findings have important implications for our understanding of post-accession administration. Sedelmeier (2011, p. 807) established, with reference to infringements of EU law, that "far from constituting an 'eastern problem', compliance in the new members has been surprisingly good". However, our research indicates that the EU8 were not just avoiding infringements but that they were—at least under Cohesion policy—matching or exceeding the EU15 record. This challenges the contention of Falkner (2010) that the CEE countries fall within a "world of dead letters" with respect to compliance with EU law.

Further, the research indicates that administrative capacity, as a rationalist mediating factor of Europeanization, has been underestimated. While previous research has established the importance of administrative capacity in the pre-accession period, this article demonstrates that this applies also in the post-accession period, contradicting expectations of a downgrading in European coordination systems (Dimitrova & Toshkov, 2009). While previous research has found variable administrative institution-building (Dimitrova, 2002), our findings reveal consistency in performance and capacity across the EU8, attributable partly to the EU regulatory framework. Thus, this paper supports the arguments of Scherpereel (2010), Meyer-Sahling and Yesilkagit (2011) and others that the shock therapy of pre-accession aid and post-accession Cohesion policy enabled the EU8 to overcome the legacy of Communist administrative traditions and introduce new norms and ways of working (in the form of organizational structures, human resource management, administrative procedures and tools)—at least in this policy domain.

The emphasis in the literature on the rationalist properties of administrative capacity (largely as a constraining structural factor) obscures the dynamics of capacity evolution and the role of learning. This article has highlighted the dynamic nature of administrative capacity and the way in which, over a short space of time, the structures, systems and procedures were adapted in response to experience through learning-by-doing. In part, these had measurable impacts on the productivity of administrative services. Contrary to conventional conceptualizations and understandings of administrative capacity, the implication is that capacity-building can in fact act as a mechanism of socialization over time.

The caveat is that the Europeanization of administrative capacity may be specific to Cohesion policy and that the development of administrative capacity in this area may be isolated from the wider government administration in the form of "islands of excellence" (World Bank, 2006; Dimitrova & Toshkov, 2009). In fact, the empirical research found that many staff were young, well educated, internationally minded and imbued with a sense of entrepreneurship (working in a new policy domain) and European ideals (the policy's role in promoting "European solidarity"). There is also some evidence for spillovers into domestic domains (Bachtler *et al.*, 2009a).

Furthermore, the EU8 administered Cohesion policy in 2004–2006 with centralized management systems and through programmes with relatively simple structures and a limited number of spending priorities. Administrative performance in 2007–2013, involving larger and more complex programmes, delivered through many more implementing bodies—including regional authorities in some cases—may be a different story. The progress with administrative capacity identified could be halted or reversed in 2007–2013 by bureaucratic or politicized implementation processes in other parts of the administrative system. Indeed, some of the preliminary information becoming available on the 2007–2013 period indicates serious problems in areas such as organizational structures (e.g. separation of managing authorities and audit bodies), the quality of project selection, staff retention and public procurement in some countries.

There are important policy lessons. Notwithstanding the progress made in developing administrative capacity, it is notable that administrative systems were more effective in meeting the regulatory and financial obligations that involve procedural compliance. Arguably, these could be more readily accommodated in administrations that still retained elements of hierarchical and bureaucratic systems of public management inherited from the Communist era. The lower benchmarking scores are associated with those administrative functions—programming, project appraisal and selection, integration of evaluation—that require public administrations organized and run according to principles of new public management/governance and specifically a concern with the content and effects of policies. This indicates a continued deficiency in the culture of public administration.

This article provides some validation of EU pre-accession aid. Although the experience of managing PHARE and ISPA had limited transferability to Cohesion policy—and did not involve many middle-ranking and junior staff in managing authorities and implementing bodies—it provided significant exposure to perceived "good practice" in Cohesion policy management, the principles underlying effective administrative capacity and contacts with counterpart administrators abroad.

Finally, this article should inform the current debate about improving institutional capacity for managing Cohesion policy. The regulatory encouragement given to Member States in 2007–2013 to reinforce their administrative capacity for implementing the Funds is strengthened in the legislative proposals for 2014–2020. One of the 11 proposed thematic priorities is "enhancing institutional capacity and an efficient public administration" and the Commission is proposing to include conditions relating to administrative capacity in its "partnership agreements" with Member States (EC, 2011). The Commission's draft concept of how capacity should be measured is, however, still rudimentary (DG Regio, 2011, p. 25). Developing more effective benchmarks for measuring and monitoring the progress of administrative performance and capacity is a critical task when the next programmes are launched in 2014.

Acknowledgements

The authors acknowledge the role of the European Commission (DG Regio) in funding the evaluation research on which this paper is based and the contribution of Jiří Blažek, Jonas Jatkauskas, Damjan Kavaš, Martin Obuch, Karol Olejniczak, Kristiina Tõnnisson to the country research and their constructive feedback—as well as from Ilona Palné Kovacs—on an earlier version of this paper. They are also grateful for the helpful comments provided by two anonymous reviewers. The usual disclaimer applies.

Notes

1. The administration of expenditure commitments in 2004–2006 continued until the end of 2008.
2. Czech Republic, Estonia, Hungary, Latvia, Lithuania, Poland, Slovakia and Slovenia.
3. For further methodological detail, see Bachtler *et al.* (2009b) and Oraže (2009).
4. A commitment of funds to a project needs to be paid out within two years or else is lost to the programme.

References

Applica, Ismeri Europa & WIIW (2009) *Ex Post Evaluation of Cohesion Policy Programmes 2000–2006 Co-financed by ERDF—Financial Implementation of Structural Funds*, Report to the European Commission (DG Regio), Applica, Ismeri Europa, WIIW.

Bachtler, J. & Gorzelak, G. (2007) Reforming EU Cohesion policy: A reappraisal of the performance of the Structural Funds, *Policy Studies*, 28(4), pp. 309–326.

Bachtler, J. & McMaster, I. (2008) EU cohesion policy and the role of the regions: Investigating the influence of structural funds in the new member states, *Environment and Planning C: Government and Policy*, 26(2), pp. 398–427.

Bachtler, J., Downes, R., McMaster, I., Raines, P. & Taylor, S. (2002) *Transfer of EU Regional Policy to Countries of Central and Eastern Europe: Can One Size Fit All?* Future Governance Paper, 10. London: ESRC Research Programme on Future Governance: Lessons from Comparative Policy, Economic and Social Research Council.

Bachtler, J., Polverari, L. & McMaster, I. (2009a) *The "Added Value" of Cohesion Policy in the EU15—Ex Post Evaluation of Cohesion Policy Programmes Co-financed by the ERDF 2000–06*, Final Report to the European Commission (DG Regio), European Policies Research Centre and Metis GmbH.

Bachtler, J., Polverari, L., Oraže, H., Clement, K., Tödtling-Schönhofer, H., Gross, F., McMaster, I. & Naylon, I. (2009b) *Management and Implementation Systems for Cohesion Policy—Ex Post Evaluation of Cohesion*

Policy Programmes Co-financed by the ERDF 2000–06, Final Report to the European Commission (DG Regio), European Policies Research Centre and Metis GmbH.

Barca, F. (2009) *An Agenda for a Reformed Cohesion Policy: A Place-based Approach to Meeting European Union Challenges and Expectations*, Independent Report prepared at the request of Danuta Hübner, Commissioner for Regional Policy.

Bollen, F., Hartwig, I. & Nicolaides, P. (2000) *EU Structural Funds beyond Agenda 2000: Reform and Implications for Current and Future Member States* (Maastricht: European Institute of Public Administration).

Börzel, T. & Risse, T. (2000) When Europe hits home: Europeanization and domestic change, *European Integration online Papers (EIoP)*, 4(15), 24 pp. Available at http://eiop.or.at/eiop/texte/2000-015a.htm (accessed 30 August 2012).

Bossaert, D. & Demmke, C. (2003) *Civil Services in the Accession States, New Trends and the Impact of the Integration Process* (Maastricht: European Institute of Public Administration).

Bossaert, D., Demmke, C., Nomden, K. & Polet, R. (2001) *Civil Services in the Europe of Fifteen. Trends and New Developments* (Maastricht: European Institute of Public Administration).

Bruszt, L. & Verdes, B. (2011) *Fostering Developmental Agency from without Aiding Transnationalizing Local Alliances between State, Civil Society and Business*, Paper to the RSA Cohesion policy network, November 28–29, Vienna.

Bulmer, S. J. & Radaelli, C. M. (2004) *The Europeanisation of National Policy? Queens Papers on Europeanization*, 1. Queens University, Belfast.

Cappelen, R., Castellacci, F., Fagerberg, J. & Verspagen, B. (2003) The impact of EU regional support on growth and convergence in the European Union, *Journal of Common Market Studies*, 41(4), pp. 621–644.

Cerami, A. (2008) Europeanization and social policy in Central and Eastern Europe, in: F. Bafoil & T. Beichelt (Eds) *Européanisation. D'Ouest en Est*, pp. 137–168 (Paris: L'Harmattan Coll. Logiques Politiques).

Demmke, C., Hammerschmid, G. & Meyer, R. (2006) *Decentralisation and Accountability as a Focus of Public Administration Modernisation. Challenges and Consequences for Human Resource Management* (Maastricht: European Institute of Public Administration).

DG Regio (2011) *The Programming Period 2014–2020—Monitoring and Evaluation of European Cohesion Policy (European Regional Development Fund and Cohesion Fund)—Concepts and Recommendations, Guidance Document*, Directorate-General for Regional Policy, European Commission, Brussels.

Dimitrova, A. (2002) Enlargement, institution-building and the EU's administrative capacity requirement, *West European Politics*, 25(4), 171–190.

Dimitrova, A. (2010) The European Union and the European States, *Public Administration Review*, 70(2), 326–327.

Dimitrova, A. & Toshkov, D. (2007) The dynamics of domestic coordination of EU policy in the new member states: Impossible to lock in?, *West European Politics*, 30(5), pp. 961–986.

Dimitrova, A. & Toshkov, D. (2009) Post-accession compliance between administrative co-ordination and political bargaining, *European Integration Online Papers*, 13(2), 18 pp. Available at http://eiop.or.at/eiop/index.php/eiop/article/view/2009_019a/137 (accessed 30 August 2012).

EC (2005) *16th Annual Report on the Implementation of the Structural Funds (2004)*, European Commission, Brussels, COM(2005) 533 final.

EC (2007) *18th Annual Report on the Implementation of the Structural Funds (2006)*, European Commission, Brussels, COM(2007) 1456 final.

EC (2008) *19th Annual Report on the Implementation of the Structural Funds (2007)*, European Commission, Brussels, COM(2008) 2649 final.

EC (2009) *20th Annual Report on the Implementation of the Structural Funds (2008)*, European Commission, Brussels, COM(2009) 617 final.

EC (2011) *Cohesion Policy 2014–2020: Investing in Growth and Jobs* (Luxembourg: Publications Office of the European Union).

ECA (2007) Annual Report Concerning the Financial Year 2006, Notice from the European Court of Auditors, Luxembourg, Official Journal of the European Union.

ECA (2008) Annual Report Concerning the Financial Year 2007, Notice from the European Court of Auditors, Luxembourg, Official Journal of the European Union, November 10, 2008.

ECA (2009) Annual Report Concerning the Financial Year 2008, Notice from the European Court of Auditors, Luxembourg, Official Journal of the European Union, November 10, 2009.

ECA (2010) Annual Report Concerning the Financial Year 2009, Notice from the European Court of Auditors, Luxembourg, Official Journal of the European Union, November 9, 2010.

ECA (2011) Annual Report Concerning the Financial Year 2010, Notice from the European Court of Auditors, Luxembourg, Official Journal of the European Union, November 10, 2011.

Ederveen, S., Gorter, J., De Mooij, R. & Nahuis, R. (2002) *Funds and Games: The Economics of European Cohesion Policy*, Occasional Paper no. 3, European Network of European Policy Research Institutes, Brussels.

Ederveen, S., De Groot, H. & Nahuis, S. (2006) Fertile soil for structural funds? A panel data analysis of the conditional effectiveness of European Cohesion policy, *Kyklos*, 59(1), pp. 17–42.

Epstein, R. & Sedelmeier, U. (2008), Beyond conditionality: international institutions in postcommunist Europe after enlargement, *Journal of European Public Policy*, 15(6), pp. 795–805.

Falkner, G. (2010) Institutional performance and compliance with EU law: Czech Republic, Hungary, Slovakia and Slovenia, *Journal of Public Policy*, 30(1), pp. 101–116.

Falkner, G., Treib, O. & Holzleithner, E. (2008) *Compliance in the Enlarged European Union: Living rights or Dead Letters?* (Aldershot: Ashgate).

Fatzer, G. (2005) Nachhaltige OE und Transformationsprozesse – Zwischen Lerngeschichten und Netzwerkentwicklung, in: G. Fatzer (Ed.) *Nachhaltige Transformationsprozesse in Organisationen*, pp. 17–28 (Cologne: EHP Verlag).

Featherstone, K. & Papadimitriou, D. (2008) *The Limits of Europeanization: Reform Capacity and Policy Conflict in Greece* (Basingstoke: Palgrave Macmillan).

Featherstone, K. & Radaelli, C. M. (Eds) (2003) *The Politics of Europeanization* (Oxford: Oxford University Press).

Goetz, K. H. (2001) Making sense of post-communist central administration: Modernization, Europeanization or Latinization?, *Journal of European Public Policy*, 8(6), pp. 1032–1051.

Grabbe, H. (2006) *The EU's Transformative Power: Europeanization through Conditionality in Central and Eastern Europe* (Basingstoke: Palgrave Macmillan).

Héritier, A., Knill, C. & S. Mingers (1996) Ringing the Changes in Europe. *Regulatory Competition and the Redefinition of the State. Britain, France, Germany*, 341 pp. (Berlin and New York: Walter de Gruyter).

Hille, P. & Knill, C. (2006) "It's the bureaucracy, stupid": The implementation of the acquis communautaire in EU candidate countries, 1999–2003, *European Union Politics*, 7(4), 531–552.

Horvat, A. (2005) *Why does Nobody Care About the Absorption? Some Aspects Regarding Administrative Absorption Capacity for the EU Structural Funds in the Czech Republic, Estonia, Hungary, Slovakia and Slovenia before Accession*. WIFO Working Papers 258/2005.

Hughes, J., Sasse, G. & Gordon, C. (2003) EU enlargement, Europeanisation and the dynamics of regionalisation in the CEECs, in: M. Keating & J. Hughes (Eds) *The Regional Challenge in Central and Eastern Europe. Territorial Restructuring and European Integration*, pp. 69–88 (Brussels: P.I.E.-Peter Lang).

Hughes, J., Sasse, G. & Gordon, C. E. (2004) *Europeanization and Regionalization in the EU's Enlargement to Central and Eastern Europe: The Myth of Conditionality* (Basingstoke: Palgrave Macmillan).

Kalman, J. (2002) *Possible Structural Funds Absorption Problems: The Political Economy View with Application to the Hungarian Regional Development Institutions and Financial System*, Local Government and Public Service Reform Initiative, Open Society Institute, Budapest.

Knill, C. (2001) *The Europeanisation of National Administrations: Patterns of Institutional Change and Persistence* (Cambridge: Cambridge University Press).

Knill, C. & Lenschow, A. (2005) Compliance, competition and communication: Different approaches of European governance and their impact on national institutions, *Journal of Common Market Studies*, 43(3), pp. 583–606.

McAleavey, P. (1995) Policy implementation as incomplete contracting: The European regional development fund, PhD thesis, Florence: European University Institute.

McMaster, I. & Novotný, V. (2006) Rise and decline of industry in Central and Eastern Europe: A comparative study of cities and regions in eleven countries, *Journal of Regional Science*, 46(3), pp. 574–576.

Mendez, C. & Bachtler, J. (2011) Administrative reform and unintended consequences: An assessment of the EU Cohesion policy "audit explosion", *Journal of European Public Policy*, 18(5), pp. 746–765.

Meyer-Sahling, J.-H. (2009) Varieties of legacies: A critical review of legacy explanations of public administration reform in East Central Europe, *International Review of Administrative Sciences*, 75(3), pp. 509–528.

Meyer-Sahling, J.-H. & Yesilkagit, K. (2011) Differential legacy effects: Three propositions on the impact of administrative traditions on public administration reform in Europe East and West, *Journal of European Public Policy*, 18(2), pp. 311–322.

Milio, S. (2007) Can administrative capacity explain differences in implantation performances? Evidence from structural funds implementation in Southern Italy, *Regional Studies*, 41(4), pp. 429–442.

NEI (2002) *Sector Report Implementation. Assessing the Administrative Capacity Needed by the Candidate Countries to Effectively Manage the Structural Funds*, Final Report to the European Commission, Rotterdam.

OECD (2001) *Public Sector Leadership for the 21st Century*. Executive Summary. Online publication. Available at http://www.oecd.org/dataoecd/0/34/2434104.pdf (accessed 31 August 2012).

Oraže, H. (2009) *The Assessment of Effectiveness, Continuity and Spillover Effects of Management and Implementation Systems in the EU10—Ex Post Evaluation of Cohesion Policy Programmes Co-financed by the ERDF 2000–06*, Final Report to the European Commission (DG Regio), European Policies Research Centre and Metis GmbH.

Radaelli, C. (2000) Whither Europeanization? Concept stretching and substantive change, *European Integration Online Papers*, 4(8), 28 pp. Available at http://eiop.or.at/eiop/pdf/2000-008.pdf (accessed 30 August 2012).

Radaelli, C. (2003) The Europeanization of public policy, in: K. Featherstone & C. Radaelli (Eds) *The Politics of Europeanization*, pp. 27–56 (Oxford: Oxford University Press).

Risse, T., Cowles, M. & Caporaso, J. (2001) Europeanization and domestic change: Introduction, in: T. Risse, M. Cowles & J. Caporaso (Eds) *Transforming Europe. Europeanization and Domestic Change*, pp. 1–20 (Ithaca, NY: Cornell University Press).

Scherpereel, J. (2010) EU Cohesion Policy and the Europeanization of Central and East European Regions, *Regional & Federal Studies*, 20(1), pp. 45–62.

Schmidt, V. A. (2002) Europeanization and the mechanics of economic policy adjustment, *Journal of European Public Policy*, 9(6), pp. 894–912.

Schimmelfennig, F. & Sedelmeier, U. (2004) Governance by conditionality: EU rule transfer to the candidate countries of Central and Eastern Europe, *Journal of European Public Policy*, 11(4), 669–687.

Schimmelfennig, F. & Sedelmeier, U. (2005) *The Europeanization of Central and Eastern Europe* (New York: Cornell University Press).

Sedelmeier, U. (2011) Europeanisation in new member and candidate states, *Living Reviews in European Governance*, 6(1), 52 pp. Available at http://www.livingreviews.org/lreg-2011-1 (accessed 30 August 2012).

SIGMA (1998) *Sustainable Institutions for European Union Membership*. SIGMA Papers No 26. United Nations Online Network in Public Administration and Finance.

Steunenberg, B. & Kaeding, M. (2009) "As time goes by": Explaining the transposition of maritime directives, *European Journal of Political Research*, 48(3), pp. 432–454.

Šumpíková, M., Pavel, J. & Klazar, S. (2004) *EU Funds: Absorption Capacity and Effectiveness of Their Use, with Focus on Regional Level in the Czech Republic*, 12th NISPAcee (The Network of Institutes and Schools of Public Administration in Central and Eastern Europe) Annual Conference Central and Eastern European Countries Inside and Outside the European Union: Avoiding a New Divide.

SWECO (2010) *Regional Governance in the Context of Globalisation*, Final Report to the European Commission (DG Regio), SWECO International, Stockholm.

Toshkov, D. (2008) Embracing European law: Compliance with EU directives in Central and Eastern Europe, *European Union Politics*, 9(3), pp. 379–402.

World Bank (2006) *EU-8. Administrative capacity in the New Member States: The Limits of Innovation?* Report 36930-GLB. OECD: Washington.

Zubek, R. (2005) Complying with transposition commitments in Poland: Collective dilemmas, core executive and legislative outcomes, *West European Politics*, 28 (3), pp. 592–619.

Urban–Rural Interactions in Latvian Changing Policy and Practice Context

LAILA KŪLE

Faculty of Geography and Earth Sciences, University of Latvia, Riga, Latvia

ABSTRACT *This article aims at a better comprehension of urban–rural interactions as a spatial concept and its utilization for spatial and regional policies. Based on literature review and on interviews with planners and experts, the article explores how the concept of urban–rural interactions is defined, characterized and structured. The understanding of urban and rural, how they are connected provides a basis for capturing complexities and development of urban–rural interactions. The study, reviews urban–rural policies and practises in Latvia. Contemporary built-up areas and lifestyles are influenced by imprints of past urban–rural interactions. Aspects of contextuality, cross-sectorality and informality have to be taken into consideration when urban–rural interactions are applied to the policy field. The article introduces a typology to capture both the diversity and particularity of places in terms of urban–rural connectivity. An insight is given how the current Latvian local government territorial structure can contribute to building target-oriented urban–rural partnerships.*

1. Introduction

The recent Europe-wide territorial cohesion's consultations renewed attention towards urban–rural relationships as a policy option. The aim of the article is to explore the concept of urban–rural interactions and provide insight to policies and practises with relevance to urban–rural linkages based on the example of Latvia. The article is based on a review of literature and relevant policy documents, and on the statements of the interviewed Latvian planners and experts at national level institutions and local municipalities. The understanding of urban–rural relations depends upon the context of how urban/rural places, and their population and activities are framed and regulated in each society and policy regime. The development of Latvia's urban–rural interactions is influenced by the country's turbulent history and long dependency periods. After the re-establishing of the independence in 1991, the development of Latvian national spatial and regional policy had been influenced by the European and the Baltic Sea Region spatial policy documents, at least by their rhetoric. Latvia shares its past policies as applied with other post-Soviet countries, although the country has distinctive cultural differences. The constitutional setting, main institutions and the property ownership structure of the Latvian Republic of 1918 were re-established in 1991. Institutions and policies have been democratized, modernized and adapted to the market economy. Latvia became a member of the EU in 2004. Soviet period policies have been replaced, however, some remnants can still be found in texts of policy-makers and more often in social memory. Both practises and policies are path-dependent and carry elements from the past; contemporary landscapes, human settlements and land use structures are evidences of policies implemented during the turbulent Latvian history, and thus, a challenge for planners of today.

In the framework of national response to the Europe-wide debate on territorial cohesion, the Latvian national survey on urban–rural relations has been carried out under the supervision of the State Regional Development Agency (Kūle *et al.*, 2009). The aim of the study was to widen a knowledge base on urban–rural interactions and to explore how this concept could be utilized for policies supporting regional development in the Latvian context. Results of the study indicated that multisectoral practises of urban–rural interactions are embedded in local communities, and thus, contribute to their social identities. Technical and social infrastructure and mobilities of social agents are contributing to balancing urban and rural development, and thus, to territorial cohesion. The term "urban–rural interactions" was not widely known in Latvia in 2008 when interviews were held. The study found that measures that can be referred as a support to urban–rural interactions are implemented under other titles and scattered over several sectors. Distribution and accessibility of service provision, outdoor recreation and local food-related activities have been highlighted by the interviewed Latvian planners as policy issues to be labelled as urban–rural interactions and not adequately covered by the mainstream policies. The paper begins with two conceptual parts about urban–rural interactions; it continues with a brief review how ideology and political regimes had been influencing policy measures of urban–rural interactions in the case of Latvia. The following two parts of the paper are devoted to the rural–urban mobility in Latvia taking into account historical context and policies that controlled or facilitated these movements. The article introduces a typology that was prepared to capture both the diversity and particularity of places in terms of urban–rural connectivity (Kūle *et al.*, 2009). The paper ends with the review of policy application challenges with the aim to stimulate mutually positive urban–rural interactions. An insight is given as to how the current Latvian national level development planning is contributing or missing opportunities to build new and support existing target-oriented urban–rural partnerships.

2. Measuring Urban–Rural Interactions

Studies on the concept of urban–rural interactions have recognized it as a complex, indistinctive, vague, multidimensional and highly contextual issue. It comprises both understanding of places and how they are interconnected (boundaries, locations, structures, patterns, flows and networks). Uncertainty in measuring urban–rural relations is caused by the fact that indicators are often data driven and scale-relevant. "Data on flows between different areas, or areas of different types, are scarcely to be found" (SPESP, 2001, p. 5) and thus, often the focus is on few isolated aspects of urban–rural relations, for instance, human mobility or the food production-consumption cycle. Statistical, mapping, analytical and policy-making needs require that the complexities and irregularities of the real world are generalized in clear-cut units. Difficulties to obtain information on urban–rural flows are a worldwide problem (Hugo *et al.*, 2003). Unified agreement on the urban–rural definition beyond the national states' boundaries is missing (ECE-FAO-Eurostat-OECD, 2005). The change of urban–rural administrative boundary or status is not only a statistical but also a social issue. Attitudes towards the change of place meaning and identity depend on ideological and geographical context, and prevailing existing urban–rural bias. "The rural–urban dichotomy is imputed with an array of ideological elements, all with different amplitudes and linkages to current and historical discourses" (Andersson *et al.*, 2009, p. 2). Rigg (1998, p. 504) highlights practical difficulties associated with the process of urban–rural categorization: incorrect registration of a residence and the definition of a household that ignores multispatiality; multiple residence, cyclical migrations, various sources of incomes, including additional, casual and informal; short-term versus long-term perspective, ignorance of an individual lifespan context and other realities of life. Despite the deficiencies, urban and rural as categories and typologies are used for various administrative, legal, academic or popular purposes (Schaffter *et al.*, 2010, p. 3). "Categorization—whether binary or not—is more than an aid to coping with complexity, however; it is also a means for creating our identities, again both individual and collective" (Cloke & Johnston, 2005, p. 1). Urban–rural category making is a part of a self-identification process, experienced as informal primary socialization in early childhood, children culture and the content of text books. Urban–rural disparities are basis for widely exploited urban–rural stereotypes. Both disparities and stereotypes can become development potentials, barriers or forces for urban–rural interactions. Individual memories of urban–rural experiences (work, life, leisure and movements) are a part of life story narratives and self-reference and thus, influence decision-making processes by adults (Beitnere, 2003). Increased human mobility (neo-nomads), multilocal living and new kinds of rural–urban lifestyles, rural industries, services, governance and regulation challenge traditional rural–urban dichotomy and fixed place identities (Andersson *et al.*, 2009). Exiting urban–rural data do not capture informal, voluntary and emergent activities, unless field studies are conducted or social agents consulted. Even micro-scale, meaningful urban–rural interactions at everyday-life level can act as catalyser and driver of local development, particularly in remote areas. It is crucial that policy-makers can have an access to such evidence-based information and knowledge of urban–rural interactions.

3. Understanding Urban–Rural Interactions: From Structures to Complementarity

The understanding of urban–rural interactions depends on the comprehension of binary concepts of urban and rural. They are social constructions (Cloke & Johnston, 2005) and thus, discursive. Contemporary social agents are constructing and de-constructing urban and rural places that are embedded in natural and historical social–cultural processes and spatial structures. Physical and mental boundaries between urban and rural are used to frame social and environmental problems, to compartmentalize research disciplines, policy branches and institutions. Within the discourses of social agents, urban and rural places are fixed and express a position on an urban–rural continuum (Pahl, 1966). Potter and Unwin (1995, p. 68) stress that there is "the essential need to treat 'urban' and 'rural' as complementary, and not mutually exclusive categories". Urban–rural interactions, that are both spatial and temporal, expose the content in process. Being in process they "induce urban–rural change and thus indicate the transformative 'gap' between states or dispositions" (Shields, 1997, p. 3). Urban–rural relations as a type of geographical interactions (Alaev, 1983, p. 82) can be expressed as exchanges of matter, energy and information by overcoming a certain distance that split these interconnected components; while humans are defined as matter, energy and information all together. Alaev describes geographical interactions through types (intensity, directions and rhythm/cyclic) and channels of the geographical interactions and by involved agents and a territory where their contacts take place. Even global flows and networks "could not operate without bonding with certain territories and cities", although they are "less stable than past notions of 'embeddedness'" (Dematteis, 2001, p. 114). There is no common view on changes if barriers to geographical, including urban–rural interactions are removed. Alaev (1983) conceptualizes empirical findings that certain energy/power is needed for geographical interactions, however, if power from one side reaches certain threshold, one geographical object could diffuse, spread or merge into another. It means that power expressed in the size of population or territory and economical, administrative or political dimensions matters for urban–rural interrelations. Dematteis citing Hannerz (1996) believes that by removing barriers, connections are multiplying; territorial and social fragmentation at microterritorial scale is increasing. Spatial development proves that the direction of flows matters, and not only mainstream urban–rural flows, but their alternative direction interactive actions are crucial for local-level change and developments. With the technology driven intensification of communications, urban and rural places and their images are often regarded as commodities and less dependent from specific place-based features and boundaries. Powerful symbolic and ideological significance constitutes places of consumption, their authentic elements and cultures, they are becoming associated "less with belonging to a particular place" and "more with opportunities and attractiveness of places" (Marsden *et al.*, 1993, p. 9; Bascom, 2001). The complex geographical space, "causal relationships of physical proximity" is substituted with "single metaphorical representation" (Dematteis, 2001, p. 120). Therefore, urban and rural are more often recognized through cultural mappings, story-lines and discourses, not formal data. Globally or nationally recognized culture driven meanings and symbols are becoming a relevant force for activating urban–rural interactions.

Various studies reveal that urban–rural interactions depend from and differ at geographical, historical, cultural and socio-economic contexts and by specific characteristics (Davoudi & Stead, 2002; Bengs & Schmidt-Thomé, 2005; Caffyn & Dahlström, 2005; Zonneveld & Stead, 2007). Urban–rural interrelationships mean visible and invisible flows of people, capital, goods, information and technologies between urban and rural areas; physical and socio-economic connections (Preston, 1975). Urban–rural relations can be characterized by time-space and qualitative and quantitative dimensions. Particular aspects to be analysed include: (1) urban–rural boundaries, (2) spatial structures—distances, locations, patterns and hierarchies of geographic (physical) and socio-economic (relational) space, (3) human activity nodes and flows in between and (4) power relations, values and attitudes. Salingaros (1998, p. 53) notes that humans are capable of identifying existing, even hidden connections and to establish new connections. Urry (2004, p. 28) argues that social relationships create multiple connections that are not fixed or located in place. Social agents are place-based and thus, disposed in urban–rural dichotomy through their material and body dimensions, although their perception can change through their circulating and mobile existence. Rosado (2008) highlights that the premise of context (value system) determines content (urban–rural reality) and provides better understanding of wholeness in urban transformations. Rosado points that the hidden urban connections, even if they are not visible and not measured, cannot be ignored. Urban and rural places are being conceived, observed, consumed and transformed not only by "locals" but by "others" from the region, the nation or from abroad. Urban–rural complemental cooperation has to strengthen urban and rural place identities. Social agents with "multiple possible options and choices available" during their life courses should be provided with the knowledge of the field (context) where urban–rural interactions have taken place rather than details (content) of these interactions (Rosado, 2008, p. 2094).

Having a Marxist view Khorev (1971, p. 372) perceives "urban" and "rural" as traditional partners in exchanging production and as the oldest type of social and territorial division of labour. Exchange between specific assets of urban and rural places occurs through mutual urban–rural investment flows of various kinds of capital (financial, physical, knowledge and health). Khorev argues that "linkages between urban and rural are built-up not only on the economical foundation but also on the superstructure, including political, ideological, cultural aspects, in such way that city steers village". He notes that rural modernization reduces an urban–rural gap in the quality of life; due to the human mobility and the spread of information, particularly by television, qualitative social change is observed since the end of the 1950s (1971, p. 381); and that the urban–rural boundary is already blurring. The most important reasons are: (1) the diffusion of rural non-agricultural activities and employment, (2) the increase of suburban-type settlement forms and urban–rural commuting and (3) the spread of urban life style in rural settlements (Khorev, 1971, p. 372). Through everyday, weekly or seasonal human interactions (commuting, experience, information and commodity exchange) physical and socially constructed urban–rural borders are changing, particularly in expanded city regions (Hidle et al., 2009). Modernization paradigm changed the way urban–rural linkages are being perceived and interrelated with the other binary dimensions of nature society (Andersson et al., 2009; Woods, 2009). Urban–rural flows and structures in between are becoming complex and their spatial reach is widening and at the same time "pure" urbanness and ruralness are being more valued and consumed. Human experience needs both connections (being in travel, changing places and activities, all kinds of mobilities and social transformations, inclusion, cohesion and integration) and isolation (solitude, tranquillity, escape, shelter, fixity, persistence, identity, continuity and protection) as long as they are based on free will of social agents and not caused by imposed actions of political powers or socio-economic contexts linked with inequity and injustice. In their article on isolating connections and connecting isolations. Clark and Clark (2009) suggest that a relationship of complementarity is needed and that can be easily referred to urban and rural places. Places of connections defined in spatial or time frames (specific regulation areas, hubs, corridors, meeting points, trading places, events and places of knowledge and cultural exchange, learning, training and innovations, leisure and outdoor recreation, places of temporal (seasonal) work and housing opportunities) need to be created and supported. Such places of connections are vital in both ends of urban–rural continuum—remote rural areas with disperse population and in central parts of cities, where the linkages to ruralness are loosing in power games of market forces, but still needed for human existence and well-being.

4. Urban–Rural Interactions Under Communist Ideology and Totalitarian Policy Regimes

Central and Eastern Europe's landscapes and social memory still carry elements from the communist regimes. One of the communist ideology postulates was that the cities should lead the countryside and that urban–rural relationships should change from being exploitative to mutually beneficial. Wegren (2001) argues that urban bias has dominated Soviet politics. In Latvia by 1972, collective farmers average income including income from private plots had surpassed that of urban workers (Misiunas & Taagepera, 1983, p. 220). This proves that under a less totalitarian regime, comparatively well-educated rural population's voice leads to more equal urban–rural distribution of welfare and services. As initiated in this period, several urban–rural policy measures are positively assessed by interviewed Latvian experts—like support to rural services and public transport, culture, outdoor and field sport activities, subsidized work of urban skilled and urban youth work and leisure in rural areas.

In the Soviet Union urban–rural policy measures were considered a part of social spatial and regional planning. Khorev (1981, p. 203) lists several aims: (1) to strengthen the regional growth and the unity of the urban–rural system, (2) to diminish regional and urban–rural social disparities, (3) to regulate commuting, demographic and migration processes, (4) to strengthen education and (5) to strengthen multifunctionality of cities and "peasant-urbanite" social group. A belief that discrepancies inherited from the capitalist society, including rural–urban, will be abolished in future (Bonner, 1998) goes back to the main principles of Marxism (Marx & Engels, 1969[1848]). These principles received more attention with Khrushchev's "revolutionary romanticism" ideas. Urban living and industrial work became ideal types and future models of Soviet spatial policies. Communist propaganda used the images of urbanized rural places and green cities, and healthy and happy faces of urban youth and intelligencia working in agriculture or contributing to rural social and cultural life. Simultaneously "capitalist" (individualism and ethnic) rural values were concealed. During his speech in the 22nd Congress of the Communist Party in 1961 Nikita Khrushchev declared: "our human settlements need to conform to the notion of 'green cities', 'garden cities'. They will comprise all good, that is in the contemporary city—houses with utilities, arterial roads, communal, children care, culture and sport institutions, with all good, that is in rural areas—rich greenery, water bodies and clean air" (cited in Stramentov, 1963, p. 3). In many aspects the reality of the ordinary citizens' everyday-life was often contrary to the Soviet rhetoric—numerous social and political problems were ignored. In spatial development "urbanity through compactness under the principle of concentration" (Engel, 2006, p. 187) was realized in cities and rural centres. Soviet policy-makers often overturned the traditional "form" and "content" of policies or built structure (Engel, 2006, p. 185). In rural urban look-like, people still continued farming in their private plots and in socialistic agricultural enterprises. Formal approach to urban growth control stimulated the growth of collective farms centres on urban–rural edges. The exchange of labour force between urban and rural places fulfilled several aims that were declared in the Soviet Union's Constitution of 1977 (used up to 1991): strengthening social homogeneity by removing barriers of social classes that exist between city (town) and village, between mental and physical work and between ethnic groups. Soviet policies having spatial implications included forced ownership change, the scale-increase of production, rural industrialization, the abolishment of traditional rural settlements and life styles, support to agro-towns and central (perspective) villages, multistory housing construction in rural areas, the spread of urban services and lifestyles, support to mobile services (shops) and artist performances, voluntary and involuntary short and longer-term urban–rural exchange of young, educated and skilled labour force and Soviet administrator class, improvement of urban–rural commuting and public transport and construction of new settlements in adjacent rural areas of cities which growth were restricted, creation of new settlements, and expeditions or mobile settlements in areas rich with natural resources (Engel, 2006, pp. 181–182). Soviet policies were selective and ignored numerous aspects of the human rights and needs (particularly consumption). The implementation of policies supporting positive urban–rural interactions was highly dependent upon local leaders and a regional context.

The Soviet policy regime change in the 1960s encouraged the Latvian local communist elite to re-establish elements of the pre-war urban–rural policy measures implemented by authoritarian Latvian president Kārlis Ulmanis (1877–1942) (Latvijas Valsts prezidenta kanceleja, 2013). In the 1930s the practicality and the meaning at everyday level were considered the best policy tools to diminish a distrust and income disparities between urban and rural population and to facilitate urban–rural cooperation. Increased human mobility, improved public health, a better access quality food and leisure, but particularly gardening and forests were considered as a "bridge" between urban and rural. Numerous arguments were listed for sending urban children to rural areas: healthier environment, closer connections with nature, better food, physical activities, to learn about agricultural activities and rural life style, to provide additional activity to farmers and to increase a trust and cooperation between urban and rural population. The notion prevailed that urban–rural gaps can be diminished only if there is a mutual understanding between urban and rural inhabitants. Several elements of the pre-war urban–rural policies were reintroduced in Latvia's territory under the Soviet regime and its ideological frames. Creative urban people were moving or commuting to work in wealthy collective farms, thus, continuing the policies of the pre-war Latvia when rural residential properties, often as second homes, were donated or rented to creative class. From 1971 to 1991 the Latvian youth work and leisure voluntary programme LOTOS ("Latviiskii otriad truda i otdykha starsheklassnikov"—in Russian) was implemented in schools with the aim to accommodate youth groups in collective farms, where work in agriculture were combined with an open-air leisure. The programme had similarities with a national programme, launched in 1935 and subsidising summer vacations in farms for children having a residence in the largest 15 cities and towns. The programme was cooperation among individual farmers, children guardianship committees of urban and rural municipalities and national social care and public health institutions (Valdības Vēstnesis, 1938). The "summer vacations" children regions' were created to coordinate partnerships between involved cities and rural municipalities (Brīvā Zeme, 1938).

5. Urban–Rural Human Movements

Human movements have a particular role in urban–rural interactions as the outcome is not only change of population size and characteristics but also change of perception, attitudes, knowledge and experience. The context of past population movements and the current large scale international labour force out-migration are crucial to understanding urban–rural population flows in contemporary Latvia. Schwartz (2006) characterizes Latvian identity as a tension between inward- and outward-looking story-lines, which she describes as "peasant nation", agrarianism and agrarian ethnospace versus "seafarers nation", internationalism and "the bridge between East and West" located in the multicultural trading crossroads. It can be characterized as a territory of places of isolations and connections (Clark & Clark, 2009) that interlinked through urban–rural interactions. Such spatial model has great potential for development, however, it should be modernized—adapted to current technological changes and the open European market. Latvian territory has been under intensive population movements caused by many wars and political regime changes; current population is still affected by the consequences of the WWII and the forced Sovietization. One-third of its pre-war two million population was lost and replaced by immigrants from other parts of the Soviet Union (Misiunas & Taagepera, 1983; Eglīte, 2009). Forced movements included the deportations of 1949, targeted explicitly to rural population (Bleiere, 2005). There were voluntary rural-to-urban or vice versa population movements as a survival strategy to escape political repressions during German and Soviet occupations by "being lost" from registrars. Private property restitution in the 1990s facilitated a return to pre-war family residences; as a result many skilled urbanites became farmers (Beitnere, 2003).

Urban–rural movements within Latvia's territory were less restricted than in the pre-war territory of the Soviet Union. Latvian population, including rural, received internal Soviet passports; except the 68 thousand at least that were imprisoned or deported (Eglīte, 2009). In the Soviet Union, the internal passport system was reintroduced in 1932 to stop an enormous inflow of rural population to cities, thus, elements of the Russian Empire' serfdom and population movement control were revived. Before fixing urban–rural population there was a campaign to "clean-up" cities from "capitalist elements". Passport-bearers were requested to be registered at age of 16 in the militia at his/her permanent place of residence and to receive a stamp in the passport (Russian "propiska" or Latvian "pieraksts"). In the pre-war territory of the Soviet Union, members of collective farms ("kolkhozniks") had not received passports up to 1974, even afterwards their movements often were controlled by local officials (Zaslavsky, 1980). Rural female migrants came to the cities illegally while young men after army service could obtain passports; other individual strategies on how to depart from the movement restrictions, were to enrol in a higher education establishment; by marriage; through extended family; and to get a job which carried a residence permit or housing privileges. Scarce population was fixed in vast and harsh areas where the land and natural resources were. Soviets used urban–rural population movement control for several purposes: to attach residents to bounded places; to keep people in collective farms; to control large cities' growth; to control the criminal influx (up to 101 km from the city—the distance became a symbol for remoteness); to control population movement in the border zones, to distribute scarce public services and commodities of food and other consumption products and etc. (Shelley, 1984; Buckley, 1995). "The 'propiska' system had not prevented millions of people from living where they wanted to live in the Soviet era, but it created an incentive for not registering one's real permanent address with the authorities" (Arel, 2002).

Latvian experts stressed that most effective was a policy that restricted a minimal dwelling space per inhabitant. In 1940s, the social residential norms were imposed on Latvian residents. The policy was abolished in 1993, until then 12 m^2 of free residential area for Riga and Jurmala (an adjacent resort city) and 9 m^2 for the rest of Latvia were needed per inhabitant to receive residence registration, except these who were extended family members. Urban–rural resident categories in the residential registration system were eliminated in Latvia in 2003. Since then inhabitants were free to choose their residential address and it is only required communication with governmental institutions. As a result, many extended families were split between urban–rural places, or they still continued to keep their rural residence as a summer-cottage. Within the northern European and the Soviet summer-cottage cultures, many families in Latvia have second homes. Garden allotments in Riga were introduced at the beginning of the nineteenth century. As the result of the Agrarian Reform in 1920–1937 garden colonies were created in both urban and rural places, mostly in the Riga region; allotments were distributed not only to persons with gardening skills, but also to railway personnel, members from creative professions (university personnel, artists and writers) and state administrators (Loks, 1930, p. 553). Due to the Soviet realities, summer-cottages and garden allotments were not only used for leisure, but also as private space and food production site (Lovell, 2002; Caldwell, 2004). In 1995, there were 32 thousand allotments inside the city (Riga City Council, 2001); since then the number is decreasing. Although data and policies at a national level are absent, local municipalities are informed regarding second homes, summer-cottage villages or garden allotments, and are concerned on issues relating to infrastructure and service provision to their seasonal population. The current economic crisis showed that easily available household plots for food production both in urban and rural areas defuse social tensions and "uncertainty in the economy" (Southworth, 2006, p. 469).

6. Estimations of Urban–Rural Population Movements in Latvia

Data indicate that the intensity of inter-regional, including urban–rural migration has increased in Latvia since the declaration of places of residence was introduced in 2003. However, since then data on urban–rural migration flows are no longer available. Although long promised, there is still little integration between different national data bases to capture human mobilities. However, project-based surveys exist. Urban–rural human movements historically have been perceived as the relation between Riga and its region, and the rest of the country. In 2011, the number of registered (declared) inhabitants was 2.23 million; the census of 2011 revealed that 2.07 million people have actual residence in Latvia, many of the younger population having moved (CSBL, 2012). In the beginning of 2011, Riga had 32% and the Riga planning region—49% of all registered population in Latvia. There are 76 cities and towns in total, where 67.5% of the population have their residences (CSBL, 2012). The urban–rural ratio has not changed significantly since the 1980s. Population decrease in remote rural areas is compensated by population growth in rural areas adjacent to large cities, mainly Riga. Between 1993 and 2002, 31 to 55 thousand people each year have been involved in internal migration; in total 369 thousand people changed their place of residence in the decade; population movement towards urban areas dominated, with tendency over a decade to increase, while migration to rural areas had tendency to decrease (Table 1) (Krisjane, 2007, p. 151). Rural and small town residents are changing their place of residence more often, Riga residents are moving outside their municipality least often (Table 2).

A dense road network and short distances make commuting easy. However, urban unemployment, low-skilled rural population, deteriorating local road quality, the rising

Table 1. Internal migration in Latvia (1993–2002)

Population movements	Distribution, %
Rural-to-urban	28
Urban-to-rural	30
Rural-to-rural	11
Urban-to-urban	31
Total	100

Source: Krisjane (2007), data from CSBL.

cost of transportation, inadequate public transport routes and schedules for job commuters (designed for service-related travel) sets limits to commuting.

7. Typology of Places in Relation of Urban–Rural Connectivity

In recent years Latvian policy-making has changed the perception as to how municipalities are grouped for the purpose of regional development policy-making. In 2008–2009, specific territories were identified according to urban–rural connectivities: (1) larger cities and rural areas in close proximity, (2) territories (corridors) of flows (transport of people, goods, energy, capital and information) and (3) places with specific particularities (development potentials) that contribute to intensification of urban–rural interactions (areas with strong branding potential, natural and cultural amenities, natural resources, areas of not-wanted land uses and administrative and functional boundaries) (Kūle, 2010). Such analytical grouping of territories were used to describe municipalities or their parts in order to reveal existing practises of urban–rural interactions, as well as to propose future policies on how to support activities that can stimulate growth. How such policies will be designed and implemented depends upon governance structures, including the existing administrative structure of Latvia. As a result of amalgamation, the number of local municipalities decreased from 522 to 119, and five planning regions (Figure 1) were established as the result of the territorial reform of 1998–2010. Latvian municipalities are treated equally in accordance with the Law on self-government (1994), with no reference as to their urban or rural character. In 2009, the legal definition

Table 2. Urban–rural distribution of residents and migrants in Latvia (1993–2002)

Type of settlements	Total population, %	Incoming migrants, %	Outgoing migrants, %
Rural	31	42	39
Urban, including	69	58	61
Riga	33	16	21
Large cities (Daugavpils, Jelgava, Jurmala, Liepaja, Rezekne and Ventpils)	17	17	15
District centres (towns) (in total 20)	12	14	15
Other towns (in total 50)	7	11	10
Total	100	100	100

Source: Krisjane (2007), data from CSBL.

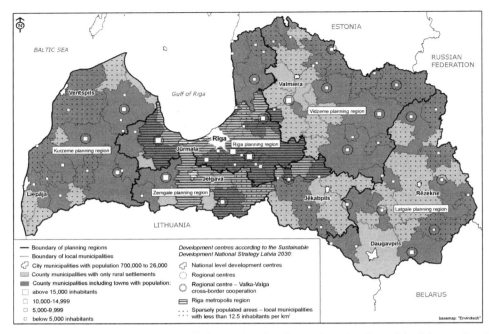

Figure 1. Urban–rural spatial structure in Latvia: planning regions, local municipalities, national and regional development centres (Saeima, 2010), other towns, Riga metropolis region (SRDA, 2011) and sparsely populated areas in 2011 (map graphics by Andris Ločmanis; data from CSBL, 2012, own calculations).

of rural area was removed from the law. There are legal definitions of city and village; however, in practice many settlements do not meet the criteria. Several urbanized villages, particularly in the Riga region, are larger in size than historical small towns. For policy needs ad hoc definitions are used more often.

8. From Urban–Rural Interactions to Partnerships: Policy Application Challenges

The application of urban–rural interactions in policy-making is faced with various challenges. The concept can be employed in different ways—as a framework for analysis, a developmental challenge, a driving force, and an objective and measures of spatial and regional development. International and Latvian policy documents indicate that urban–rural interactions are not recognized as a distinctive analytical category. Urban–rural relationships as a policy option are listed by the European Spatial Development Perspective alongside with polycentric urban systems (CSD, 1999). Urban–rural relationships are seen as a policy instrument that, if adequately designed, can provide better connectivity, and thus, an access to affordable and quality infrastructures and services (EC, 2010, p. 7). There is a possibility of urban and rural symbiosis as urban and rural are "mutually supportive if there are positive partnerships that can capture the full benefits for both urban and rural areas" (CBSS, 2011, p. 10). Urban–rural relationships aiming to overcome territorial divides, development gaps and utilizing full potentials of regions (VASAB, 2009) are directly related with improved metropolitan and multilevel governance, territorial (cross-border, transnational and inter-regional) cooperation, stakeholder involvement and partnership building, as well as place-related innovations and knowledge transfer.

The Latvian National Development Plan (LNDP) 2007–2013 states that importance of "polycentric urban and rural structures" and "urban–rural cooperation with an aim to provide accessibility of services as close to inhabitants as possible" (CM, 2007). Although there are no measures directly aimed at urban–rural partnerships, there are numerous measures that at least in its rhetoric support urban–rural interactions. Rural and entrepreneurship aid measures have been designed based on the flexible urban–rural divide and ad hoc definitions of eligible rural areas. Thus, the food-industry became eligible in cities, while suburbanized rural municipalities were excluded from several rural development measures. Regional aid measures at a national level were not designed for trans-municipal cooperation or multipartner projects aiming at urban–rural partnerships; even though Latvian planning regions, local municipalities and public institutions have good experience in such projects in the Baltic Sea region programme. Urban–rural interactions are mentioned in the document approving priorities for the draft LNDP 2014–2020 (Jankovskis et al., 2012), besides other development directions under the priority "territories supporting growth"—accessible services and infrastructure (defining acceptable minimal level), no-agricultural rural industry, rural cooperation, high-value use of natural capital, decentralized concentration and the utilization of unique territorial potentials. How the development of urban–rural interactions will be implemented is not yet specified—for instance, through support to governance, entrepreneurial activities, culture or social development, or through the utilization of vacant public properties (school, railway stations, and culture, religious and commercial buildings) and land in remote areas. The draft LNDP (PKC, 2012) states that urban–rural partnerships is an option to provide better balanced living and working conditions and an access to basic services and mobility opportunities. Several concrete measures are suggested that can lead to minimizing urban–rural disparities; it includes a policy measure "to define and implement the minimal package of public services for two levels (1) national (9 cities) and regional (21 towns) centres and (2) services in 'rural areas' (including all other urban–rural area)". Subsidies to periphery-to-centre work-related commuting are proposed along with support to rural services, transport and information and communication infrastructure and to subsidize jobs of young skilled in areas outside Riga. Training, innovations, direct marketing, local and green procurement, rural horizontal and vertical rural cooperation, support to agriculture and food-industry clusters, small harbours (PKC, 2012) can be also be referred as tools towards positive urban–rural interactions. There is no reference (PKC, 2012) to urban–rural partnership building that might involve various types of urban and rural social actors (public, private and non-government) organized in (1) multilevel general-purpose governance of territorial jurisdictions or (2) goal-oriented/task specific/flexible and functional associations of specialized jurisdictions (Hooghe & Marks, 2003).

There is a belief that possibilities exist to rebalance town-country relations in demographic, image-related and economic and social policy aspects (Piveteau, 2006). Urban–rural partnerships refer to initiatives to formulate, adapt and implement integrated policy in which a joint regional potential is utilized (SPESP, 2001). Urban–rural partnerships address the policy side of urban–rural relations and cover issues of governance, particularly regional, and cooperation along with vertical (multilevel government) and horizontal (multiactor) lines. Horizontal networks are found in spatial strategies, which have an attempt to coordinate urban and rural areas and strengthen local rural capabilities (content), increase knowledge, trust and interdependences, while vertical networks are found in sectoral policies, for instance, agriculture and goes beyond local markets and regional and national settings (Kneafsey *et al.*, 2001). Urban–rural relationships are "the precondition for a partnership, or at least, a good starting point to form a partnership" (Kawka, 2009, p. 62). Several objectives for urban–rural partnerships have been identified (modified from SPESP, 2001): to strengthen territorial governance, to promote multisectoral and inter-institutional cooperation, to coordinate investments, to diversify the economy, to increase the level of the decision-making, to avoid fragmentation in planning and management, to balance settlement structure, to improve accessibility and service provision, to mobilize and to enhance endogenous resources. Urban–rural interdependencies are not replacements to compartmentalized urban and rural policies; but it is believed that this concept will provide innovative, alternative or additional approaches aimed at benefiting both urban and rural areas, bringing policy efficiency, synergies and sustainability and providing solution for areas that are the mixture of urban and rural (Caffyn & Dahlström, 2005).

Typologies of urban–rural interactions are requested by policy-makers to improve policy targeting and to challenge existing urban–rural divides. For this purpose, it is advised to use the ad hoc systems (Voas & Williamson, 2001). Current attempts to classify urban–rural interrelationships are related to analytic purposes (Miller, 1971; Preston, 1975; Davoudi & Stead, 2002), and reflect rather urban–rural variety than connectivity. The typology of urban–rural relationships has been proposed by the European study (SPESP, 2001, p. 5): home-work relationships, central place relationships, relationships between metropolitan areas and urban centres in rural and intermediate areas, relationships between rural and urban enterprises, rural areas as consumption areas for urban dwellers, rural areas as open spaces for urban areas, rural areas as carriers of urban infrastructure and rural areas as suppliers of natural resources for urban areas. However, based on data (non)-availability, the study, grouped European regions differently—according to the size of main cities, urban networks and population density. Critical arguments against such typologies are several. They are based on doubts to isolate rural from urban and beliefs that all spatial units are connected in some way and that such typologies are scale dependent or sensitive to geographical or socio-economic contexts (Champion & Hugo, 2004). Other arguments against urban–rural typologies are based in the belief that only cities can be considered as growth centres thus, ignoring the variety of rural spaces and their capabilities to attract urban-based flows (Buciega *et al.*, 2009).

The new Latvian pattern of amalgamated municipalities provides opportunities to develop urban–rural partnerships (1) within municipally and (2) with neighbouring and (3) more distant municipalities. The study of rural–urban relations revealed inadequate coordination between places and policy fields as a main obstacle for developing more successful urban–rural partnerships (Kūle *et al.*, 2009). The outdoor recreation (transport issues, clean-up of littering and use of natural resources) are organized at ad hoc local activity, as national or regional policy is missing. Interviewed local experts revealed that in "soft" issues (social, culture and education) local municipalities have tendency to cooperate with other local municipalities that are equal in size and interests (Kūle *et al.*, 2009). Several urban–rural partnerships are based on the ownership structure. The Latvian Agrarian Reform of 1920–1937 nationalized large estates—land was distributed to farmers, while 84 manor houses were nationalized and used in a new creative way—for diversified high quality agricultural activities, agricultural research, educational establishments, sanatorium, orphanages and children's summer camps (Loks, 1930); many of these activities have been continued until today. As an example, Riga cooperation with rural areas takes place in providing social services. As the continuation of the policies of 1930s, Riga City's children and social care institutions use premises in rural municipalities (Ādaži, Rencēni and Lauderi). Centre-periphery, proximity or urban–rural aspects in these situations do not play an important role. Concerning the hard infrastructure issues, local municipalities are obliged to cooperate with adjacent larger urban areas due to the efficiency upon proximity and size, and due to fixed technical infrastructure networks. The urban–rural issues are being highlighted at national and regional levels by the Latvian policy documents, although until now mostly as a political rhetoric. There are unutilized opportunities to establish and develop urban–rural partnerships particularly in relations to local food, public health, recreation and other services.

9. Conclusions

New technologies and increased human mobility are changing spatial patterns and characteristics of rural–urban interactions. However, the concepts of rural and urban will remain vital for everyday-life, social and place identity and for understanding of local environment. Dominating political regimes frame how urban and rural places are constructed, and how human and material flows between urban and rural areas are regulated. Thus, urban–rural interactions are deeply rooted in local culture, microlevel practices and the land ownership structure. The general principles of governance level policies in relation to urban–rural partnerships have been repeated by different political regimes. The Soviet policies tend to control and promote urban–rural population movements, while more democratic ante-bellum political regimes and contemporary policies in Latvia focus on urban–rural land use and activities over urban–rural boundaries. Contemporary Latvian policy-making rejects urban–rural population involuntary movements and restrictions, while there is a proposal to subsidized voluntary urban–rural movements as a part of regional aid. Land use policies of urban and rural areas need to accommodate "other" and temporal (seasonal) uses to permit urban–rural connections: urban agriculture and forestry, allotment gardens and summer-cottages, places of outdoor recreation, rural urban-type settlements and non-agricultural activities. Spatial policies of urban and rural territories need to accommodate both places of connection and places of isolation.

There is a belief that urban–rural partnerships can bring impetus and additional growth both at local and regional levels. The role of regional and national level institutions to facilitate urban–rural cooperation over municipal boundaries is crucial. However, designing and implementing such measures requires place-specific approaches. Both rural and urban potentials, needs and development restrictions have to be assessed and considered at all levels of spatial planning. Dialogue with local and regional communities is essential to identify the complexities of urban–rural interactions and potential for urban–rural partnership building and policy interventions.

Typologies of territories identified according to urban–rural connectivity can be used for analytical and policy purposes. The size of urban areas and the proximity between urban and rural areas, and the specific development particularities as accelerants of urban–rural interactions matter most. Not only urban regions, but also development corridors and specific "other" land use areas in rural areas are places of urban–rural connectivity. Policy instruments contributing to additional growth in both urban and rural places should include mainstream rural-to-urban, as well as "counterflow" urban-to-rural movements of labour, firms, investments, knowledge, skills and innovations. Policy measures designed to facilitate rural–urban interactions can bring complementarity to existing sectoral policies, better provision of public services, new business opportunities, additional skills and knowledge and the improved quality of life both for rural and urban residents. Challenges are associated with data-related uncertainties. More benefits should be gained by rural communities from seasonal population with urban connections; policy instruments should take into account urban–rural multiresidences of individuals and firms, particularly those that are involved in creative activities. The multiplicity of urban–rural interactions is linked with a higher local-level economic performance (Kūle *et al.*, 2009). Not covered by public policies "other" activities will largely contribute to an informal sector as it is observed at the moment. The rural aid should be better coordinated with spatial and sectoral policies, not only at the design phase but also at the implementation and monitoring phases. There is an unutilized development potential in outdoor recreation, youth policies, culture, public health, social care and poverty reduction that can be used as stimulus for building urban–rural partnerships, with the aim of bringing jobs to rural areas and inter-mutual attitude change. Policy tools used in the past can provide examples for urban–rural contemporary policy measures, as it is easier to "sell" activities with a positive social memory. Although being complex, urban–rural interactions can provide a basis for policy measures with support for urban–rural population mobilities, and to use place-specific development potential at its full capacity beyond urban–rural physical and mental boundaries.

References

Alaev, Ė. B. (1983) *Sotsial'no-ėkonomicheskaia geografiia* (Moskva: Mysl').

Andersson, K., Eklund, E., Lehtola, M. & Salmi, P. (2009) Introduction: Beyond the ruralurban divide, in: K. Andersson, E. Eklund, M. Lehtola & P. Salmi (Eds) *Beyond the Rural–Urban Divide: Cross-Continental Perspectives on the Differentiated Countryside and Its Regulation*, pp. 2–21 (Bingley: Emerald).

Arel, D. (2002) Demography and politics in the first post-Soviet censuses: Mistrusted state, contested identities, *Population*, 57(6), pp. 801–827.

Bascom, J. (2001) "Energizing" rural space: The representation of countryside culture as an economic development strategy, *Journal of Cultural Geographies*, 19(1), pp. 53–73.

Beitnere, D. (2003) *Pašreference latviešu kultūras paradigmā* (Riga: LU Filozofijas un socioloģijas institūts Rīgas Stradiņa universitāte).

Bengs, C. & Schmidt-Thomé, K. (Eds) (2005) *Urban–Rural Relations in Europe: ESPON 1.1.2 Final Report* (Helsinki: Centre for Urban and Regional Studies Helsinki University of Technology).

Bleiere, D. (2005) Repressions against farmers in Latvia in 1944–1953, in: V. Nollendorfs & E. Oberländer (Eds) *The Hidden and Forbidden History of Latvia under Soviet and Nazi Occupations 1940–1991*, pp. 242–255 (Riga: Institute of the History of Latvia).

Bonner, K. (1998) Reflexivity, sociology and the rural–urban distinction in Marx Tonnies and Weber, *Canadian Review of Sociology and Anthropology*, 35(2), pp. 165–189.

Brīvā Zeme (1938) Vasaras bērnu rajoni, *Brīvā Zeme*, March 25, p. 3.

Buciega, A., Pitarch, M.-D. & Esparcia, J. (2009) The context of rural–urban relationships in Finland, France, Hungary, the Netherlands and Spain, *Journal of Environmental Policy & Planning*, 11(1), pp. 9–27.

Buckley, C. (1995) The myth of managed migration: migration control and market in the Soviet Period, *Slavic Review*, 54(4), pp. 896–916.

CM (Cabinet of Ministers) (2007) National Strategic Reference Framework (NSRF) 2007–2013, 23 October. Available at www.esfondi.lv (accessed 18 July 2011).

IMPACTS OF EUROPEAN TERRITORIAL POLICIES IN THE BALTIC STATES

Caffyn, A. & Dahlström, M. (2005) Urban-rural interdependencies: Joining up policy in practice, *Regional Studies*, 39(3), pp. 283-296.

Caldwell, M. L. (2004) *Not by Bread Alone: Social Support in the New Russia* (Ewing, NJ: University of California Press).

CSBL (Central Statistical Bureau of Latvia) (2012) Central Statistical Bureau of Latvia Databases. Available at http://www.csb.gov.lv/en (accessed 18 May 2012).

Champion, T. & Hugo, G. (2004) Introduction: Moving beyond the urban-rural dichotomy, in: T. Champion & H. Graeme (Eds) *New Forms of Urbanization: Beyond the Urban-Rural Dichotomy*, pp. 3-24 (Aldershot: Ashgate).

Clark, E. & Clark, T. L. (2009) Isolating connections—Connecting isolations, *Geografiska Annaler B*, 91(4), pp. 311-323.

Cloke, P. & Johnston, R. (2005) Deconstructing human geography's binaries, in: P. Cloke & R. Johnston (Eds) *Spaces of Geographical Thought: Deconstructing Human Geography's Binaries*, pp. 1-4 (London: Sage).

CSD (Committee on Spatial Development) (1999) *European Spatial Development Perspective* (Luxembourg: Office for Official Publications of the European Communities).

CBSS (Council of the Baltic Sea States) (2011) *Strategy on Sustainable Development 2010-2015 adopted by the CBSS Committee of Senior Officials on 26 January 2011* (Stockholm: CBSS Secretariat).

Davoudi, S. & Stead, D. (2002) Urban-rural relationships: An introduction and a brief history, *Built Environment*, 28(4), pp. 269-277.

Dematteis, G. (2001) Shifting cities, in: C. Minca (Ed.) *Postmodern Geography: Theory and Praxis*, pp. 113-128 (Oxford: Blackwell).

ECE-FAO-Eurostat-OECD (2005) *Meeting on Food and Agricultural Statistics, Rome, 29 June-1 July 2005*. Available at http://www.unece.org/stats/documents/2005.06.agri.htm (links, Latvia) (accessed 18 July 2011).

Eglīte, P. (2009) A brief overview of 20th century Latvian migration studies, *Folia Geographica*, 14, pp. 81-87.

Engel, B. (2006) Public space in the Blue cities in Russia, *Progress in Planning*, 66(3), pp. 147-239.

EC (European Commission) (2010) *Conclusions of the Fifth Report on Economic, Social and Territorial Cohesion* (Brussels: European Commission).

Hannerz, U. (1996) *Transnational Connections* (London: Routledge).

Hidle, K., Farsund, A. A. & Lysgard, H. K. (2009) Urban-rural flows and the meaning of borders, *European and Regional Studies*, 16(4), pp. 409-421.

Hugo, G., Champion, A. & Lattes, A. (2003) Toward a new conceptualization of settlements for demography, *Population and Development Review*, 29(2), pp. 277-297.

Hooghe, L. & Marks, G. (2003) Unraveling the central state, but how? Types of multi-level governance, *American Political Science Review*, 97(2), pp. 233-243.

Jankovskis, J., Kauliņš, J., Krieviņš, M., Sīmane, M., Stūre, I., Vesperis, V., Vilks, P. & Zvīgulis, J. (2012) Nacionālā attīstības plāna 2014-2020.gadam prioritāšu pamatojuma ziņojums. Pārresoru koordinācijas centrs. Available http://www.mk.gov.lv (accessed 10 April 2012).

Kawka, R. (2009) Growth and innovation through urban-rural partnership, in: W. Strubelt (Ed.) *Guiding Principles for Spatial Development Germany*, pp. 57-73 (Berlin: Springer).

Khorev, B. S. (1971) *Problemy Gorodov* (Moscow: Mysl').

Khorev, B. S. (1981) *Territorial'naia organizatsiia obshchestva* (Moskva: Mysl').

Kneafsey, M., Ilbery, B. & Jenkins, T. (2001) Exploring the dimensions of culture economies in rural West Wales, *Sociologia Ruralis*, 41(3), pp. 296-310.

Krisjane, Z. (Ed.) (2007) *The Geographic Mobility of the Labour Force* (Riga: University of Latvia).

Kūle, L. (2010) Urban-rural interactions in Latvia, *Regional Insights*, 1(1), pp. 12-14.

Kūle, L., Osis, U., Stalidzāne, I., Tisenkopfs, T., Timofejevs, A. & Timofejevs, K. (2009) *Pētījums "Latvijas pilsētu un lauku mijiedarbības izvērtējums"* (Riga: Konsorts, Valsts reģionālās attīstības aģentūra).

Latvijas Valsts prezidenta kanceleja (2013) *Kārlis Ulmanis: Latvijas Valsts prezidents 1936-1940*. Available at http://www.president.lv/pk/content/?cat_id=910 (accessed 12 February 2013).

Loks, J. (1930) Piešķiršanas komisijas darbība rūpniecības un citu valsts fonda objektu lietās, in: A. Alberings (Ed.) *Latvijas Agrārā reforma*, pp. 552-556 (Rīga: Zemkopības ministrija).

Lovell, S. (2002) Soviet exurbia: Dachas in postwar Russia, in: D. Crowley & S. E. Reid (Eds) *Socialist Spaces: Sites of Everyday Life in the Eastern Bloc*, pp. 105-121 (New York: Berg).

Marsden, T., Murdoch, J., Lowe, P., Munton, R. & Flynn, A. (1993) *Constructing the Countryside* (London: University College of London).

Marx, K. & Engels, F. (1969[1848]) *Manifesto of the Communist Party* (Moscow: Progress Publishers).
Miller, V. P. (1971) Towards a typology of urban–rural relationships, *The Professional Geographer*, 23(4), pp. 319–323.
Misiunas, R. J. & Taagepera, R. (1983) *The Baltic States: Years of Dependence 1940–1980* (Berkeley: University of California Press).
Pahl, R. E. (1966) The rural–urban continuum, *Sociologia Ruralis*, 6(4), pp. 299–329.
PKC (Pārresoru koordinācijas centrs) (2012) Nacionālā attīstības plāna 2014–2020. gadam 1.redakcija. Available at http://www.nap.lv (accessed 25 May 2012).
Piveteau, V. (2006) Town-country relations, a new issue in public policies, in: N. Bertrand & V. Kreibich (Eds) *Europes's City-Regions Competitiveness*, pp. 50–60 (Assen: van Gorcum).
Potter, R. B. & Unwin, T. (1995) Urban–rural interaction: Physical form and political process in the Third World, *Cities*, 12(1), pp. 67–73.
Preston, D. (1975) Rural–urban and intersettlement interaction: Theory and analytical structure, *Area*, 7(3), pp. 171–174.
Riga City Council (2001) *Rīgas vides pārskats* (Riga: Riga City Council).
Rigg, J. (1998) Rural–urban interactions, agriculture and wealth: A Southeast Asian Perspective, *Progress in Human Geography*, 22(4), pp. 497–522.
Rosado, C. (2008) Context determines content: Quantum physics as a framework for "wholeness" in urban transformation, *Urban Studies*, 45(10), pp. 2075–2097.
Saeima (2010) Sustainable Development Strategy of Latvia until 2030, 10 June. Available at http://www.latvija2030.lv (accessed 18 July 2011).
Salingaros, N. A. (1998) Theory of the urban web, *Journal of Urban Design*, 3(1), pp. 53–72.
Schaffter, M., Fall, J. J. & Debarbieux, B. (2010) Unbounded boundary studies and collapsed categories: Rethinking spatial objects, *Progress in Human Geography*, 34(2), pp. 254–262.
Schwartz, K. Z. S. (2006) *Nature and National Identity after Communism: Globalizing the Ethnoscape* (Pittsburgh, PA: University of Pittsburgh Press).
Shelley, L. I. (1984) Urbanization and crime: The Soviet experience, in: H. W. Morton & R. C. Stuart (Eds) *Contemporary Soviet City*, pp. 113–128 (New York; M.E. Sharpe).
Shields, R. (1997) Flow as a new paradigm, *Space and Culture*, 1(1), pp. 1–7.
Southworth, C. (2006) The dacha debate: Household agriculture and labor markets in post-socialist Russia, *Rural Sociology*, 71(3), pp. 451–478.
SRDA (State Regional Development Agency) (2011) *Development of Regions in Latvia 2010* (Riga: State Regional Development Agency).
Stramentov, A. E. (1963) *Vedenie v gorodskoe stroitel'stvo* (Moskva: Gosudarstvennoe izdatel'stvo literatury po stroitel'stvu, akhitekture i stroitel'nim materialam).
SPESP (Study Program on European Spatial Planning) (2001) *Final Report* (Bonn: Federal Ministry of Transport, Building and Housing).
Urry, J. (2004) Connections, *Environment and Planning D, Society and Space*, 22(1), pp. 27–37.
Valdības Vēstnesis (1938) Noteikumi par pilsētu iedzīvotāju bērnu novietošanu atpūtā pie lauku iedzīvotājiem1938.gada vasarā, *Valdības Vēstnesis*, April 4.
Vision and strategies around the Baltic Sea (VASAB) (2009) *Vilnius Declaration: Towards Better Territorial Integration of the Baltic Sea Region*. Available at http://www.vasab.org/conference/page/67 (accessed 18 July 2011).
Voas, D. & Williamson, P. (2001) The diversity of diversity: A critique of geodemographic classification, *Area*, 33(1), pp. 63–76.
Wegren, S. (2001) *Democratization and Urban Bias in Post-Communist Russia* (Washington, DC: National Council for Eurasian and East European Research).
Woods, M. (2009) Rural geography: Blurring boundaries and making connections, *Progress in Human Geography*, 33(6), pp. 849–858.
Zaslavsky, V. (1980) Socioeconomic inequality and changes in Soviet ideology, *Theory and Society*, 9(2), pp. 383–407.
Zonneveld, W. & Stead, D. (2007) European territorial cooperation and the concept of urban–rural relationships, *Planning Practice & Research*, 22(3), pp. 439–453.

Europeanization and De-Europeanization of Estonian Regional Policy

GARRI RAAGMAA*, TARMO KALVET** & RAGNE KASESALU[†]

*Department of Geography, University of Tartu, Tartu, Estonia, **Department of Public Administration, Tallinn University of Technology, Tallinn, Estonia, [†]Advisio OÜ, Tartu, Estonia

ABSTRACT *Over the last two decades, the role of the EU can be considered highly important in advancing institutional reforms and overall development in Estonia. The article focuses on Estonian regional policy (RP) and analyses whether it has gone through Europeanization (i.e. convergence with EU regulations and values, or followed its own development path). The institutional cycle model of territorial governance is used for establishing the analytical framework. The research was largely carried out as a second-person action research and used interviews over the period of 1990–2011. The article concludes that Estonian RP shows considerable dynamics as public and political support to RP, administrative structures and policy tools have changed. Europeanization of Estonian RP was most visible in 1994–1998, when an institutional framework was created, in parallel with intensive learning from the West. Overall, in 1999–2004 the application of EU cohesion policy tools took place with significant convergence. After joining the EU in 2004, national RP programmes were reduced, the institutional framework was frozen and a selective application of EU rules and the use of EU cohesion policy measures for achieving some personal political agendas started, driving Estonian RP away from common European values.*

1. Introduction

According to the most general definition, regional policy (RP) has to reduce regional or spatial disparities in economic well-being. The main causes of regional problems are changes in economic structure—a new industry tends to avoid old industrial areas (Hall, 1988). Because of extensive transition from the socialist system to a market economy and restructuring of the economic systems, the situation in Central and Eastern European (CEE) countries is particularly *"demanding a RP response"*, including reforms of territorial and administrative structures, the new RP legislation and the implementation of spatially targeted incentives (Bachtler & Downes, 1999, p. 793).

Estonia, like most CEE countries, replaced the earlier spatial planning and policy schemes during the 1990s by learning from their Western counterparts. The role of the EU can be considered highly important in advancing institutional reforms and overall development. Requests for the preparation of national development plans and strategies have been significant push factors for better planning and Structural Funds have enabled greater investment than earlier (Kalvet, 2010, 2011). Estonia is generally described as a successfully converging (with the EU) economy (cf Tiits *et al.*, 2003) but with significant and growing regional differences: GDP of the capital region of Tallinn has been growing faster than in other regions (Figure 1) and only Tartu, a university town and centre for South Estonia, has GDP *per capita* slightly over the national average (Statistics Estonia, 2011). As first described by Raagmaa (1996, p. 695), three types of problem areas in Estonia can also be distinguished in 2011: high growth in the capital city region resulting in overconcentration and lack of infrastructure; declining industrial areas in North-East Estonia and single factory settlements characterized by high unemployment, underused infrastructure and emigration; and remote rural areas distinguished by a poor income base, high unemployment and out-migration of youth (see also Kalvet, 2010, 2011; Roose *et al.*, 2010).

In this paper, we analyse whether the Estonian RP has gone through Europeanization (convergence with EU regulations and values) or retained its own development path

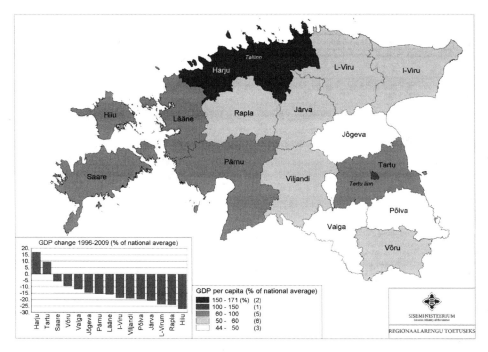

Figure 1. Regional (cities Tallinn & Tartu are given separately on the map) GDP per capita in 2009 and change 1996–2009 (% national average).
Source: Statistics Estonia, Ministry of Interior, designed by Eedi Sepp.

(divergence) and whether this has had an impact on the efficiency and effectiveness of RP. One would expect to see major convergence since the Estonian RP strategic documents refer explicitly to convergence with EU regulations and approaches, and the role of the Structural Funds is currently very important in Estonian RP—92% of regional development funding 2007–13 has been allocated from the ERDF (EE, 2012).

We first look at the theoretical concepts of regional and cohesion policies and their changes in Europe (Section 2). Following the established framework, we analyse, in Section 3, Estonian RP based on observations, statistical data, analysis of documents and the written media, and interviews carried out between 1990 and 2011. Section four discusses the effects of interventions and (de-)Europeanization processes.

2. Theories and Practices Behind Regional Policy

The concept of RP has, in recent decades, undergone a number of major development stages. Prior to the 1970s, Western RP primarily subsidized relocation of production (e.g. Perroux, 1955). RP measures have been regionalized since the early 1990s (Jauhiainen, 2008, p. 1039), the aim being to build up regionally networked innovation systems strengthening competitiveness in the global market and promoting the knowledge society via localized learning processes and increasing "sticky" knowledge grounded in social interaction (Asheim & Coenen, 2005, p. 1174). In tackling unused innovation potential, the first step to take is capacity building, both through the training of people and through the promotion of new institutions (Barca, 2009, p. 247).

Today's European RP is the expression of the EU's solidarity with its less-favoured countries and regions: to make all regions more competitive and to create more and better jobs (EUR-Lex, 2010). The main principles of EU Cohesion Policy targeted towards economic growth and creating jobs are concentration, programming, partnership and additionality, and current cohesion policy is worth 347 billion euros between 2007 and 1013 (CEC, 2010).

However, Eurostat and recent reports (CEC, 2010) indicate continuously increasing regional disparities within EU member states (Lang, 2011). Several authors outline that the cohesion policy remained embedded in the tradition of European national policies, firmly rooted in the belief that replicating top-down infrastructure, education and industrial policies, regardless of the local institutional contexts, would suffice to generate greater growth and promote economic convergence (e.g. Amin, 1999; Pike *et al.*, 2006; Rodríguez-Pose & Storper, 2006). The influence of institutions on regional development patterns has been fundamentally neglected (Rodríguez-Pose & Storper, 2006, p. 4). Even if some regional economies manage to renew themselves, then others remain locked in decline (Martin & Sunley, 2006; Reinert & Kattel, 2007; Tiits *et al.*, 2008) despite significant transfers from the EU and national budgets. Regional differences, especially in the CEE countries, are increasing (Heidenreich & Wunder, 2008; Hoffmeister, 2009; Paas & Schlitte, 2010; Petrakos *et al.*, 2005; Stryjakiewicz, 2009; Wostner, 2005) and such trends can be observed since the very beginning of the transition (Blazyca *et al.*, 2002; Buček, 1999; Manrai *et al.*, 2001; Rykiel, 1995; Weltrowska, 2002).

Olsen (2003, p. 334) called Europeanization the penetration of European-level institutions into national and sub-national systems of governance. According to Börzel and Risse (2000, p. 4), the term Europeanization describes processes of domestic change resulting from three different aspects: policies, institutions and policymaking processes; they make a distinction between a "top-down" and a "bottom-up" dimension. Lenschow (2006) defines three types of Europeanization: top-down (EU–nation state), horizontal (state–state) and round-about (state–EU–state). Europeanization in terms of developing institutions at the European level refers to both the strengthening of organizational capacity for collective action and the development of common ideas (Böhme & Waterhout, 2008).

Administrative systems have a path-dependency, such as the persistence of institutions and cultures (Nadin & Stead, 2008, p. 35). The level of public intervention, strength of spatial policies and cooperation between administrative levels and sectors, in terms of general values and norms and modes of behaviour, are characterized by a specific cultural context (Knieling & Othengrafen, 2009) which is the result of historical and existing institutional structures and legal frameworks. In the CEE, where public policies went through dramatic changes, the question is whether they are going through Europeanization or retaining their own development paths. Many authors argue that European countries, but especially EU newcomers, are increasingly influenced by European policies. Böhme and Waterhout (2008, p. 233) compared the three Structural Funds periods, 1994–1999, 2000–2006 and 2007–2013, and admit that there is a clear shift towards addressing more territorial cohesion issues. Europeanization of spatial planning and application of EU cohesion policy should by their very nature make spatial planning systems and development more coherent across Europe. Waterhout (2008) sees territorial cohesion as an integrating field for balanced development, competitiveness, sustainability and good territorial governance.

To understand the complex process of public policymaking in the context of multilevel governance, we use an institutional cycle model of territorial governance elaborated by Cotella and Janin Rivolin (2010) (Figure 2). Guiding domestic change under the direct

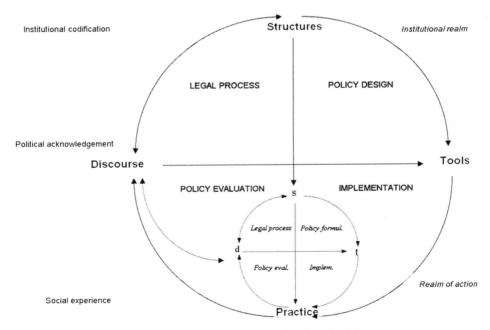

Figure 2. Institutional cycle of EU and national territorial governance.
Source: After Cotella and Janin Rivolin (2010), authors' own compilation.

influence of the EU institutional structures on the Member State's structures ("S" → "s") has been important in the redefinition of spatial planning systems in CEE countries (Cotella, 2009). The EU put pressure on those countries' governments to align their administrative structures more coherently with EU policy requirements (Cotella & Rivolin, 2010), but also to create and implement new local tools ("s" → "t") that are coherent with the EU measures. The EU tools shape local practices ("T" → "p") through financial incentives which are conditioned by the additionality principle and by other conditions. An interesting feature in both mechanisms is a discourse ("D" ↔ "d"): how the general public and politicians acknowledge the need for changes and new policies. In the context of permanent time pressure, administrators are pragmatic and try to avoid additional time-consuming tasks (like public debates) and any other changes that may threaten stability and create extra workload. Power embedded in the institutionalized routines, which shape the actions and thoughts of members of the organization, thereby creating organizational stability and also encapsulating organizational know-how, may be mobilized to resist new organizational rules (Burns & Scapens, 2000, p. 23). However, structures can only be sustainably upgraded via changing discourse and values of institutional stakeholders (Cotella & Rivolin, 2010). New policies and strategies become institutionalized and legalized and become converted into "tools" only when existing institutions are capable and willing to make changes, to improve their capacity and ability to carry out policies: the level of professionalism, communicability, etc. The approval of the new regulation does not automatically stand for implementation of new rules. Changes in people's minds and capacity building take time and if new ways for resolving problems have not been discussed and practised, in a real situation we may expect people to act using their previously obtained knowledge, routines and relations. Thus, there is a reason to argue that forced application of EU policies suitable to the Western European democracies supported by powerful NGOs may in many ways lead to different results in CEE countries.

In CEE countries, after temporary decentralization of the state bureaucracies at the beginning of 1990s, power concentrated in central agencies. Due to the long-term financial dependence on the central government, only a handful of larger local authorities managed to invest in the creation of their own programming capacity. Most local governments rely on the central government (Yanakiev, 2010, p. 55). Growing internal differences in the CEE countries and concerns expressed in Barca's report from 2009 show that different approaches in policy discourses need to be tackled: neither national nor regional/local authorities share the same values with the Commission and EU-level designed policies and discourses may acquire quite different forms in local tools and practices.

2.1 Typology of Cohesion Policy Adaption

We compiled a framework for analysing the Europeanization of national RP (Table 1). The question is: how have European cohesion policies been adopted within the national frameworks with a particular reference to (1) the commitment of key individuals, (2) discourse, (3) structures and (4) tools?

Option "A" describes the situation where the application of RP is harmonious with the EU policies: (1) majority of political leaders and civil servants both approve the EU approach; (2) there is an active debate about the EU policy principles, their aims and expected results; (3) new structures are established, financed and developed, and also

Table 1. Typology of regional/cohesion policy adaption and Europeanization

	Institutional dynamism, application of new rules	Path-dependency, institutional status quo
Political support to Europeanization and approval of new spatial planning rules and policies	A. *Convergence*: Europeanization of national and EU spatial policies, active public debate	B. *Partial "Yes, Minister" type of convergence, selective application of EU rules*: Public policy based on earlier cultural legacies and institutions, using EU tools for strengthening existing institutional structures, centralization, no public debate
Political establishment not interested in making changes	C. *Partial "Old-barnyism" type of convergence, political mimicry*: Partial convergence, selective application of EU rules, similarly labelled institutions and tools work to different purposes than in EU, using EU measures for fulfilling own political agendas, no persistent public debate	D. *Divergence*: Differentiation according to earlier traditions and new ambitions, public statements opposing Europeanization

Source: Authors.

(4) new policy measures are created and linked with the EU measures. This is the essence of true Europeanization.

Option "B" refers to partial convergence with EU policies where (1) public policy *seems* coherent with the EU approach but the institutional set-up will remain largely unchanged; (2) there is some public debate about the EU policies but it focuses on issues of minor importance or a limited number of topics, e.g. only transport infrastructure; (3) the existing institutional establishment will rather reinforce its positions, and new structures, if created, will depend on existing ones; (4) new policy measures are predominantly created for getting maximum cash inflow from the EU measures. This option can be characterized by the slogan "Yes, Minister" (From the BBC TV show and book "Yes, Minister" where politicians are willing to make changes but existing bureaucracy keeps its positions (BBC, 2011)).

Option "C" also refers to partial convergence, where (1) civil servants—who are learning from their Western colleagues—are interested in carrying out changes, but politicians either do not understand the value or are intentionally against changes because they do not see political benefits. If there is (2) a public discussion, it is channelled into discussing secondary issues and/or populism. (3) To an extent, institutional changes are made as requested by the EU, but they remain underfinanced and consequently understaffed. (4) New policy tools and institutions might be created too, but the EU funds will be spent without a real comprehensive strategy underpinning them. Simultaneously both politicians and ministerial civil servants (have to) declare positive changes but in reality it is merely mimicry. This option might be called old-barnyism ("Rehepaplus" in Estonian. The term appears in Kivirähk's (2000) novel *Rehepapp ehk november* (Old Barny, or November) containing an account of the chronicles of a nameless village in the eighteenth to nineteenth century. Old-barnyism acquired the meaning of "constantly thinking of the easiest way to appropriate something to one's own use").

Option "D" may emerge when (1) the political establishment declares that coherence with the EU is not a priority, and that a different national interest exists. (2) Publicly they may even raise slogans that stress national interest and the threat of losing independence, thus explaining the rejection of reform initiatives and justifying these exceptional positions through the public voice. (3) However, they may create new institutions in order to get access to the EU funds but (4) relevant institutions and policy measures rather support already existing establishments instead of structural reforms. This is de-Europeanization.

2.2 Research Questions and Methods

National RP and linkages to EU policies will be analysed from four aspects. The first relates to the RP discourse and questions the capacity in which EU cohesion policy and national RP have been discussed. Research questions we seek to answer include: Is there a public and parliamentary discussion about national territorial development, cohesion and RP? Is RP on the agendas of political parties? What kind of legal achievements are there in the field of RP? Are there attempts to contribute to EU-level discussion? Second, research questions explore the RP institutional structures and dynamism: What institutions have been created for RP design and implementation? Do they follow EU policy principles? Are national institutions across the range of administrative levels capable of implementing national and EU policies? Is there a common uniform government agenda or are ministerial strategies separated? The third aspect analyses the RP tools: What measures are designed for RP? Are these tools coherent with the EU measures? Are the application procedures clear and efficient? Finally, in terms of RP practice: Who are the main players in RP implementation? What are the results?

The following empirical section is constructed as a chronological narrative compiled as a result of a collegiate and consultative participatory action research (Cornwall & Jewkes, 1995, p. 1669) based mainly on meetings and interviews with persons active in Estonian RP. Studying RP with the action research method can be considered a novelty. So far action research has mainly been used in rural and spatial as well as in development and anthropological studies (e.g. Fricke & Totterdill, 2004; Wiggering *et al.*, 2010) at the micro-level. Action research is applicable when there are a small number of stakeholders which allows the formation of a communicative space (Kemmis, 2001, p. 100). As contributors to this paper have been directly involved in making and/or evaluating Estonian RP since the early 1990s, they have knowledge in their files and memo(rie)s which is not available in written form. Our participation would qualify as a second-person action research (Reason & Torbert, 2001), as we have been part of the process, but we present empirical material mostly through a third-person research approach. Given the small size of the national RP expert community, we do not use excerpts from personal interviews and conversations in order to provide confidentiality of sources.

3. RP in Estonia

The first-time Estonian principles of RP were formulated was in 1988 (IME, 1988) but were not implemented in their entirety (Jauhiainen & Ristkok, 2000). The first RP document, where RP was defined as "an activity of the state targeted to achieve a balanced development of all the regions of the country", was adopted by the Government on 14 March 1991 (see Appendix 1). The policy was designed by young semi-academic persons who had learned from European experience.

The conservative government that came to power in 1992 was primarily struggling with macro-stability. The few existing RP measures were cut off as RP was seen to be irrational in the market economy. The 1992–1994 period has been called "neoliberal" by Jauhiainen and Ristkok (2000) as politicians showed no initiative. This was actually "civil servants' RP" since they took the initiative for reorganization of institutions and planning of new measures: a training programme for business consultants, programmes for islands and border areas development and the settlements policy as well as establishing three regional Business Centres in the most problematic regions.

A new cabinet under Moderates (now Social Democrats) adopted the concept of RP and created the position of the Minister of Regional Affairs (MRA) by the end of 1994. The Council of Regional Policy was established for the co-ordination of sector policies. The new Planning and Building Act was passed and a national spatial planning "Eesti 2010" process, which used a novel knowledge creation and scenario method (Adams, 2006, p. 166), commenced. This period was also characterized by active public discussions, the RP discourse was increasingly important on the political agenda. The new centrist government launched six new territorially targeted development programmes in 1995 and established the Estonian Regional Development Agency (ERDA), created the foundation of crisis settlements and other initiatives in 1997. The record amount of National funding totalled over 8.7 million euros in 1998 (Figure 3). As Estonia started negotiations to accede to the EU, PHARE (Programme of Community aid to the countries of CEE) measures opened. The preparation of the Strategy of Regional Development supported by PHARE began in 1997 and applied a wide participatory approach involving the most interested stakeholders from across the different levels of administration. RP-related issues were also widely discussed in the media, and the Strategy was approved in 1998.

The new conservative government cut RP funds severely at a time of 1999 economic crisis. As the Ministry of Economic Affairs became responsible for the implementation of RP, some of its officials questioned "wasting money in the periphery", decreasing RP resources by 54%. The RP institutional set-up fell apart: the Council of the Regional Development was discontinued, ERDA was merged with *Enterprise Estonia* and public investment decisions partly made by regional authorities were exclusively concentrated in the hands of ministries. Politicizing of the executive apparatus started: officials were compelled to join the minister's party or were replaced by "loyal" people. County governors were politicized too with a few exceptions. The "civil servants' RP" returned: a new Department of Regional Development, responsible for RP design, was established at the Ministry of Interior and the Regional Development Strategy was approved once again with minor amendments in 1999. An attempt at territorial administrative reform, which aimed to restructure state regional governance and reduce the number of municipalities to about 100 units, failed.

In 2000–2001, PHARE aid for Estonia totalled 62.8 million euros and Instrument for Structural Policies for Pre-Accession (ISPA) 65.1 million euros, which was considerably higher than national RP allocations. Oppi and Moora (2004) studied distribution of these measures and concluded that the EU projects were received by local governments with a higher socio-economic potential and located in the more developed parts of Estonia. In

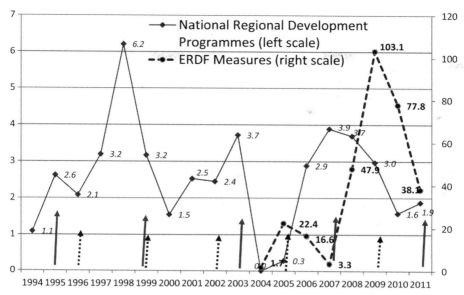

Figure 3. Estonian RP programme allocations (national and ERDF) in MEUR 1994–2011. Arrows indicate parliamentary and dotted arrows municipal election years.
Source: Ministry of Interior & Enterprise Estonia, authors' own compilation.

general, the absorption capacity for Structural Funds in most local governments was low because of a lack of competent staff for preparing projects (Tatar, 2010, p. 221). Despite the alarming experience—concentration of resources in richer municipalities and making small ones dependent on external consultancy (Oppi & Moora, 2004) —EU regional development measures in 2004–2006 were mainly designed as open-grant competitions.

The EU Single Programming Document for the 2004–2006 period was prepared under the leadership of the Ministry of Finance. Public discussion was held at a very general level about the dilemma "asphalt versus brains" and whether Estonia would be capable of absorbing all the funds. The Ministry of Finance dominated all phases of the RP decision-making, thus assigning local and regional actors only a subordinate role (Kettunen & Kungla, 2005, p. 367): most territorially targeted programmes were abandoned, the link between regional development strategy and sector policy actions weakened and county level governance basically disappeared. Uniformly designed grant-schemes resulted in the disappearance of "a larger picture" in RP which gradually declined as one of the sector policies.

RP was not used in the political rhetoric of the new conservative government in 2003. The MRA as the second Minister at the Ministry of Interior strengthened his position, but because of disagreements with ministers of finance the national RP programmes decreased to zero in 2004. The MRA also made attempts to reform both local and regional administration but encountered strong opposition. The 2005–2015 Regional Development Strategy (Regional Development Strategy of Estonia 2005–2015, 2004) was compiled and approved without any public discussion and involvement.

The application of the EU Structural Funds started in 2004. Within an ERDF measure of "Local Socio-economic Development", a sub-measure "The Development of Local

Physical Environment" was designed for improving local services, increasing efficiency of local public infrastructures, improving local employment and living quality as well as better use of local resources. In fact, 83% of 30 million euros was invested in municipal schools and kindergartens (Urb, 2011). Another 13.8 million euros for "improving regional competitiveness" was invested in museums, theme parks, promenades, etc., labelled mainly as tourism development (Figure 4). None of the projects supported restructuring of manufacturing industry (EE, 2012).

An economic boom and a steadily growing budget made possible several new national RP initiatives since 2005. The EU 2007–2013 cohesion policy brought 389 MEUR ERDF money under the "Integrated and Balanced Development of Regions". The largest share (37%) was designated for the measure "Improvement of Local Public Services" at a lower co-financing rate (15%) for investing mainly in schools, kindergartens and nurseries. The measure for "Improving Regional Competitiveness" initially continued to invest mainly in tourism: 2 industrial areas were supported in 2008, 3 in 2009 and 14 in 2010 (EE, 2012)—so policy finally adapted to the crisis conditions.

After the 2007 elections, the post of the MRA was given to the conservative party, whose most well-known initiative was the idea of establishing self-governing counties and cities as the only tier of local administration. Once again, this was rejected by coalition partners. The MRA initiated some concrete solutions for industrial development and local service provision, but the overall RP framework has not been changed despite severe crisis and massive outmigration from industrial and rural regions (Kalvet, 2010, 2011).

Thus, despite the EC guidelines that "Cohesion Policy represents the single largest source of financial support at EU level for investment in growth and jobs, designed to enable all regions to compete effectively in the internal market" (CEC, 2009, p. 1) most ERDF measures (90%) (EE, 2012) at the disposal of the Ministry of Interior were not focused on industrial competitiveness but, following the overwhelming interests of small municipalities, were targeted at renovating schools, kindergartens, museums and the like (EE, 2012). In contrast to the pre-accession period (which learned from the European experience) where regionally targeted RP programmes were introduced for the purpose of local restructuring and increasing local institutional capacity, Estonian RP within the EU has become distant from European values.

4. Effects of Interventions and the Reasons for De-Europeanization

The regional development strategy document, currently in force, concluded that regionally balanced development in Estonia has remained unachievable because of scarce financial resources and modest coordination of sector policies (Regional Development Strategy of Estonia 2005–2015, 2004, p. 6). This is still true. The percentage of the population living in Harju county was 41.2% in 2011, thus above the base value of 41% set in the strategy, and is increasing by an average of 0.5% annually. The share of Harju County in the total GDP was 53% in 1996 and 61.1% in 2009 and the trend is growing. As primary sector employment is expected to decline along with labour-intensive manufacturing, a further concentration of economic activities in the capital region is probably occurring (Eamets et al., 2009).

Various evaluations conclude that RP has made very little progress in increasing regional economic competitiveness outside the two larger city regions and the impacts of ERDF interventions have ignored the regional dimension and focus (Kalvet, 2010, 2011). When, during the 2004–2006 programming period, 21% of structural measures

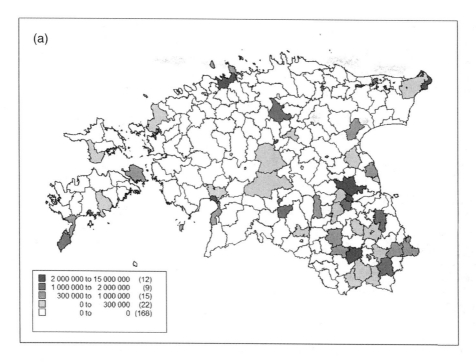

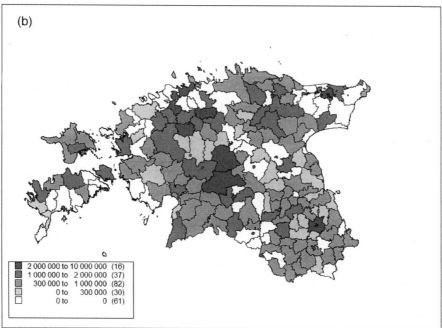

Figure 4. The distribution of ERDF regional development grants by municipalities in MEUR 2004–2010: (a) Regional competitiveness improvement programme and (b) grants for development of local public services.
Source: Ministry of Interior & Enterprise Estonia, authors' own compilation.

were directed to the capital city region (41% of population), then during the 2007–2013 EU structural measures implementation period, 46% of resources are planned for the capital city region. Yet, within the framework of 2004–2009 development programmes for enterprise, tourism, technology and innovation Tallinn received 43% of projects with 52% of funding and Tartu, respectively, 17% and 28% (total 80%) and per capita differences between counties are almost fivefold. County-level development organizations managed projects worth just over 10 million euros which is less than 2% of the resources allocated by Enterprise Estonia (600 million euros) during 2004–2009 (Noorkõiv, 2010, pp. 66–67).

How have the main principles of EU cohesion/RP been implemented? The first principle "concentration" is mainly applied in Cohesion Fund infrastructure projects. ERDF regional development measures are all distributed via grant schemes applicable to municipalities and NGOs. As the average size of projects remains modest, the "concentration" and also "programming" principles are hardly achievable. Because of very small local governments (55% have less than 2000 inhabitants) and their limited co-operation, the application of "partnership" principle is insufficient as well. "Additionality" has been applied but co-financing is primarily requested from beneficiaries.

On the positive side, experts have cited the increased importance of strategic planning and the inclusion of evaluations as part of the policy cycle with the explicit requirement of such activities in the EU (Kalvet, 2010). The Estonian Ministry of Finance ordered mid-term evaluations of the Structural Funds (2007–2013) in 2009 (Ernst & Young Baltic *et al.*, 2009) and 2011 (CPD, 2011) but these reports are rather general and do not cover national RP measures. The Ministry of Interior has ordered several studies about spatial changes (e.g. Ahas *et al.*, 2010; Eamets *et al.*, 2009) and made two attempts to evaluate the immediate RP impact but both public bids made in 2006 and 2010 were cancelled at the selection stage. This means that the Estonian RP has been evaluated only on the basis of allocated resources and general statistics without analysis of institutional capacity of applicants and immediate effects.

The Regional Development Strategy Action Plan (Regional Development Strategy of Estonia 2005–2015, 2004) was mostly ignored by the other ministries. The RP discourse itself remained hidden until the very end of 2011 when the issue of widening regional differences was raised by the President of Estonia (Ilves, 2012). The RP institutional set-up remained greatly unchanged after 2004. The local development plans have been drawn up in a way which secures investments for local construction sites. The focus on infrastructure building can be explained by lack of municipal resources and also by socialist legacy: mayor's capability is measured by investments brought into the community (Raagmaa & Kroon, 2005, pp. 214–5).

Thus, accession to the EU ignited hidden agendas which at least partly drove Estonia away from the EU cohesion policy principles and aims. Since 2004, RP gradually obtained "old-barnyism" nature, evading EU "subsidiarity", "partnership" and "concentration" principles and regional development as one of the horizontal policy priority: ministries and municipalities used ERDF funds without comprehensive strategies and aim to achieve the cohesion effect.

Political will of the leading bodies in the government has been decisive in RP formulation and implementation. The conservatives who led the Cabinet in 1992–1994 paid little attention to RP and significantly diminished the funds for RP in 1999. Since 2007, when conservatives had the post of the MRA, no remarkable results and improvements in RP can be reported. This is in contrast to the periods of 1994–1998 (social democrats, centrists) and 2006–2007 (rural party) when MRAs succeeded to extend RP (Figure 3).

There is a lack of joint collaborative action and trust between administrative levels. Efficient partnership would require relevant institutional set-up but currently it is scanty at the county level and is hampered by disagreements between power groups locally often dictated by national party offices. A combination of centralized state agencies and tiny municipalities are, according to several state institutions (e.g. National Audit Office, Chancellor of Justice) in the interest for the ruling coalition. The same power-"trap" applies in municipalities where a trend of authoritarianism can be followed: whereas in 67% of municipalities with less than 1500 inhabitants, the biggest party gathered over 50% of votes in the local council in 2005 (Sootla & Kattai, 2010), by 2009 this number stood at 73% (Sootla, 2011). This confirms Barca's argument (2009, p. 21): "These local elites /.../ can often choose the economic institutions that best suit their own interests, in doing so, acting as 'rent-seekers', exploiting their power to extract a return way beyond their contribution to value-added". Both local and national elites have been interested in the reduction of power at the regional level. A free rein in the utilization of ERDF resources enabled the central government to replace investments previously funded through tax revenues and to reduce personal income tax rate from 26% to 21%.

Lack of finance and capacity has forced the heads of municipalities to lobby in the ministries and Parliament. Almost 51% of the respondents of the municipal survey think that the process is unfair and 39% have not enough knowledge of this matter. Many believe that when funds are distributed relationships matter the most (Tatar, 2010, p. 213). The ruling parties have put that dependency situation into use to increase their power locally, often the receipt of national investments is made dependent on party membership.

Public policy has been centralized with limited fiscal decentralization (OECD, 2011, pp. 55–58). Administrative silos have hindered the implementation of RP and the current administrative structure is a major obstacle to regional development—on the one hand, highly centralized and disintegrated central government ministries/agencies and, on the other hand, a diverse system of local governments that are too small to act as partners in the implementation of RP. The ability to apply for funds is determined by local budgets which are financially dependent on the state: development projects can hardly be co-financed beyond any necessary operational costs. The inter-governmental system in Estonia confers *de jure* autonomy to local governments but is *de facto* financially constrained (Kriz, 2008, p. 180; Tatar, 2010, p. 214). Local governments themselves see two main restrictions on using the Structural Funds: the absence of required co-financing and an overly expensive process for preparing project applications (Tatar, 2010, p. 215). Thus, financially weaker municipalities, especially after the last crisis which reduced revenues by 10–20%, and due to the limits on taking out loans are unable to apply for EU grants (Figure 4). Rural areas have largely received grants from tiny national sources, although, they can also apply for funding from rural development, incl. LEADER, and fisheries measures.

5. Conclusion and Discussion

Regional development theory has turned towards the institutional approach which places a considerable importance on innovation, regional governance structures and leadership (Stimson *et al.*, 2009). Following that shift, the RP is supposed to build up regionally networked innovation systems and promote the knowledge society via localized learning processes (Asheim & Coenen, 2005). However, latest reports (Barca, 2009, CEC, 2010) indicate that in many countries regional development policy remained embedded in traditional hierarchical settings and the widely discussed Europeanization has remained unachievable.

This paper studied Estonian RP since its very beginning in the late 1980s. We used the framework given by Cotella and Janin Rivolin (2010) for analysing the following components: (1) discourse, the activity and grasp of discussions; (2) institutions and their dynamism; (3) tools, whether they are coherent with the EU measures; and (4) practices—whether the measures are suitable and effective in reducing regional differences and strengthening regional competitiveness. We created a typology of cohesion policy adoptions in which we focused on partial convergence led by civil servants or politicians, respectively "Yes, Minister" and "old-barnyism" types. The empirical section was constructed as a chronological narrative compiled as a result of a collegiate and consultative participatory action research using statistics, literature and notes taken during the meetings and interviews with persons active in RP.

Adoption of European rules has had different speeds and forms in Estonia. Institutional dynamism was most visible during the periods 1994–1998 when the Estonian RP was institutionalized and in 1999–2003 when EU cohesion policy tools were adopted. The first period featured eager learning from European experience—this was a true horizontal Europeanization accompanied by active public discussion and adoption of European RP institutions and tools. The following "Yes, Minister"-type period was characterized by scarce public discussions, the changes were driven by civil servants following EC top-down requirements resulting in the reduction of national spatially targeted programmes and standardization of RP procedures. The third period, from 2004 and especially 2008 onwards, has mainly been focusing on "absorption". There was no remarkable discussion about the concrete regional/cohesion policy aims and measures in the media, participation in the EU-level discussion was scanty (see Adams *et al.*, 2013) and took place mainly at the ministerial and experts level.

During the 2000s, the lower levels of territorial governance gradually lost their development capacity due to financial centralization and politicization. At the same time, political elites in a way "hijacked" the Structural Funds attempting to finance social and cultural objects from the ERDF. Construction of the Estonian National Museum in Tartu as a tourism site was finally denied by the EC but dozens of schools, kindergartens and local museums were renovated largely using the ERDF. The "old-barnyism" practised by both national and local elites drifted national practices away from the EU cohesion policy principles and induced a level of indifference towards the need for economic restructuring of regions. Since enterprise development and innovation support were largely concentrated in the two larger cities while other regions primarily received funds for social and tourism infrastructure, the structural problems of rural and old industrial areas persisted. Hence, regions outside these two cities faced extremely high unemployment rates and massive outmigration of working age population during the 2008 economic crisis.

Summing up, this paper confirms the statement made by Böhme and Waterhout (2008, p. 231) that spatial planning in Europe does not converge or harmonize, but rather translates into various processes and formats "as a consequence of deeply embedded differences between European nations in terms of political, professional and administrative cultures and structures" (Stead & Cotella, 2011, p. 13). The institutional frameworks elaborated and in function in Western Europe, are apparently less applicable to CEE because of (1) a different socio-economic situation and lack of finances; (2) little experience of democracy, participatory culture and a non-governmental sector which is still weak; (3) traditional dependency on the (central) state and weak local/regional administrative structures and (4) path-dependency of using know-how from the socialist period in policymaking.

The Estonian case first of all pinpointed the threat of institutional lock-in and an urgent need for regional and local capacity-building; otherwise, there is no chance for multilevel governance, partnership and place-based policymaking. The second lesson told that without a thorough policy discussion the institutional change, inclusion of new knowledge and good practices would not be sustainable and allowed "pragmatic" politicians and civil servants to neglect important policy principles. Thirdly, it became evident that RP tools which attempted a one-size-fits-all approach in the form of standardized grant schemes, arguably saving administrative costs, actually increased regional differences even further because of extra costs of project preparation and extensive paperwork and therefore eliminated weaker regions from the circle of potential applicants. Fourthly, as the ministerial evaluation reports lack qualitative and case analysis and are unable to measure the real cohesion effect, it is extremely important to carry out ex-post evaluations of RP and to learn from the on-going practices.

Acknowledgements

We thank all interviewees and our special thanks go to the officials of the Ministry of Interior and Enterprise Estonia who generously supported us with recent data and gave very proficient comments. We are also grateful for the constructive comments of the two anonymous referees.

This research has been supported by the European Social Fund through the Estonian Research and Innovation Policy Monitoring Programme and co-funded by the Target Funding Project No. SF0180052s07 "Factors influencing spatial mobility of population and the impact on the regional development" of the Ministry of Education and Research of Estonia and by the Estonian Science Foundation (grant ETF8423).

References

Adams, N. (2006) National spatial strategies in the Baltic States, in: N. Adams, J. Alden & N. Harris (Eds) *Regional Development and Spatial Planning in an Enlarged European Union*, pp. 155–181 (Surrey: Ashgate).
Adams, N., Cotella, G. & Nunes, R. (2013) The engagement of territorial knowledge communities with European spatial planning and the territorial cohesion debate: A Baltic perspective, *European Planning Studies*. doi: 10.1080/09654313.2013.772735
Ahas, R., Silm, S., Leetmaa, K., Tammaru, T., Saluveer, E., Järv, O., Tammiksaar, E., Aasa, A., Tiru, M. & Tähepõld, A. (2010). Regionaalne pendelrändeuuring. Lõpparuanne [Study of regional commuting. Final report]. Tallinn: Siseministeerium. Available at https://www.siseministeerium.ee/public/Regionaalne_pendelrndeuuring_11.06.2010.pdf (accessed 22 August 2012).
Amin, A. (1999) An institutionalist perspective on regional economic development, *International Journal of Urban and Regional Research*, 23(2), pp. 365–378.
Asheim, B. T. & Coenen, L. (2005) Knowledge bases and regional innovation systems: Comparing Nordic clusters, *Research Policy*, 34(8), pp. 1173–1190.

Bachtler, J. & Downes, R. (1999) Regional policy in the transition countries: A comparative assessment, *European Planning Studies*, 7(6), pp. 793–807.
Barca, F. (2009) An agenda for a reformed cohesion policy. A place-based approach to meeting European Union challenges and expectations. DG REGIO. Available at http://ec.europa.eu/regional_policy/archive/policy/future/pdf/report_barca_v0306.pdf (accessed 15 May 2011).
BBC (2011) Episodes from "Yes Minister". Available at http://www.bbc.co.uk/programmes/b009v0dc/episodes/2011 (accessed 23 September 2011).
Blazyca, G., Heffner, K. & Helinska-Hughes, E. (2002) Poland—can regional policy meet the challenge of regional problems?, *European Urban and Regional Studies*, 9(3), pp. 263–76.
Böhme, K. & Waterhout, B. (2008) The Europeanization of spatial planning, in: A. Faludi (Ed.) *European Spatial Research and Planning*, pp. 225–248 (Cambridge, MA: Lincoln Institute of Land Policy).
Börzel, T. & Risse, T. (2000) When Europe hits home. Europeanization and domestic change, *European Integration Online Papers (EioP)*, 4(15). Available at http://eiop.or.at/eiop/pdf/2000-015.pdf
Buček, M. (1999) Regional disparities in transition in the Slovak Republic, *European Urban and Regional Studies*, 6(4), pp. 360–364.
Burns, J. & Scapens, R. W. (2000) Conceptualizing management accounting change: An institutional framework, *Management Accounting Research*, 11(1), pp. 3–25.
CEC (Commission of the European Communities) (2009) European Cohesion Policy in Estonia. Available at http://ec.europa.eu/regional_policy/sources/docgener/informat/country2009/et_en.pdf (accessed 13 February 2010).
CEC (Commission of the European Communities) (2010) Investing in Europe's future: Fifth Report on Economic, Social and Territorial Cohesion, European Commission. Available at http://ec.europa.eu/regional_policy/sources/docoffic/official/reports/cohesion5/index_en.cfm (accessed 16 August 2011).
Cornwall, A. & Jewkes, R. (1995) What is participatory research?, *Social Science & Medicine*, 41(12), pp. 1667–1676.
Cotella, G. (2009) Exploring the territorial cohesion/economic growth multidimensional field: Evidences from Poland, in: T. Markowski & M. Turala (Eds) *Theoretical and Practical Aspects of Urban and Regional Development*, pp. 71–95 (Warsaw: Polish Academy of Science, Committee for Spatial Economy and Regional Planning).
Cotella, G. & Janin Rivolin, U. (2010) Institutions, discourse and practices: Towards a multi-dimensional understanding of EU territorial governance. Paper presented at the XXIV AESOP Congress Space is Luxury, Helsinki, 7–10 July.
CPD (2011) *Inimressursi arenduskava (IARK) prioriteetse suuna 5 Suurem haldusvõimekus tulemuslikkuse hindamine ja mõjude analüüs. Hindamisaruande lõppversioon* (Tallinn: CPD arenduskeskus).
Eamets, R., Terk, E., Paas, T., Kaldaru, H. & Varblane, U. (2009) in: G. Raagmaa (Ed.) *Report Eesti regioonide majandusstruktuuri muutuste prognoos* (Tallinn: Siseministeerium).
EE (2012) Enterprise Estonia. Toetatud projektide andmebaas [Database of supported projects]. Available at http://www.eas.ee/et/eas/sihtasutusest/toetatud-projektid/toetatud-projektid-alates-2004a-aprill
Ernst & Young Baltic, Poliitikauuringute Keskus Praxis, Säästva Eesti Instituut, Balti Uuringute Instituut (2009) Struktuurivahendite rakenduskava hindamine. Uuringuaruanne [Evaluation of the operational plans on the use of Structural Funds. Research Report]. Available at http://www.eas.ee/images/doc/sihtasutusest/uuringud/ettevotlus/struktuurivahendite_rakenduskava_hindamine_2009.pdf (accessed 16 August 2011).
EUR-Lex (2010) Consolidated versions of the treaty on European Union and the treaty on the functioning of the European Union, *Official Journal of the European Union. C 83*, Vol 53, 30 March. Available at http://eur-lex.europa.eu/LexUriServ/LexUriServ.do?uri=OJ:C:2010:083:FULL:EN:PDF (accessed 23 August 2012).
Fricke, W. & Totterdill, P. (Eds) (2004) *Action Research in Workplace Innovation and Regional Development* (Amsterdam: Benjamins).
Hall, P. (1988) The geography of the fifth Kondratieff, in: D. Massey & J. Allen (Eds) *Restructuring Britain. Uneven Re-development: Cities and Regions in Transition*, pp. 6–47 (London: Hodder and Stoughton).
Heidenreich, M. & Wunder, C. (2008) Patterns of regional inequality in the Enlarged Europe, *European Sociological Review*, 24(1), pp. 19–36.
Hoffmeister, O. (2009) The spatial structure of income inequality in the enlargened EU, *Review of Income and Wealth*, 55, pp. 101–127.
Ilves, T.H. (2012) *President Toomas Hendrik Ilvese kõne Eesti Vabariigi 94. aastapäeval*. Available at http://arvamus.postimees.ee/750756/president-ilves-moelgem-ja-moistkem-tana-mis-on-see-meie-eesti-elu (accessed 26 February 2012).

IMPACTS OF EUROPEAN TERRITORIAL POLICIES IN THE BALTIC STATES

IME kontseptsioon (1988) (Tallinn: IME-Probleemnõukogu).
Jauhiainen, J. S. (2008) Regional and innovation policies in Finland—towards convergence and/or mismatch?, *Regional Studies*, 42(7), pp. 1031–1045.
Jauhiainen, J. S. & Ristkok, P. (2000) Regional development and policy in Estonia, in: J. Owsinski & M. Johansson (Eds) *Global-Local Interplay in the Baltic Sea Region*, pp. 365–384 (Warsaw: Ofycina Naukowa).
Kalvet, T. (2010) *Country Report on Achievements of Cohesion Policy: Estonia. Expert Evaluation Network Delivering Policy Analysis on the Performance of Cohesion Policy 2007–2013* (Brussels: DG Regional Policy).
Kalvet, T. (2011) *Country Report on Achievements of Cohesion Policy: Estonia. Expert Evaluation Network Delivering Policy Analysis on the Performance of Cohesion Policy 2007–2013* (Brussels: DG Regional Policy).
Kemmis, S. (2001) Exploring the relevance of critical theory for action research: Emancipatory action research in the footsteps of Jürgen Habermas, in: P. Reason & H. Bradbury (Eds) *Handbook of Action Research: Participative Inquiry and Practice*, pp. 91–102 (London: Sage).
Kettunen, P. & Kungla, T. (2005) Europeanization of sub-national governance in unitary states: Estonia and Finland, *Regional and Federal Studies*, 15(3), pp. 353–378.
Kivirähk, A. (2000) *Rehepapp ehk November* (Tallinn: Varrak).
Knieling, J. & Othengrafen, F. (Eds) (2009) *Planning Cultures in Europe: Decoding Cultural Phenomena in Urban and Regional Planning* (Farnham, Surrey: Ashgate).
Kriz, K. A. (2008) Local government finance in Estonia, in: Z. Sevic (Ed.) *Local Government Finance Reform in Central and Eastern Europe*, pp. 161–183 (London: Edward Elgar).
Lang, T. (2011) Urban resilience and new institutional theory: A happy couple for urban and regional studies?, in: B. Müller (Ed.) *Urban regional resilience*, pp. 15–24 (Heidelberg: Springer).
Lenschow, A. (2006) Europeanization of public policy, in: J. Richardson (Ed.) *European Union: Power and Policy-making*, 3rd ed., pp. 55–71 (London: Routledge).
Manrai, L., Lascu, D., Manrai, A. & Babb, H. (2001) A cross-cultural comparison of style in Eastern European emerging markets, *International Marketing Review*, 18(3), pp. 270–285.
Martin, R. & Sunley, P. (2006) Path dependence and regional economic evolution, *Journal of Economic Geography*, 6(4), pp. 395–437.
Nadin, V. & Stead, D. (2008) European spatial planning systems, social models and learning, *disP*, 172(1), pp. 35–47.
Noorkõiv, R. (2010) Regional development and the human environment, in: M. Lauristin (Ed.) *Human Development Report 2009*, pp. 49–72 (Tallinn: Eesti koostöö kogu).
OECD (2011) Public governance reviews. Estonia. Towards a single government approach. Assessment and recommendations.
Olsen, J. P. (2003) Europeanization, in: M. Cini (Ed.) *European Union Politics*, pp. 333–348 (Oxford: Oxford University Press).
Oppi, T. & Moora, E. (2004) The failure of EU Regional Policy in Estonia? Conference Proceedings of the 12th NISPAcee Conference Central and Eastern European Countries Inside and Outside the European Union: Avoiding a New Divide in Vilnius, Lithuania, 13–15 May.
Paas, T. & Schlitte, F. (2010) Regional income disparities and convergence in EU: Catching up or falling behind?, in: J. W. Kramer, G. Prause & J. Sepp (Eds) *Baltic Business and Socio-Economic Development*, pp. 630–651 (Berlin: Berliner Wissenschafts-Verlag).
Perroux, F. (1955) Note sur la de pole de croissance, *Economie Applique*, 7, pp. 307–320, Available at http://www.ismea.org/ismea/eapp.arch.html
Petrakos, G., Psycharis, Y. & Kallioras, D. (2005) Regional inequalities in the EU new member-states: Evolution and challenges, in: J. Bradley, G. Petrakos & I. Traistaru (Eds) *The Economics and Policy of Cohesion in an Enlarged European Union*, pp. 45–64 (New York: Springer).
Pike, A., Rodrigues-Pose, A. & Tomaney, J. (2006) *Local and Regional Development* (London: Routledge).
Raagmaa, G. (1996) Shifts in regional development of Estonia during the transition, *European Planning Studies*, 4(6), pp. 679–699.
Raagmaa, G. & Kroon, K. (2005) Central places versus networks: The future of collective farms built community infrastructure in Estonia, *Geografiska Annaler*, 87B(3), pp. 205–224.
Reason, P. & Torbert, W. R. (2001) The action turn: Towards a transformational social science, *Concepts & Transformations*, 6(1), pp. 1–37.

Regional Development Strategy of Estonia 2005-2015 (2004). Tallinn: Siseministeerium. Available at https://www.siseministeerium.ee/public/Eesti_regionaalarengu_strateegia_2005_2015_eng_tolge.doc (accessed 2 December 2011).

Reinert, E. & Kattel, R. (2007) European eastern enlargement as Europe's attempted economic suicide? Working Papers in Technology Governance and Economic Dynamics, 14 (Tallinn: Tallinn University of Technology).

Rodríguez-Pose, A. & Storper, M. (2006) Better rules or stronger communities? On the social foundations of institutional change and its economic effects, *Economic Geography*, 82(1), pp. 1–25.

Roose, A., Raagmaa, G. & Kliimask, J. (2010) Rural development trajectories in the Estonian periphery: Impacts of the EU Cohesion Policies, in: *Regional Responses and Global Shifts: Actors, Institutions and Organisations*, pp. 162–163. Annual International Conference of Regional Studies Association in Pecs, Hungary, 24–26 May.

Rykiel, Z. (1995) Polish core and periphery under economic transformation, in: P. Korcelli (Ed) *Geographia Polonica*, Vol. 66, pp. 111–124 (Warszawa, Poland: Wydawnictwo Akapit Press). Available at http://rcin.org.pl/Content/4188/WA51_13383_r1995-t66_Geogr-Polonica.pdf

Sootla, G. (2011) Personal consultation (11 August 2011).

Sootla, G. & Kattai, K. (2010) Estonia: Challenges and lessons of the development of local autonomy, in: J. Loughlin, F. Hendriks & A. Lidström (Eds) *The Oxford Handbook of Subnational Democracy in Europe*, pp. 576–595 (Oxford: Oxford University Press).

Statistics Estonia (2011) Statistical database. Available at http://pub.stat.ee/px-web.2001/dialog/statfile1.asp

Stead, D. & Cotella, G. (2011) Differential Europe: Domestic actors and their role in shaping spatial planning systems, *The Planning Review*, 47, disP 186, 3, pp. 13–21.

Stimson, R., Stough, R. & Salazar, M. (2009) *Leadership and Institutions in Regional Endogenous Development (Horizons in Regional Science)* (Cheltenham: Edward Elgar).

Stryjakiewicz, T. (2009) The old and the new in the geographical pattern of the Polish transition, *Geographica*, 40(1), pp. 5–24.

Tatar, M. (2010) Estonian local government absorption capacity of European Union structural funds, *Halduskultuur—Administrative Culture*, 11(2), pp. 202–226.

Tiits, M., Kattel, R., Kalvet, T. & Kaarli, R. (2003) *Competitiveness and Future Outlooks of the Estonian Economy* (Tallinn: Research and Development Council).

Tiits, M., Kattel, R., Kalvet, T. & Tamm, D. (2008) Catching up, Forging ahead or Falling behind? Central and Eastern European development in 1990–2005, *Innovation: The European Journal of Social Science Research*, 21(1), pp. 65–85.

Urb, J. (2011) Sotsiaalse infrastruktuuri arendamine Eestis Euroopa Liidu toetuste abil [Social infrastructure development with EU support], Unpublished manuscript, MA dissertation, University of Tartu, Tartu.

Waterhout, B. (2008) *The Institutionalization of European Spatial Planning* (Amsterdam: IOS Press).

Weltrowska, J. (2002) Economic change and social polarization in Poland, *European Urban and Regional Studies*, 9(1), pp. 47–52.

Wiggering, H., Knierim, A., Ende, H.-P. & Pintar, M. (Eds) (2010) *Innovations in European Rural Landscapes* (Berlin: Springer).

Wostner, P. (2005) The dynamics of regional disparities in a small country: The case of Slovenia, in: D. Felsenstein & B. A. Portnov (Eds) *Regional Disparities in Small Countries*, pp. 169–185 (Heidelberg: Springer).

Yanakiev, A. (2010) The Europeanization of Bulgarian regional policy: A case of strengthened centralization, *Southeast European and Black Sea Studies*, 10(1), pp. 45–57.

Appendix 1. Stages of Estonian RP: discourse, institutions, tools, results and type of RP

Period	Political acknowledgement, discourse, public debate, legal acts	Institutions, reforms, main processes and stakeholders	Tools, resources	Practice, results	Type of RP, Europeanization
Pre-1992	IME programme	Regional Development Department (Ministry of Economic Affairs)	Corporate tax reliefs according to development zoning	No effect	A/(C)
	No public discussion	Administrative decentralization—reestablishment of first tier local authorities			Horizontal
	Government Directive No 54 on regional-political division and regional incentives				Europeanization
1992–1993	No public discussion	Department of Local Government and Regional Development (State Chancellery)	Regional development agencies	Small and medium size enterprise (SME) development in rural regions	A
	Administrative territorial reform package passed	Board of Local Government and Regional Development (Ministry of Interior)	Combining foreign aid with budget allocations		"Civil servants' RP"
			First regional development allowances		Horizontal
					Europeanization

(*Continued*)

Appendix 1. Continued

Period	Political acknowledgement, discourse, public debate, legal acts	Institutions, reforms, main processes and stakeholders	Tools, resources	Practice, results	Type of RP, Europeanization
1994–1998	The concept of RP approved (1994)	The Council of RP established	Regional development programmes financed from the budget	SME development	A
	Active discussion in the media	Department of Local Government and Regional Development (Ministry of Interior Affairs)	First EU aid	Regional development projects, several successful cases	Horizontal and (later) top-down
	The Planning and Building Act passed	Estonian Regional Development Foundation established		Learning "EU-type" project management	Europeanization
	National spatial plan "Eesti 2010" process started (1995)	State county governments and their regional development departments established	Maximum amount of national regional development measures		
	The Regional Development Strategy process (1997–1998) and approval		Free zones in economically declining regions established		
1999–2003	Minister of Interior publicly denies RP and invites people to migrate to Tallinn	Estonian Regional Development Foundation and Enterprise Estonia merged and transferred to the Ministry of Economy	Regional development programmes reduced but continuously financed from the budget	SME development	A/B
	New "silent" approval of the Regional Development Strategy	New Department of Regional Development (Ministry of Interior)	Much larger EU PHARE and INTERREG measures available	Regional development projects with minor importance	"Second civil servants' RP"
	Discussions about (failed) territorial administrative reform (1999–2000)	The RP council brought to a halt			Top-down
	National spatial plan finally approved (2000) and put on the shelf	Centralization and politicization of counties			"Yes, Minister" Europeanization
	Preparations for application of EU structural tools, designing measures				

				C	
2004–2011	RP disappears from the political agenda and public discussion	Ministry of Finance sets institutional framework for the use of EU measures	Extensive ERDF financed grant based measures applied (92% from all financial allocations)	Replacing national social infrastructure investments with ERDF	"Old-barnyism"
	Regional Development Strategy 2005–2015 approved without public debate (2004)	Enterprise Estonia + two regional offices + Enterprise Estonia subordinated and financed "independent" county development centres responsible for cohesion/RP application	National regional development measures reduced since 2007	Very few projects focused on industrial development and enterprise restructuring until 2010 outside large cities, tourism development only	
	Failed attempts to pass Regional Development Act	Politicization of local authorities			De-Europeanization
	Media and parliamentary discussion about administrative reform: several failed attempts to restructure regional and local administrations		Innovation and enterprise development programmes under the Ministries of Education and Economic Affairs, ignoring RP targets		
	Regional Development strategy not followed by other ministries		EU rural development measures, LEADER under the Ministry of Agriculture, partly duplicating national RP measures		

Source: Authors.

Urban Policies for the Creative Industries: A European Comparison

KÜLLIKI TAFEL-VIIA, ANDRES VIIA, ERIK TERK & SILJA LASSUR

Estonian Institute for Futures Studies, Tallinn University, Tallinn, Estonia

ABSTRACT *Although the development of creative industries (CI) has formed into extensive and significant phenomenon in European cities, the conceptualization and generalization of these practices and policies is still rather weak. In addition to the attempts to explain the formation of these kinds of practices in the cities and discuss the path-dependent character of CI policies, the challenging task is to identify the main alternatives and inherent logic of CI policies, especially due to the existing rich and diverse experiences of European cities. This article aims to build a typology of the policy practices relating to CI. We make use of an "ideal types" approach, which focuses on determining a limited number of parameters to characterize alternative CI policies in different (European) cities; this is based on how one kind of CI policy practice can be distinguished from another. The article examines how the CI policies in four post-socialist cities (three of which are located in the Baltic region) contrast with the policies found in a range of other cities in Europe.*

1. Introduction

Recognizing that cultural and creative fields are important for the economic vitality of cities together with the wider socioeconomic changes have forced cities to rethink their responsibilities and change their policy perspectives. Since the 1980s, the development of creative industries (CI) can be recognized in local-level policies (Hesmondhalgh & Pratt, 2005). The approaches to CI and related practices spread over the borders of (European) cities and countries, which allows us to explain these kinds of developments as certain type of phenomenon of European economic, social and cultural homogenization (Delanty & Rumford 2005; Rascaroli & O'Donovan, 2010). Some authors underline that the broad diffusion of the UK approach to CI (Creative Industries Mapping Document, 1998) has brought homogeneous type of developments into policymaking (Costa *et al.*, 2008; Prince, 2010) and emphasize the influence of policy transfer mechanisms on CI policies. Despite these kinds of developments, the conceptualization of CI policies has been still rather weak until now. Several studies have concentrated on international comparisons of CI policies (Kovacs *et al.*, 2007; Foord, 2008; Evans, 2009), but the problems in comparing and the lack of comparable data in terms of both qualitative parameters (Taylor, 2006; Foord, 2008; Evans, 2009; Chapain & Comunian, 2010) and quantitative parameters (Allin, 2000; Creigh-Tyte, 2005; KEA, 2006; Baycan-Levent, 2010; Chapain & Comunian, 2010) have been repeatedly recognized. Also the empirical bases used have been rather narrow. In most of these cases, attempts tend to be limited to indicating a resemblance to the UK model (Birch, 2008; Flew & Cunningham, 2010) or the Scandinavian model (Birch, 2008; Power, 2009). Such generalizations of CI policy practices are insufficient and of little use to policymakers making grounded policy choices; their weak explanations also contribute little to building CI policy theory. This forces the authors to argue that there is a shortage of knowledge about the parameters applicable for research exercises that focus on generalizing the CI policy practices of cities. Because of the path-dependent character of CI policy—links to a particular urban environment and the peculiarities of the local cultural affairs and cultural initiatives—this raises the question about whether there can be a limited number of CI policy alternatives used to characterize CI policies in different (European) cities. This topic enters into the discussions on Europeanization and policy convergence in the field of CI by raising the question, as to whether the developments towards a single model of European CI policy can be recognized, or whether a distinct post-socialistic or Baltic approach is apparent.

In this article, we aim to build a typology of CI policy practices. To achieve this, we focus on defining the combination of policy parameters that determine the policy alternatives in developing CI in European metropoles by exploring policy practices in 11 European cities: Amsterdam, Barcelona, Berlin, Birmingham, Helsinki, Oslo, Riga, Stockholm, Tallinn, Vilnius and Warsaw. Most of these cities are capital cities and share certain characteristics, such as playing a central role in the economy and being the centre of CI in their region and country, making them a strong candidate for this study. At the same time, the cities are radically different in terms of historical background and the maturity of their policies; three cities in the Baltic States and Warsaw are newcomers in terms of both the development of market economy support policies and CI policies. Differences in historical backgrounds and in the developmental of CI policies, and the fact that they are located in different geographical regions, provide the additional conditions necessary to test the universality of the policy parameters being developed. When focusing on building CI policy typology, we follow an "ideal types" approach, which is especially concerned with defining the limited number of crucial parameters that distinguish one alternative choice (policy practice in our context) from another. The discussion is premised on the findings of "Creative Metropoles"—an international qualitative study that mapped public policies on CI in 11 European cities. The study was carried out in 2009.

2. Factors Determining CI Policy Choices – "Ideal Types" Approach

This article seeks to conceptualize CI policies from the perspective of determining the main alternatives for developing CI. We make use of a tradition derived from sociology and based on Max Weber's construction of "ideal types". According to Weber, "ideal types" are:

formed by the one-sided accentuation of one or more points of view and by the synthesis of a great many diffuse, more or less present and occasionally absent concrete individual phenomena, which are arranged according to those one-sidedly emphasized viewpoints into a unified analytical construct. (Weber, 1904/1949, p. 147)

Weber (1904/1949) has stressed that "the ideal type concept /.../ is not a description of reality but it aims to give unambiguous means of expression to such a description. /.../ It is a conceptual construct which is neither historical reality nor even the 'true' reality". Although Weber perceived "ideal types" as something purely theoretical and artificial, this approach addresses at least three important issues that are valuable in building conceptual models or typologies: CI policy alternatives in our case. First, it emphasizes the importance of the holistic approach. Ideal types are complex constructs that represent holistic configurations of multiple dimensions. They are intended to "provide an abstract model, so that deviation from the extreme or ideal type can be noted and explained" (Blalock, 1969). Second, it highlights the importance of a limited number of main parameters in determining the construct. Ideal types are defined according to the endpoints of a continuum. It amounts to a simplified model constructed on a small number of parameters. However, this also comes with at least one cost: nuances are lost in the search for overall patterns (Huy, 2001). Third, this approach highlights the importance of inherent logic. It follows an intellectual tradition that presupposes that a certain level of congruence exists among certain attributes (policy practices in our case) and that this congruence produces a finite number of unique combinations that are believed to determine the relevant outcome (Greenwood & Hinings, 1996). The internal consistency within an ideal type explains why certain kinds of combinations of different parameters have been reached as a result (Doty & Glick, 1994). Morgan (2006) argues that ideal types are useful as a benchmark device and can thus, help us clarify what we are looking for (Shiner, 1975). Similarly, Nadin and Stead (2013) discuss the use of ideal types in planning policy as idea-constructs that help put the chaos of social reality in order.

According to Doty and Glick (1994), the ideal types approach presumes that the development of formal typologies is composed of two parts: (a) the description of ideal types, and (b) the set of assertions that relate the ideal types to the dependent variable. Using the ideal types approach means that certain dimensions have to be found, the combination of which enables the set of ideal types to be described. Earlier discussions on CI and its policies enable us to highlight the following four categories that are relevant when analysing CI policies: (1) aspirations driving CI policies; (2) strategic choices for developing CI; (3) types of intervention; and (4) governance and the institutional architecture of support. These four, represent categories where different patterns and choices can be distinguished in the CI policy practices of cities (see also Table 1).

Various studies indicate that the *aspirations driving CI policies* vary in different cities and countries. The economic-centred aspiration tends to dominate (Foord, 2008; Evans, 2009). Several other policy rationales can also be found: social inclusion, the development of social capital, community cultural programming, the creation of tourist venues and visitor economies, the development of infrastructure (transport and information and communication technology (ICT)) and city branding (Jansson & Power, 2006; Rutten, 2006; Foord, 2008; Evans, 2009). Based on cities' practices and on previous studies, four broader streams of rationales can be distinguished. The first group of aspirations relates to economic renewal, which indicates that CI are considered the key new growth sector

Table 1. Four main categories, where different patterns and choices can be distinguished in the CI policy practices of cities

Categories	Variants			
Aspirations driving CI policies	Economic renewal	Increasing urban (spatial) attractiveness	Social regeneration	Enhancement of internationalization
Strategic choices for developing CI	Sector-based approach	Cluster-based approach		Integral approach
Types of intervention mechanisms	Measures related to supporting entrepreneurship and enhancing business capacity	Measures facilitating access to finance for creative businesses and taxation measures	Measures enhancing demand for CI	Measures related to developing spaces for CI	Mechanisms supporting and developing "soft" infrastructure and networks
Governance and institutional architecture of support of CI	Creation of new forms of governance	Division of support between local, national and regional levels	Supporting cooperation between different public-sector units	Involvement of third and business sector representatives, and citizens in policy-making

Source: Compiled by the authors.

of the economy and the main source of future growth in employment (Garnham, 2005). Increasingly, the development of CI is linked with nourishing innovation and supporting developments towards a knowledge economy (Foord, 2008); this expands the influence of the development of CI beyond the CI sector and to the entire economy. It is therefore, not solely an economic approach, but rather a comprehensive approach to creativity, where creativity is strongly related to the development of different fields. The second group relates to increasing urban (spatial) attractiveness by focusing on the development of space/place. This is often based on local heritage and on historical or cultural resources, with a focus on redeveloping run-down and deprived areas (Power & Jansson, 2006). For decades, culture has been a significant component in economic and physical regeneration strategies in many West European cities (Lavanga, 2006). The third stream—"social regeneration"—encompasses topics such as fostering social cohesion and reducing inequality, while also stimulating cross-cultural cooperation and cultural diversity (Florida, 2002; Evans, 2005; Rutten, 2006; Baycan-Levent, 2010). It proceeds from the criticism of the social costs of urban strategies aimed at satisfying only economic objectives (Bayliss, 2007), and based on the argument that "strengthening social cohesion improves people's mental and physical well-being"; it thus, nourishes economic competitiveness in general (Landry, 2000). The fourth dominating rationale is associated with the enhancement of internationalization. The practices from the 1980s, which were rooted in aggressive place marketing initiatives (Kearns & Philo, 1993), were often based on a local heritage of historical or artistic resources. One of the most prominent examples of remaking and marketing a place is the Guggenheim Museum in Bilbao. More recent developments attach value to the formation of localized complexes of cultural and/or CI that will then export their outputs far and wide (Power & Jansson, 2006).

The second category—*strategic choices for developing CI*—reflects the general strategy taken in developing mechanisms to support CI. Here, three options can be distinguished: a sector-based approach, a cluster-based approach and an integral approach. The domination of the UK approach in CI policy practices—the "list-based approach" (Flew & Cunningham, 2010)—has influenced cities and countries to choose a sector-based approach (Costa et al., 2009) when developing CI. Some of the key concepts used to explain CI are also based on defining CI by defining certain groups of creative sectors, such as the "cultural economy" (Scott, 2001) or the "creative economy" (Howkins, 2002). In terms of policy, this means that CI is treated as an insulated sectoral policy (alongside other policies). The sector-based approach follows the industrial economy and supply chain logic, where CI policies are often derived uncritically from other industry sectors (e.g. resource or manufacturing), whose dynamics differ from those in the creative sectors (Hearn et al., 2007). Another option that can be distinguished is the cluster-based approach, which is founded on the understanding that creative activities often take place in clusters (Porter, 1998; Porter & Stern, 2001). New approaches to CI (e.g. value creating ecology) emphasize that the constellation of CI firms are dynamic; there, the value flow is multi-directional and works through clusters of networks (Hearn et al., 2007). CI clusters have also been seen as important in cultivating urban density (Shoales, 2006) and maintaining a high degree of product innovation (Yusuf & Nabeshima, 2005). The most recent studies on CI policies (Foord, 2008; Evans, 2009) also reveal the increasing importance of cluster development in CI supporting strategies. The third option is the integral approach, where CI is developed in a wider sense or context. This option proceeds from approaches such as the *creative city* (Landry, 2000), which can be described as all-embracing by capturing a variety of fields related to urban development (Landry *et al.*, 2005), or the concept of the *experience economy* (Pine & Gilmore, 1999), which stresses the customer point of view, not only of developing CI, but also of general growth in the economy. The integral approach to CI may take the form of CI being developed together with knowledge and science city clusters, where the emphasis is on infrastructure and generic content industries (Evans, 2009) or development being allied to the broad support of culture and creativity, which surpasses the boundaries between various policy fields (Trip & Romein, 2010). In principle, this approach is based on the idea that the activities supporting CI have cross-sectoral scope and that there are no sector-based priorities (Arge Creativ Wirtschaft Austria, 2009).

The third category concerns *types of intervention mechanisms*. CI policy is linked to many other policies, and thus, comprises a complex of various measures related to industry development and the enhancement of research, development and innovation, support for culture and the arts, and the provision of tools for promoting urban planning, network building and other initiatives (O'Regan & Ryan, 2004; Hearn *et al.*, 2007). There is on-going debate about whether or not to include support for non-profit cultural and creative organizations and activities within CI policies (Power & Jansson, 2006). The answer depends largely on the general approach to CI and the rationales set for CI policy. The other important discussion relates to the predominance of supply-side and scarcity of demand-side instruments. The focus on supply-side drivers that specifically follow the "value chain model"—which is based on the one-way logic of causation: producer–commodity–consumer (Hartley, 2008)—has been found to be difficult to apply when developing CI. The organizational model for CI is a network interaction (Hartley, 2005) of micro and small producers rather than the supply chain hierarchy of Fordist industries (van der Borg & Russo, 2006). The rise in user created content (OECD, 2007) and digital media (KEA, 2006) has also led to the realization of the importance of demand-side instruments in supporting CI. Previous studies (Rutten, 2006; Braun & Lavanga, 2007; Hearn *et al.*, 2007; Costa *et al.*, 2008; Foord, 2008; Evans, 2009) indicate that five basic groups of measures can be distinguished: (1) measures related to supporting entrepreneurship and enhancing business capacity, (2) measures facilitating access to finance for creative businesses (such as various funds and foundations targeted at financing CI) and taxation measures (such as tax breaks and exemptions), (3) measures enhancing demand for CI, (4) measures related to developing spaces for CI and (5) mechanisms supporting and developing "soft" infrastructure and networks, such as including nurturing the involvement of citizens through cultural and creativity programmes and including creative individuals in urban development.

The fourth parameter, where cities have chosen different paths, relates to *governance and the institutional architecture of support for CI*. Because of the inter-disciplinary nature CI policy, it is a field of responsibility for several policy institutions. There have been an increasing number of discussions in the theoretical discourse about whether the traditional structures of governance are suitable for CI, owing to its peculiar patterns of operation (Balducci, 2004; Kunzmann, 2004; Lange, 2009). CI challenges the structures and practices of governance in several ways, including blurring the borders between the parties at the governance level and the intertwining of relationships (Jessop, 1995; Rhodes, 1996), an increased need for cooperation in cross-sectoral policies (Potts & Cunningham, 2008; Throsby, 2008; O'Connor, 2009) the deinstitutionalization of public-sector and private-sector partnerships (Lange, 2009), and the increasing significance of mediating institutions (Costa *et al.*, 2009). It has been argued that CI is also creating new (network-based) forms of governance (Kalandides, 2007; Lange, 2008). Practices by cities indicate that institutional and governance arrangements in supporting CI include solutions such as (1) creating new (decentralized, network-like) forms of governance, (2) dividing support between local, national and regional levels, (3) supporting cooperation between different public-sector units and (4) involving third-party and business-sector representatives and citizens in policymaking (Rhodes, 1996; Mulcahy, 2006; Costa *et al.*, 2008).

All in all, although we can distinguish and list certain alternatives regarding CI policy, only limited degree of convergence tendencies regarding CI policy aspirations, making of strategic choices, types of intervention and governance can be recognized. We can rather speak about multiplicity of choices when it comes to practices of policymaking in the field of CI. Still, as CI is a complex of various other policies, Europeanization-related developments arise to the extent that these are topical in other fields supported by immediate policy guidelines or even EU level policy tools (e.g. cross-border cooperation and innovation policy). What is important to emphasize is that these four categories and the different policy options described under these parameters are determined mainly from CI policy practices in cities or countries with long-term experience in developing CI. Newcomers like Eastern and Central European cities or countries cannot rely on long-term practices when it comes to developing CI. Differences in their historical, as well as institutional environment and economic background place them in a substantially different situation compared with Western developed countries (Tomić-Koludrović & Petrić, 2005; Primorac, 2006; Jürisson, 2007) in terms of following contemporary thought in developing CI.

3. Methods of Data Collection and Analysis

The information presented in this article is based on the findings of "Creative Metropoles" (Creative Metropoles—Public Policies and Instruments In Support of Creative Industries, 2010), an international comparative study carried out in 2009. The authors of this article were members of the research team that developed the methodology for the study and carried out the analysis. The study encompassed 11 European cities: Helsinki, Oslo Stockholm, Amsterdam, Barcelona, Berlin, Birmingham, Tallinn, Riga, Vilnius and Warsaw. The study aimed to examine the development of CI policies in those cities. The data was collected using a qualitative, structured and semi-open questionnaire. The questionnaire was completed by local researchers in each of the 11 cities to ensure that the most relevant and up-to-date information was being used.

The questionnaire consisted of 37 questions divided into four sections: (1) general architecture of support, (2) measures supporting the development of CI, (3) the criteria behind strategic choices in CI policy, (4) background statistical data. Cultural policy instruments and supporting measures were excluded from the study. About half the questions were open-ended questions; the remainder had a finite set of predetermined answers. The questionnaire also contained ranking-type answers, where a 10-point scale was used.

Analysis of the data was carried out in four general phases. An initial analysis of the results was carried out by the research team. The answers were analyzed by city and by topic, using text analysis methodology. The cities were divided into two groups, based on the stage of the development of their CI policies: (1) cities with more established CI policies (West European and Nordic cities) and (2) "newcomers" such as post-Socialist cities. The parameters that determine the choices in CI policies were singled out by finding those kinds of policy choices that play a more dominant role in conceptualizing the central pillars of CI policy and form the basis for distinguishing between the cities. The ideal types of CI policy were ascertained through the following process. Initially, different combinations of the alternatives were tested in several rounds by exploring the possible exclusion of different alternatives. In the next phase, we aimed to find the most reasoned inherent logic behind these combinations. In this iterative process, combinations were compared with real practices in cities. Next the integral combination of alternatives was explained by finding reasonable titles for each combination—the "ideal type" and a full description for each type. Finally, the cities' CI policies were described according to the ideal types, by first finding the cities with the greatest resemblance to the ideal types and then those that deviated from the ideal types. The outcomes of the analysis were sent back to the researchers and officials in the cities in order to confirm that the results had been interpreted correctly. The findings of the analysis were discussed at several interactive workshops (organized within the project) to obtain wider feedback. Based on the feedback and discussions, the findings were specified and summarized by the research team members.

4. Empirical Typology of Cities' CI Policy Practices—Findings of the International Comparative Study

We introduce the findings of the study in three parts. First, the parameters that determine the CI policy models ("ideal types") are presented. Second, the three "ideal types" are described. Third, the CI policy practices of 11 European cities are introduced (based on the ideal types of CI policy).

4.1 The Parameters Defining CI Policies—Ideal Models of CI Policy

We start by describing the parameters that determine the policy choices in CI policies that the study was able to identify. In the study, the cities were asked several questions about aims, measures and the general architecture of support for CI policy (Table 2).

Responses to these questions made it possible to identify the three key parameters that determine the main CI policy choices: (1) general focus of CI policy, (2) strategic choices for developing CI, and (3) cooperation types in CI policy development between different levels of administration. Each parameter includes alternative variants of possible action. The following describes the alternatives of the three parameters in more detail. *The general focus of CI policy* encompasses three main options. First, it may be oriented clearly towards qualitative effects of creativity and creative activities. This might mean that the whole city environment is made more attractive, there is a diversified and creative atmosphere and a vibrant city life. This policy is oriented less towards achieving immediate economic effects (such as turnover, profit and increased employment) from enterprises in the CI sectors. The second option relates to having a clear focus on developing entrepreneurship in CI sectors and the CI as an economic sector. The central aims are often related to the viability of creative enterprises, and to their growth and economic contribution. However, the findings indicate that economic development often runs parallel to the stimulation of general creativity. The third concerns the opportunity to regenerate urban space arising from CI development. Here, the cities' practices relate to the

Table 2. Questions relating to the architecture of support for CI policy

Questions
(a) Please provide a list of the strategic documents in force (strategies, action plans, etc.) that are aimed at supporting CI or which include activities related to CI. Please start with the most relevant.
(b) Please provide a short overview (nature and main goals) of the documents listed.
(c) Please indicate the focus of CI policy on the given scale (economic, spatial, social, inward/outward).
(d) Please describe the overall aim of your city's CI policy.
(e) Please describe the division of support architecture between state, regional and local (your city) level in supporting CI.
(f) Please indicate which overall approach to supporting CI dominates in your city. Selecting from the following: sector-based, cluster-based, CI sector supported as a whole.
(g) Please describe the explicit role (the extent of activities) the city has in developing and supporting CI.
(h) Please describe the organizational structure of support for CI. Please name and describe the structural units of the city, the special organizations and the actors responsible for supporting (implementing) CI at city level.
(i) Please describe the model of cooperation with businesses and the third sector: the division of work/tasks between the public sector, the business sector and the third sector.
(j) Please describe the level of international cooperation in the field of CI development.
(k) Please indicate who initiates the goals for CI policies in your city. (List of five possible variants given.)
(l) Please name the 10 most relevant measures (grant schemes, support tools, investments, regulations, etc.) in force in your city.
(m) What are the strategic choices in CI development: priority sectors, clusters, other types of strategic choices.
(n) What is the explanation behind prioritization decisions (historical, uniqueness, international trends, lobby, strong education and R&D activities, strong enterprises, etc.).
(o) How do CI priorities relate to your city's other priorities in other fields.

Source: Study "Creative Metropoles. Situation analysis of 11 cities"; compiled by the authors.

large-scale regeneration of urban space (such as brownfield regeneration or the revitalization of a waterfront) and their interconnection with the development of CI. In many cities, the concentration of CI in some districts of the city has resulted from the fact that former brownfield or other industrial areas and waterfronts became vacant when the CI were growing. *Strategic choices for developing CI* also contains three possible options. The first is clearly the sectoral focus, which may relate to developing the CI sector or concentrating on developing some prioritized sub-sectors of CI. The second relates to the development of clusters, not only CI clusters but also wider clusters where the CI (sub-)sectors are connected to other sectors (such as tourism). In the third option, selection according to sectors or clusters is considered irrelevant; support is given to different initiatives or actions, which are then expected to bring more or less direct positive influences on the development of CI in the city. *Cooperation types in CI policy development between different levels of administration* contain two main alternatives. First, the dominant actor in developing the city's CI policy is the municipality itself. Second, higher institutional levels (regional and/or state) have an important influence on the development of the city's CI policy, so there is a high degree of interconnection between the CI policies of the city and those of other levels.

The findings from this study of 11 cities confirm the main categories illuminated in earlier studies on CI policies. However, the findings also reveal important differences that enable us to specify our understanding of the main pillars that constitute the alternatives in CI policies. Social regeneration and internationalization were not found to be central to CI policy, but rather elements that may (and usually do) accompany other vital components. Rather, they perform, respectively, as parts of an inward and outward dimension that complements or specifies the main focus of CI policy. The spectrum of measures in use has a supporting rather than a determining effect on CI policy alternatives. The differences in measures depend first and foremost on the development stage of the CI policy. Similarly, the importance of different kinds of new governance arrangements (such as networks and the involvement of different parties) may perform a supporting, but not a determining role in defining the main alternatives of CI policies. The alternative is determined by the division of the administrative levels involved, which is largely dependent on the country's whole administrative system.

4.2 "Ideal Types" of CI Policy

Here we introduce the "ideal types" of CI policy, determined through a combination of the alternatives of the three key parameters of policy choices. These are CI entrepreneurial city, city in regeneration (or city with a new face) and cultural creative city. The following describes the inherent logic of each "ideal type" in more detail (see also Table 3).

With the first type, *CI entrepreneurial city*, the basic emphasis is on the direct economic effect of enterprises and activities within the CI sectors. The CI policy is business-oriented. The goal is the establishment of economically sustainable enterprises within CI sectors. It is expected that at least some of them grow from being small and medium-sized enterprises to financially viable providers of employment for the city. Creating links between CI and other enterprises may also be one of the elements of the CI support policy. CI policies are implemented by municipalities in cooperation with entrepreneurs' organizations that represent the CI sectors. The role of the state in these policies is insignificant. In the second model, *City in regeneration/City with a new face*, CI policy is space-oriented. A large number of development activities related to CI are directed towards the renewal of spatial structural elements by providing them with new functions. Following that model means, at least in extreme cases, changing the entire

Table 3. Three "ideal types" of CI policy

	CI entrepreneurial city	City in regeneration/ city with a new face	Cultural creative city
General focus	Business-oriented	Space-oriented	Culture-oriented
Strategic choice	Sector-based	Cluster-based	Developing CI in wider sense
Cooperation between administrative levels and main administrative agent	City	State—region—city	Region—city

Source: Study "Creative Metropoles. Situation analysis of 11 cities"; compiled by the authors.

position of the city: developing an entirely new face. Policy is strongly oriented towards (urban) planning and supporting cluster development (CI clusters as well as mixed clusters that include CI). This model presumes there is capacity to make major decisions and large financial allocations. Therefore, the role of the state and/or the regional authorities is more important. In the third model, *Cultural creative city*, CI policy is predominantly culture oriented. The spectrum of the support policy is broad; in the ideal case, this would cover all activities related to culture and creativity. The CI support policy addresses, for example, the development of a creative atmosphere and cross-cultural initiatives, as well as supporting creative entrepreneurship. It is presumed that cultural creativeness will indirectly but significantly contribute to the economy and other aspects of urban life. This model depends strongly on the self-organization mechanisms and grass-roots level initiatives of the creative sector. The main levels involved in CI policy governance are cities in cooperation with regions.

4.3 *CI Policy Practices of 11 Metropoles according to the Three "Ideal Types"*

Here we describe the CI policy practices of 11 European cities, based on the three "ideal types" of CI policy. The results of the study enable us to conclude that three cities—Amsterdam, Birmingham and Berlin—represent the clearest choice of the three "ideal types". The other eight cities are combinations of two "ideal types" as they possess the characteristics of each of two types (see also Figure 1). In the following section, we first introduce the three clearest examples and then look briefly at the position of the remaining eight.

Berlin provides the closest match to the "CI entrepreneurial city". In Berlin, CI is approached as an economic sector (the CI sector is clearly defined as an economic sector). Enhancing business capacity can be considered the driving force behind CI policy. CI is defined as covering creative companies, which are mostly profit oriented and deal with the creation, production and (medial) distribution of cultural/creative goods and services. One of the aims of Berlins CI policy is to strengthen the CI sector's ability to attract more businesses from outside:

> Berlin's aim is to attract more businesses, investors and visitors from outside and to lead growth in the CI sector on this path. / ... / CI companies need to make use of foreign trade markets. Many of Berlin's CI sectors have a high export potential (music, design, fashion, games) and a great interest in foreign collaboration. /.../ Further, Berlin's city marketing, tourism marketing and internationalisation strategy clearly aim at attracting people from outside. (Berlin)

Berlin's cultural policy strategy even aims to help the cultural and CI to expand their sales and to increase market share in the city. Berlin has also linked the development of CI with support for innovation. Most of the measures that support CI focus on enhancing business capacity and the internationalization of CI. Also, the development of spaces for CI is first and foremost aimed at supporting innovation and the creative production of small and medium-sized creative enterprises (e.g. Betahaus). Berlin has also developed venture capital schemes and other financial instruments (e.g. loans) to support access to finance for creative businesses. Berlin is autonomous in its activities and covers both the regional level and the city level; this means that the city equates to the region, and

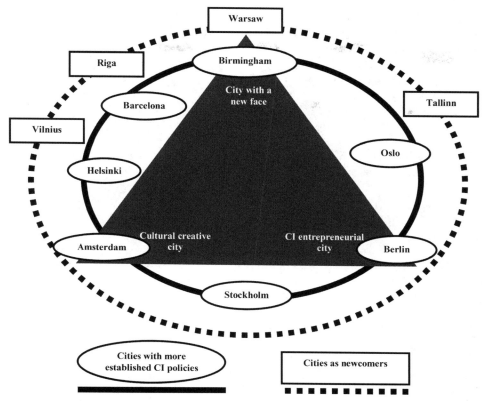

Figure 1. The 11 metropoles according to the three "ideal types" of CI policy.
Source: Study "Creative Metropoles. Situation analysis of 11 cities"; compiled by the authors.

so the city support level is the same as the regional support level. Nonetheless, the city level in Berlin plays a much stronger role in supporting CI (compared with the national level or the regional level).

Birmingham is closest to the "ideal type" of "City in regeneration/City with a new face". As Birmingham is an old industrial city, the space can be seen as the driving force behind CI policy, as there is a need to restructure the city's economy (developing public/urban space has a central role in supporting CI). Spatial aspects of creative industry policies are also integrated into Birmingham's new master plan. This city is an example of the cluster-based approach to developing CI. It has linked the development of CI with several other fields; this covers not only culture and the economy but also spatial planning and educational development. It has special programmes to support CI clusters or specific sub-sectors. For example, Birmingham finances its media cluster through a large cluster strategy programme and a special media agency. The city also actively supports cluster building (such as the Birmingham Custard Factory and Fazeley Studios) through the development of spaces for creative, media and digital businesses; it also provides under-utilized spaces for student shows, community events and public meetings. Birmingham is an example of where state-level and regional-level CI policies have a strong influence on the development of policy at city level. If, in general, the role of the regional administration is mainly complementary or mediating, then in the case of Birmingham, many support schemes for CI are provided through regional programmes. For instance, in Birmingham, the urban planning tools required for exposing cultural heritage and making use of design/architecture are supported by a regional authority. In addition, improving transport and enabling public access are examples where regional authorities work alongside the municipality. Birmingham's CI policy follows the national strategy defined by the Department for Culture, Media and Sport.

> Birmingham's CI policies follow the national strategy defined by the Department for Culture, Media and Sports. This is mainly established via development agencies on the regional level. In addition, the city has developed its own city master plan regarding social, economic and environmental development, wherein CI is a key factor. (Birmingham)

Amsterdam has the strongest connections with the "cultural creative city" type. Amsterdam's CI policy can be characterized as culture-driven or culture-focused. Cultural diversity and cultural identity are considered to be central keywords: the CI play an important role in developing and maintaining lifestyles and cultural identities within society. Amsterdam has chosen a wide-scope approach, where CI is supported in a wider sense and is connected with other sectors. The city has linked the development of CI with several different fields, not only with cultural and economical activities but also with tourism-related activities. Amsterdam expects to become internationally known as a creative city, as it develops tourism and supports business internationalization. It is also focusing on strengthening the inward focus in CI policy by considering the citizens of Amsterdam to be the main target group of CI policy and involving the citizens in the city's development. In addition, Amsterdam has highlighted the importance of strengthening the links between CI and education. Overall, Amsterdam is a city that has stated that its approach to supporting CI is broad, and it has also come up with complex programmes in the development of CI:

> The main goal is to strengthen the city's economy, and it is especially aimed at improving Amsterdam's position internationally. Creativity will be the central focus—creativity geared towards action and able to get the best from all projects and parties involved. There are five areas of action:
> (1) use and attract talent;
> (2) stimulate and facilitate from start to growth;
> (3) atmosphere and hospitality, freedom, service;
> (4) use and create space;
> (5) Amsterdam's international reputation. (Amsterdam)

Local and regional levels both play important roles in developing CI policythat relies on developing cooperation between city and region. The stronger role played by regions in developing CI is clearly evident in Amsterdam, as many support schemes are provided at regional level and/or are very tightly connected to regional funding schemes. From the city's perspective, there are efforts to influence the national agenda and objectives; Amsterdam had already started to develop CI policies in 2002, whereas the first national policies were developed in 2005. However, in Amsterdam, there is no clear division between the tasks and objectives at state and city level. Different experts and policy meetings play important roles there.

Most of the rest of the cities sit between two types: "cultural creative city" and "city with a new face". Barcelona and Helsinki and the "newcomers" Vilnius and Riga, and with certain reservations, Warsaw displays features of both of these types. In Barcelona, the development and revitalization of urban/public spaces provides important support for CI (as did the Olympic Games). Helsinki has also outlined some spatial expectations for CI, such as making urban space more interesting and creative. Several initiatives on redesigning urban spaces are characteristic of the city's CI policy. Riga's history as an industrial city now presents it with very real issues relating to regeneration. Vilnius has several on-going projects related to the renovation, regeneration and revitalization of urban space and old industrial sites. In Warsaw, there is considerable scope for projects to revitalize urban spaces. At the same time, Barcelona has good historical preconditions for being (and becoming) a widely scoped cultural international centre. Helsinki has recognized the opportunity to employ CI to make the city more attractive and creative. Barcelona and Helsinki have linked CI with developments in other fields: Helsinki with the development of ICT and innovation, and Barcelona with the development of tourism and ICT. Riga has rather good preconditions for becoming a cultural creative city in the future. It has a metropolitan atmosphere and quite a cosmopolitan historical background, which is still reflected in its diverse urban and multicultural environment. Vilnius's orientation seems to be more towards linking the development of CI to other economic sectors and towards a more indirect effect on the city's development. In terms of governance structure, Barcelona develops its CI policy in cooperation with stakeholders at the regional level; in Helsinki, the state has quite an important influence on developing CI (which is characteristic of a "city with a new face").

Two of the 11 cities share features with the "city with a new face" and "CI entrepreneurial city" types: Oslo and Tallinn. The initiative to redesign Oslo's waterfront urban space and the adoption of a cluster approach towards CI development makes it similar to the "city with a new face". Also, national-level policies have a considerable influence on developing CI in Oslo. In Tallinn, the development of CI has also, to some extent, been related to the reconstruction of urban space. Opening the city to the sea has just started and the use of CI to regenerate old industrial sites is topical. However, the scale of the changes is not as large or as coordinated citywide. As Oslo does not have the international "cultural nest" status, the city has stated that its CI policy can instead be characterized by its focus on creative business support, which makes it similar to the "CI entrepreneurial city". In Tallinn, the other policy directions related to CI seem to indicate a greater intention to support creative enterprises than to raise the general level of creativity across the whole spectrum. This, therefore, makes Tallinn more similar to the "CI entrepreneurial city".

One city—Stockholm—is a combination of two ideal types: "cultural creative city" and "CI entrepreneurial city". Stockholm is a city that has been based on a service economy for some time and the level of industrial employment has been marginal for several decades. Therefore, large-scale urban regeneration is not the issue here. The spectrum of CI is quite wide and orientations vary, yet we can recognize a leaning towards cluster policies. Stockholm follows the concept of experience industries, which focus on the consumer, and so the approach may be considered to be more business centred; this makes Stockholm similar to the "CI entrepreneurial city". The most important support structures for CI can be found at local and regional levels, making the city mainly responsible for cooperation with regional stakeholders when it comes to policy.

5. Conclusions and Discussions

This article aimed to build a typology of the policy practices relating to CI. We used the "ideal types" approach, which emphasizes that certain constructs can be built using a limited number of parameters that are tied in with inherent logic and present a holistic understanding of that particular construct.

Regarding the limitations of the study, one has to consider that the "ideal types" of CI policy have been developed according to findings on metropoles or capital cities. Capital cities contain more diversified functions; they can enjoy the preferences of, for example, capital accumulation, and attracting tourists and investors—factors that do not usually exist for smaller or non-capital cities. Therefore, one has to be careful when evaluating the CI polices of cities that are smaller or less significant, based on these types. At the same time, applying the three "ideal types" of CI policy when analysing the CI policies of smaller cities may also provide important new input for further developing these "ideal types".

We drew three significant conclusions from our study. The first is that the main differences between CI policies in different cities lie in three parameters: the focus of CI policy, the strategic choices for developing CI and the cooperation pattern between the different levels of administration. The other parameters in CI policy play supportive roles in relation to these parameters. This result enhances our former understanding of the parameters determining CI policy, at least in three senses. First, as the main focus of CI policy may be economic, cultural or space-oriented, social regeneration and internationalization aspirations are not independent focuses and may only (and usually do) accompany the main policy focuses. Rather, they perform, respectively, as parts of an inward and outward dimension that complements or specifies the main focus of CI policy. Second, the spectrum of measures in use has a supporting rather than a determining effect on the nature of CI policy alternatives. The differences in measures depend first and foremost on the development stage of CI policy. Cities with more developed CI policies have a wider spectrum of measures in force, compared with cities that are newcomers (such as capitals in the Baltic States and Warsaw in our study) in terms of CI policy. Third, the importance of different kinds of new governance arrangements (such as networks and the involvement of different parties), which have been related to CI policies, perform supportive but not determining roles in defining the main alternatives of CI policies. The alternative is determined by the division of the administrative levels involved, which is largely dependent on the country's whole administrative system.

The second is that the choices the cities make in developing CI are dependent either on the choices made at country level or on their historical and/or cultural background. Specifically, the "city with a new face" type can be achieved only when a city can make use of state-level financial support when developing CI, as the city alone cannot cope with large-scale urban regeneration. This alternative also presumes that historical reasons have made spatial regeneration topical in the city. Similarly, the "cultural creative city" type depends largely on the city being known historically as a cultural "nest" or centre, because these characteristics only develop over a long period of time. Cultural diversity also explains the broad approach to developing CI and excludes the possibility of having sectoral and sub-sectoral priorities. Again, the "CI entrepreneurial city" type is a choice the city can cope with alone (and independently from any support provided at state or regional level). This also explains why, in this alternative, CI is developed predominantly as a sectoral policy with a narrower business orientation. Altogether, these findings strengthen and expand the understanding of the path-dependent character of CI policy. It gives a reason to argue that policy transfer mechanisms play only supportive and certainly not determining role on CI policy development in Europe, at least regarding cities with longer experience in CI policymaking. The importance of path dependency in developing CI policies may also explain why the newcomers in our study (such as capitals in the Baltic States and Warsaw) do not have a common policy pattern in developing CI. This would have been expected, given that their general development models during the transition period have been rather similar (Lauristin, 2011). The finding that the position of newcomers—especially the capitals in the Baltic States—on the typology of CI polices is rather dispersed is thus, surprising. Additional research is needed to fully explain the reasons behind their different choices in developing CI.

The third is that the findings allow us to conclude that although CI policy is a complex of a large variety of different activities, choices and actions, a limited number of factors characterize the main choices and focus of CI policy. The development of "ideal types" of CI policy and the evaluation of 11 cities based on these types indicate that the variety in CI policies is concerned more with specific matters (such as measures and administrative solutions) than with the main choices driving CI policies. Although the cities' practices showed that there are more combinations of different types than a resemblance to one particular type, the choices that the cities have made are still characterized mainly by the features of no more than two "ideal types". Applying the three "ideal types" of CI policy when analysing CI policy practice thus, enables us to show which combination the cities choose and which they leave behind. Our findings indicate that if a city combines the features of the "cultural creative city" and the "city with a new face" types, it more or less discards the choices that constitute the "CI entrepreneurial city" type. Or, if the city combines the "CI entrepreneurial city" and "city with a new face" types, it minimizes the choices contained in the "cultural creative city" type. Moreover, if the city combines the "cultural creative city" and "CI entrepreneurial city" types, then the choices inherent with the "city with a new face" type are not topical for the city. These findings allow us to conclude that although the main choices and focus of CI policy can be described with a limited number of factors, the cities' practices indicate that there is only limited evidence of policy convergence. The emergence of three "ideal types" of CI policy and the fact that real practices of the cities are rather combinations of these types, give no ground to speak about developments towards a common European CI policy.

The newcomers among these studied cities have adopted (with variations) several leading CI policy instruments (e.g. development of cultural quarters, culture factories, creative incubators) that have been common in the West-European cities with longer experience in CI policy development. However, the current study did not identify a separate type of CI policy practices among the newcomers. The CI policy practices of newcomers are combinations of characteristics of these three "ideal types" and are formed dependently on the cities' historical situation, local peculiarities, objective needs and/or due to certain political aspirations. We may argue that the common features of the CI policies of the newcomers are the development and implementation mechanisms of these policies being somewhat more unpretentious and less developed than in the "old" EU cities. This can be interpreted by limited CI policy convergence and Europeanization, because these reflect engagement of "newcomers"—cities into the mainstream policy developments, especially in terms of integration of cultural and business spheres. It is the convergence across several interrelated policies like entrepreneurship support policy, public finance policies, etc, which matter, not just convergence via impact of spatial planning practices and policies. Although spatial planning practices and policies have potentially strong impact on cities' CI policies, these are quite path-dependent and place specific (compared to, e.g. entrepreneurship policies). Furthermore, implementation of (large-scale) urban regeneration initiatives is strongly influenced by city's investment capacity which is rather weak in case of post-socialist cities. The overall adoption of European culture and heritage is not much an issue, because it had been a survival strategy already during Soviet times, when belonging culturally to "West" was emphasized as much as possible.

To summarize, applying the "ideal types" approach when analysing CI policy practices allowed us to identify the main factors that constitute the CI policy alternatives and factors that have a supportive role to play. The construction of "ideal types" revealed the parameters that are inherently linked and thus, enhanced our understanding of the alternatives, which the cities (can) combine when developing CI. The findings also have important practical value, as following the "ideal types" of CI policy enables cities' CI policies to be benchmarked on a more coherent basis. The finding of the importance of path dependency in developing CI enables us to argue that the transfer of CI policy measures from one city/country to another and adopting solutions in use in other cities is even more complicated. Policy transfer lies in making use of various external practices; by combining, these cities design their own CI policy mix dependently on city's objective needs and development choices rather than adopting an integral policy pattern from another city. Therefore, the CI policy mix can be relatively different even in the cities with similar socioeconomic background. As the study revealed a distinctive post-socialist or Baltic approach to CI policy cannot be identified.

Acknowledgements

The authors would like to express gratitude to the research partners in Creative Metropoles project and all municipality partners from 11 cities involved, who contributed and shared their experience. The authors would also like to sincerely thank the referees and editors of the special issue for their valuable comments and highly appreciate their recommendations.

References

Allin, P. (2000) The development of comparable European cultural statistics, *Cultural Trends*, 10(37), pp. 65–75.
Arge Creativ Wirtschaft Austria (2009) *Third Austrian Report on Creative Industries. Summary. Focus on Creative Industries and Innovation* (Vienna: CWA).
Balducci, A. (2004) Creative governance in dynamic city regions, *DISP*, 158(3), pp. 21–26.
Baycan-Levent, T. (2010) Diversity and creativity as seedbeds for urban and regional dynamics, *European Planning Studies*, 18(4), pp. 565–594.
Bayliss, D. (2007) The rise of the creative city: Culture and creativity in Copenhagen, *European Planning Studies*, 15(7), pp. 889–903.

Birch, S. (2008) *The Political Promotion of the Experience Economy and the Creative Industries—Cases from UK, New Zealand, Singapore, Norway, Sweden and Denmark* (Denmark: Imagine and Samfundslitteratur).

Blalock, H. M., Jr. (1969) *Theory Construction: From Verbal to Mathematical Formulations* (Englewood Cliffs, NJ: Prentice Hall).

van der Borg, J. & Russo, A. P. (2006) *The Impacts of Culture on the Economic Development of Cities* (Rotterdam: Erasmus University Rotterdam, European Institute for Comparative Urban Research).

Braun, E. & Lavanga, M. (2007) *An International Comparative Quick Scan of National Policies for Creative Industries* (Rotterdam: EURICUR).

Chapain, C. & Comunian, R. (2010) Enabling and inhibiting the creative economy: The role of the local and regional dimensions in England, *Regional Studies*, 44(6), pp. 717–734.

Costa, P., Magalhães, M., Vasconcelos, B. & Sugahara, G. (2008) On "creative cities" governance models: A comparative approach, *The Service Industries Journal*, 28(3), pp. 393–413.

Costa, P., Seixas, J. & Roldao, A. (2009) From "creative cities" to "urban creativity"? Space, creativity and governance in the contemporary city. Paper presented at EURA/UAA Conference on City Futures '09—City Futures in a Globalizing World, Madrid, Spain, 4–6 June. Available at http://www.cityfutures2009.com/PDF/10_Costa_Pedro.pdf (accessed 12 April 2010).

Creative Industries Mapping Document (1998) *Creative Industries Task Force*. Available at http://www.culture.gov.uk/global/publications/archive_1998/Creative_Industries_Mapping_Document_1998.htm?properties=archive_1998%2C%2Fglobal%2Fpublications%2Farchive_1998%2F%2C&month (accessed 26 October 2008).

Creative Metropoles—Public Policies and Instruments in Support of Creative Industries (2010) *INTERREG IVC Project's Research Report*, Tallinn: Tallinn University, Estonian Institute for Futures Studies.

Creigh-Tyte, A. (2005) Measuring creativity: A case study in the UK's designer fashion sector, *Cultural Trends*, 14(2), pp. 157–183.

Delanty, G. & Rumford, C. (2005) *Rethinking Europe: Social Theory and the Implications of Europeanization* (London: Routledge).

Doty, H. D. & Glick, W. H. (1994) Typologies as a unique form of theory building: Toward improved understanding and modelling, *Academy of Management Review*, 19(2), pp. 230–251.

Evans, G. (2005) Measure for measure: Evaluating the evidence of culture's contribution to regeneration, *Urban Studies*, 42(5/6), pp. 959–983.

Evans, G. (2009) Creative cities, creative spaces and urban policy, *Urban Studies*, 46(5&6), pp. 1003–1040.

Flew, T. & Cunningham, S. D. (2010) Creative industries after the first decade of debate, *The Information Society*, 26(2), pp. 1–11.

Florida, R. (2002) *The Rise of the Creative Class. And How it's Transforming Work, Leisure, Community and Everyday Life* (New York: Basic Books).

Foord, J. (2008) Strategies for creative industries: An international review, *Creative Industries Journal*, 1(2), pp. 91–113.

Garnham, N. (2005) From cultural to creative Industries. An analysis of the implications of the "creative industries" approach to arts and media policy making in the United Kingdom, *International Journal of Cultural Policy*, 11(1), pp. 15–29.

Greenwood, R. & Hinings, C. R. (1996) Understanding radical organizational change: Bringing together the old and the new institutionalism, *Academy of Management Review*, 21(4), pp. 1022–1054.

Hartley, J. (Ed.) (2005) *Creative Industries* (Malden, MA: Blackwell).

Hartley, J. (2008) From the consciousness industry to creative industries: Consumer-created content, social network markets, and the growth of knowledge, in: J. Holt & A. Perren (Eds) *Media Industries: History, Theory and Methods*, pp. 231–244 (Oxford: Blackwell).

Hearn, G., Roodhouse, S. & Blakey, J. (2007) From value chain to value creating ecology. Implications for creative industries development policy, *International Journal of Cultural Policy*, 13(4), pp. 419–436.

Hesmondhalgh, D. & Pratt, A. (2005) Cultural industries and cultural policy, *International Journal of Cultural Policy*, 11(1), pp. 1–14.

Howkins, J. (2002) *The Creative Economy. How People Make Money from Ideas* (London: Penguin Books).

Huy, Q. N. (2001) Time, temporal capability, and planned change, *The Academy of Management Review*, 26(4), pp. 601–623.

Jansson, J. & Power, D. (Eds) (2006) *Image of the City. Urban Branding as Constructed Capabilities in Nordic City Region* (Norway: Nordic Innovation Centre).

Jessop, B. (1995) The regulation approach, governance and post-Fordism, *Economy and Society*, 24(3), pp. 307–333.
Jürisson, V. (2007) *Saving Cultural Policy* (Unpublished manuscript).
Kalandides, A. (2007) For a stricter use of the term "gentrification", *Geographies*, 13, pp. 158–172.
KEA (2006) *The Economy of Culture in Europe* (Brussels: KEA European Affairs).
Kearns, G. & Philo, C. (Eds) (1993) *Selling Places: The City as Cultural Capital, Past and Present* (Oxford: Pergamon).
Kovacs, Z., Murie, A., Musterd, S., Gritsai, O. & Pethe, H. (2007) *Comparing Paths of Creative Knowledge Regions* (Amsterdam: University of Amsterdam).
Kunzmann, K. R. (2004) An Agenda for creative governance in city regions, *DISP*, 158(3), pp. 5–10.
Landry, C. (2000) *The Creative City: A Toolkit for Urban Innovators* (London: Earthscan).
Landry, C., Greene, L., Matarasso, F. & Bianchini, F. (2005) *Age of the City—Creativity and the city*. Available at http://www.comedia.org.uk/pages/pdf/downloads/Age_of_the_City_Creativity_and_the_city.pdf (accessed 28 February 2008).
Lange, L. (2008) Accessing markets in creative industries—professionalization and social-spatial strategies of culturepreneurs in Berlin, *Creative Industries Journal*, 1(2), pp. 115–135.
Lange, L. (2009) Re-scaling governance in Berlin's creative economy, *Creative Encounters Working Paper*, 39, pp. 3–28.
Lauristin, M. (2011) Introduction. Human development during the period of transition: The challenges faced by the Baltic states, in: M. Lauristin (Ed) *Estonian Human Development Report 2010/2011. Baltic Way(s) of Human Development: Twenty Years On*, pp. 10–12 (Tallinn: Estonian Cooperation Assembly).
Lavanga, M. (2006) *The Contribution of Cultural and Creative Industries to a More Sustainable Urban Development. The Case Studies of Rotterdam and Tampere* (Amsterdam: University of Amsterdam).
Morgan, M. S. (2006) Economic man as model man: Ideal types, idealization and caricatures, *Journal of the History of Economic Thought*, 28(1), pp. 1–27.
Mulcahy, K. V. (2006) Cultural policy, in: B. G. Peters & J. Pierre (Eds) *Handbook of Public Policy*, pp. 265–279 (London: Sage).
Nadin, V. & Stead, D. (2013) Opening up the compendium: An evaluation of international comparative planning research methodologies, *European Planning Studies*. Available at http://dx.doi.org/10.1080/09654313.2012.722958 (accessed 10 December 2012).
O'Connor, J. (2009) Creative industries: A new direction? *International Journal of Cultural Policy*, 15(4), pp. 387–402.
OECD (2007) *Participative Web: User-Created Content*. (Geneva: Working Party on the Information Economy, Directorate for Science, Technology and Industry, Committee for Information, Computer and Communications Policy).
O'Regan, R. & Ryan, M. D. (2004) From multimedia to regional content and applications: Remaking policy for the digital content industries, *Media International Australia*, 102, pp. 28–49.
Pine, J.II & Gilmore, J. H. (1999) *The Experience Economy: Work is Theatre & Every Business a Stage* (Cambridge, MA: Harvard Business School Press).
Porter, M. E. (1998) Clusters and the new economics of competition, *Harvard Business Review*, (Nov–Dec), pp. 77–87.
Porter, M. E. & Stern, S. (2001) Innovation: Location matters, *MIT Sloan Management Review*, (Summer), pp. 28–36.
Potts, J. & Cunningham, S. (2008) Four models of the creative industries, *International Journal of Cultural Policy*, 14(3), pp. 233–247.
Power, D. (2009) Culture, creativity and experience in Nordic and Scandinavian cultural policy, *International Journal of Cultural Policy*, 15(4), pp. 445–460.
Power, D. & Jansson, J. (Eds) (2006) *Creative Directions—A Nordic framework for Supporting the Creative Industries* (Sweden: The Swedish Institute for Food and Biotechnology).
Primorac, J. (2006) *The Position of Cultural Workers in Creative Industries: The South-Eeastern European Perspective* (Amsterdam: European Cultural Foundation).
Prince, R. (2010) Globalizing the creative industries concept: Travelling policy and transnational policy communities, *The Journal of Arts Management, Law, and Society*, 40(2), pp. 119–139.
Rascaroli, L. & O'Donovan, P. (Eds) (2010) *The Cause of Cosmopolitanism: Dispositions, Models, Transformations* (Oxford: Peter Lang).

Rhodes, R. A. W. (1996) The New Governance: Governing without Government, *Political Studies*, XLIV, pp. 652–667.

Rutten, P. (2006) *Culture & Urban Regeneration. Cultural Activities & Creative Industries. A Driving Force for Urban Regeneration. Finding & Conclusions on the Economic Perspective.* Available at http://www.mdrl.ro/urbactII/urbact/projects/cultural_activities/UC-Perspective%20eco.pdf (accessed 12 April 2008).

Scott, A. J. (2001) Capitalism, cities, and the production of symbolic forms, *Transactions of the Institute of British Geographers*, 26(1), pp. 11–23.

Shiner, L. E. (1975) An ideal type gone astray, *Comparative Studies in Society and History*, 17(2), pp. 245–252.

Shoales, J. (2006) Alpha clusters: Creative innovation in local economies, *Economic Development Quarterly*, 20(2), pp. 162–177.

Taylor, C. F. (2006) Beyond advocacy: Developing an evidence base for regional creative industry strategies, *Cultural Trends*, 15(1), pp. 3–18.

Throsby, D. (2008) Modeling the Cultural industries, *International Journal of Cultural Policy*, 14(3), pp. 217–232.

Tomić-Koludrović, I. & Petrić, M. (2005) Creative industries in transition: Towards a creative economy, in: N. Švob-Đokić (Ed.) *The Emerging Creative Industries in Southeastern Europe*, pp. 7–24 (Zagreb: Institute for International Relations).

Trip, J. J. & Romein, A. (2010) Creative city policy: Bridging the gap with theory. Available at http://www.dur.ac.uk/resources/geography/conferences/eursc/17-09-10/TripandRomein.pdf (accessed 1 July 2011).

Weber, M. (1904/1949) "Objectivity" in social science and social policy, in: M. Weber (Ed) *The Methodology of the Social Sciences*, pp. 49–112 (Glencoe, IL: The Free Press).

Yusuf, S. & Nabeshima, K. (2005) Creative industries in East Asia, *Cities*, 22(2), pp. 109–122.

Index

Note: Page numbers in *italics* refer to figures
Page numbers in **bold** refer to tables

"acquis" in Eastern Europe 6, 32
administrative performance and capacity: adaptability in 80; assessment 77–81, **78**, **81**; conceptual framework 66–72, **68–9**, **71**; evaluation of achievements 77; financial management and control 74–6, **75**; monitoring of progress 76–7; operationalization **68–9**, **71**; programming of resources 72; project generation 72–4, **73**, **74**; reporting to commission 76; *see also* Cohesion policy
amalgamated municipalities 100
Amsterdam as "cultural creative city" type 138–9
Applied Research Projects 49
Association of Architects 47
Association of Local and Regional Government in Latvia 47

Baltic Sea Islands Network 54
Baltic Sea Region (BSR): institutional reforms 58; macro-regional strategy 18, 53; similar characteristics of 43; territorial cohesion debate 49–58, **51–2**, **55–6**; territorial development in **44**, 44–7
Barcelona as CI entrepreneurial city 139
Berlin as CI entrepreneurial city 136–7
Birmingham as "ideal type" of city 137–8
bottom-up regionalism 30, 37
bounded regions 25, 27–30, 37–8
B7 Islands Network 56

causal relationships of physical proximity 91
Central and Eastern Europe (CEE): Cohesion policy 66, 70, 72–7, **73**, **74**, **75**; communist regimes 93–4; decentralization of state bureaucracies 109; European spatial planning in 43; introduction 6; pro-development lobby in 58; regional devolution 30; regional inequality decreases 24–5; spatial planning differences 2–4; *see also* Eastern Europe; regional policy; *specific countries*
central place relationships 100
CI entrepreneurial city 135, 136–7, 141
"city with a new face" type 139
Cohesion policy: adaption 109–11, **110**; administrative adaptability 80; administrative assessment 80–1, **81**; Central and Eastern Europe 66, 70, 72–7, **73**, **74**, **75**; debates 4; financial support at EU level 114; human resources in 79–80; introduction 6; organizational structures in 78, 79; overview 33; *see also* administrative performance and capacity
Commission for the Peripheral and Maritime Regions (CPMR) 54, 56–8
Commission of the European Communities 16
Committee for Spatial Development 56
common understanding in spatial planning 47
communism 1, 83, 93–4
communities of practice 43, 48, 54, 58
Community Initiative Interreg 49
Community Support Framework 73
conceptual framework of EU conditionality 66–72, **68–9**, **71**
context (value system) 92
Council of Regional Policy 112
creative industries (CI): data collection and analysis 132–3; 11 metropoles of "ideal types" 132, 136–40, *137*; ideal models of 133–5, **134**; "ideal types" approach 127–32, **129**, **135**, 135–8, 141–2; policy practices 133–40
"cultural creative city" type 138–29
"cultural nest" status 139

INDEX

Czech Republic: administrative productivity 80; Cohesion policy 73, 74, 79; ERDF systems in 75; territorial-administrative reforms 30, 32

decommitments of structural funds **74**
de-Europeanization 114–17, *115*
democratic ante-bellum politics 101
deportations 95
distribution of power 11

Eastern Europe: "acquis" in 6, 32; Europeanization of spatial policies 31–5; governing through spatial tools 29; regional devolution 30; *see also* Central and Eastern Europe; *specific countries*
economic competitiveness 28, 32, 114, 130
economic crisis 2, 46, 96, 112, 118
economic renewal 128, 130
11 metropoles of "ideal types" 132, 136–40, *137*
"embeddedness" notions 91
"Emerging Borderland Europe" scenario 38
"Empty Empire of Rules" scenario 37
endogenous resources 100
Enterprise Estonia 116
entrepreneurs' organizations 135
epistemic distance in spatial planning 47
Estonia: Cohesion policy 73; de-Europeanization 114–17, *115*; initial planning legislation in 47; spatial planning documents in 45; territorial knowledge communities, response 50, **51–2**, 52–4; *see also* regional policy (RP), in Estonia
Estonian Ministry of Finance 116
Estonian National Museum 118
Estonian Regional Development Agency (ERDA) 112
Euclidean planning 13
European Cohesion Policy *see* Cohesion policy
European Commission 14, 34, 65, 70
European coordination systems 82–3
European Court of Auditors 70, 75
European Directorate (DG-REGIO) 18
European Groupings of Territorial Cooperation (EGTC) 57
European integration and spatial rescaling, Baltic States: introduction 10–11; macro-regions as "soft planning" 15–18, *16*, *17*; new planning approaches 12–13; territorial cooperation as "soft planning" 14–15, *15*
Europeanization: of administrative capacity 83; creative industries under 127; defined 66; regional policies and 106–7; of spatial planning 2–3, 25, 34–5, 38; three types 107

European macro-regions as "soft planning" 15–18, *16*, *17*, 19
European Observation Network for Territorial Development and Cohesion (ESPON) 33, 44, 49, 53, 57, 59
European Spatial Development Perspective (ESDP) 14, 25, 33–4, 98
European spatial planning (ESP) 42–4, 47–8, 59; *see also* territorial knowledge communities
European Territorial Cooperation 11, 14–15, 19, 49
European Union (EU): Baltic Strategy conference 4; Cohesion Fund 24, 65, 116; funding from 2; fuzzy or permeable borders, existence of 13; governing through spatial tools 29; regional processes *27*; spatial governance in 26–31, **27**, *27*
Euroregion Baltic 56
Eurostat report 107
experience economy concept 131

Fifth Report on Economic, Social and Territorial Cohesion (CEC) 43, 49
financial management and control 74–6, **75**
fluid regions 25, 28–31, 38
"fuzzy boundaries" 12, 19

globalization 25, 29, 31
governance *see* spatial governance
Green Paper on Territorial Cohesion (CEC) 16, 44, 49, 59
gross domestic product (GDP) 24, **44**, 45, 106, *106*, 114

"hard planning" 12–13
higher education budgets 46
home-work relationships 100
human-made spatial patterns 26
human movements 94–6
human resources in Cohesion policy 79–80
Hungary 7, 32, 79, 80

"ideal types" approach 127–32, **129**, **135**, 135–8, 141–2
information and communication technology (ICT) 99, 128
Innovation Circle Network 54, 56–8
institutional cycle model of territorial governance *108*, 108–9
institutional dynamism 118
Instrument for Structural Policies for Pre-Accession (ISPA) 32, 72, 83, 112
INTERREG Initiative 2–3, 14, 17–19
intervention mechanisms category 131
Ireland 50

INDEX

Khorev, B.S. 92, 93
Khrushchev, Nikita 93

Laeken European Council 49
Lamze, Arnolds 46
Latvia: Cohesion policy 73; local communist elite 94; spatial planning documents in 45–6; territorial knowledge communities, response 50, **51–2**, 52–4; urban–rural interactions 88–9, 94–7, **97**
Latvian Agrarian Reform (1920–37) 96, 100–1
Latvian National Development Plan (LNDP) 99
Latvian urban–rural policy 7
Lisbon Strategy 35
"list-based" approach 130
Lithuania 50, **51–2**, 52–4
Lithuanian Comprehensive Plan 46
Long-Term Perspective (LTP) 56, 90
LOTOS programme 94

market-based economics 45, 46
Marxism 92, 93
"Metropolitan States with Periphery" scenario 37–8
metropolitan *vs.* rural relationships 100
Minister of Regional Affairs (MRA) 112–14, 116–17
monitoring of progress 76–7
multi-level governance 29, 30, 37, 52

National Co-ordination Group 50, 54
neo-liberalism 12, 25, 43, 46, 58
Network of Eastern External Border Regions (NEEBOR) 54, 56–8
"newcomers" city type 139
Nõmmik, Salme 6

old-barnyism 110–11, 118
operationalization of administrative performance **68–9**, **71**
Operational Programme (OP) 73
organizational structures in Cohesion policy 78, 79

path-dependency of spatial planning systems 26, 39, 48
PHARE Programme 3, 32, 72, 79, 83, 112
place-based features 12, 28, 34, 91, 119
Planning and Building Act 112
Poland 7, 29, 32, 74, 79
policy application challenges 98–101
policy convergence 3–6, 127, 141–2
policy transfer mechanisms 25, 33, 38, 126–7, 141–2
polycentrism 26, 35–8

pre-accession framework 30, 32, 66–7, 70, 81–3, 114
producer–commodity–consumer causation 131

rationalist mechanisms of adaptation 67, 70
regional development: administrative structures for 79; de-Europeanization and 114; ERDF measures 116; hierarchical settings of 118; introduction 2; key stakeholders in 44, 50, 53; networked framework in 30; policy support for 89; purpose of 97; role of Structural Funds in 107, 113; sector policy actions link 113; in urban–rural interactions 98, *98*
Regional Development Strategy 113, 116
regional devolution 30
regionalism 30, 32, 37
regionalization 10, 29
regional policy (RP) in Estonia: cohesion policy adaption 109–11, **110**; effects of interventions 114–17, *115*; overview 111–14, *113*; research questions and methods 111; stages of **123–5**; theories and practices behind 107–11, *108*, **110**
region-binding 31, 38
revolutionary romanticism 93
Russia 18, 20, 54, 58, 94

SAPARD Programme 32
Single Programming Document 113
Slovakia 32, 73–7, 79–80, 82
Slovenia 73–7, 79, 82
social agents 89–92
Social Democrats 112, 117
socio-economic conditions 4, 26, 91, 100
"soft planning": macro-regions as 15–18, *16*, *17*; spatial rescaling and 12–13; territorial cooperation as 14–15, *15*
"soft security" goals 13
Sovietization 95
Soviet Union 1, 4, 93–5
spatial governance 26–31, *27*, 27, 38, 52
spatial planning, Baltic States: contributions in 6–7; Europeanization, limits of 3–4; Europeanization of 2–3; policy convergence of 5–6; replacement of 106
spatial planning, European Union: in Eastern Europe 31–5; emergence of 26–31, **27**, *27*; three scenarios for 35–8, **37**
spatial rescaling *see* European integration and spatial rescaling
State Regional Development Agency 89
statistical regression techniques 70
Structural Funds: application of 113–14; decommitments of **74**; Europeanization of

INDEX

108; management 30; midterm evaluations of 116–17; push factors for 106; role in regional development 107, 113
structural policies 30, 33

Targeted Analysis Projects 49
territorial–administrative reforms 27–8, 31–4
territorial cohesion debate 12, 49–58, **51–2**, **55–6**; *see also* urban–rural interactions
territorial cooperation spaces 14–15, *15*, 19
territorial knowledge communities: development of 44–7; enlargement of Baltic actors in ESP 47–9; GDP per capita **44**; internalization and Europeanization 46–7; pragmatism and political expedience 45–6; responses from selected interest groups 54–8, **55–6**; responses from state institutions 50–4, **51–2**; in territorial cohesion debate 49–58, **51–2**, **55–6**
Territorial State and Perspectives of the European Union document 16
top-down regionalism 30
totalitarianism 93–4
transformative "gap" 91

Treaty of Amsterdam (1997) 49
Treaty of Nice (2001) 49
Type I governance 13
typology of cohesion policy adaption 109–11, **110**
typology of places **97**, 97–8, *98*

Ulmanis, Kārlis 94
Union of Architects in Lithuania 47
urban density 130
urban planning 131, 136, 138
urban–rural interactions: under communism/totalitarianism 93–4; human movements 94–6; Latvian estimations of 96–7, **97**; measurement of 89–90; policy application challenges 98–101; typology of places **97**, 97–8, *98*; understanding of 90–2
urban space, regeneration 134

value chain model 131
Vision and Strategies around the Baltic Sea (VASAB) 44, 48–9, 56, 59

Weber, Max 127–32, **129**